Routledge Revivals

Mark Twain as a Literary Comedian

Originally published in 1979, *Mark Twain as a Literary Comedian* looks at how Mark Twain addressed social issues through humour. The Southwest provided the subject for much of Twain's writing, but the roots of his style lay principally in north-eastern humour. In the mid-1800s the northern United States underwent social changes that reflected in the writing of the literary humourists like Twain. Sloane argues that he used humour to describe conditions in the emerging middle-class urban experience and express his American vision and that Twain's views on the human, social, and political conditions, presented through his fictional characters, elevated the use of literary humour in the American novel.

Mark Twain as a Literary Comedian

David E.E. Sloane

First published in 1979
by Louisiana State University Press

This edition first published in 2018 by Routledge
2 Park Square, Milton Park, Abingdon, Oxon, OX14 4RN
and by Routledge
711 Third Avenue, New York, NY 10017

Routledge is an imprint of the Taylor & Francis Group, an informa business

© 1979 Louisiana State University Press

All rights reserved. No part of this book may be reprinted or reproduced or utilised in any form or by any electronic, mechanical, or other means, now known or hereafter invented, including photocopying and recording, or in any information storage or retrieval system, without permission in writing from the publishers.

Publisher's Note
The publisher has gone to great lengths to ensure the quality of this reprint but points out that some imperfections in the original copies may be apparent.

Disclaimer
The publisher has made every effort to trace copyright holders and welcomes correspondence from those they have been unable to contact.
A Library of Congress record exists under ISBN: 78011125

ISBN 13: 978-0-8153-9562-1 (hbk)
ISBN 13: 978-1-351-18346-8 (ebk)
ISBN 13: 978-0-8153-9563-8 (pbk)

Mark Twain
as a Literary Comedian

David E. E. Sloane

Louisiana State University Press
Baton Rouge and London

Copyright © 1979 by Louisiana State University Press
All rights reserved
Manufactured in the United States of America

Design: Patricia Douglas Crowder
Typeface: VIP Aster
Composition: LSU Press

LIBRARY OF CONGRESS CATALOGING IN PUBLICATION DATA

Sloane, David E   E   1943–
    Mark Twain as a literary comedian.

    (Southern literary studies)
    Bibliography: p.
    Includes index.
    1. Clemens, Samuel Langhorne, 1835–1910—Criticism
and interpretation.   2. Comedy—History and criticism.
I. Title. II Series.
PS1338.S55   818'.4'09   78–11125
ISBN 0–8071–0460–4

For Jane

Contents

	Acknowledgments	xi
ONE	Backgrounds	1
TWO	Literary Comedy	13
THREE	Artemus Ward as Pioneer Funnyman	29
FOUR	The Social Ethics of a Comedian	45
FIVE	Mark Twain The Development of a Literary Comedian	58
SIX	Toward the Novel	84
SEVEN	Humor and Social Criticism *The Gilded Age* and *The Prince and the Pauper*	104
EIGHT	*Adventures of Huckleberry Finn* The Literary Comedian Within the Novel	128
NINE	*A Connecticut Yankee* A Culmination of American Literary Comedy	146
TEN	*The American Claimant* and *Pudd'nhead Wilson*	168
ELEVEN	Conclusion	189
	Bibliography	201
	Index	217

Acknowledgments

MANY PEOPLE have contributed substantially to this work. Louis Budd at Duke University has been particularly valuable in helping in the search for information and the development of ideas. James M. Cox also deserves special thanks for contributing important ideas to the final work. Resources, libraries, and librarians at Duke University, Lafayette College, Rutgers University, and the University of New Haven have also been consistently helpful. Frederick Anderson and the staff of the Mark Twain Papers at the University of California at Berkeley also helped in the search for manuscript materials and letters. Lafayette College aided this work with a Summer Research Fellowship enabling me to carry on intensive research. I am also indebted to Bonnie Sloane for early encouragement and aid. Finally, I am grateful to the University of New Haven for both grant support and the warm encouragement needed to bring the work to completion.

Mark Twain as a Literary Comedian

ONE

Backgrounds

THE SOUTHWESTERN HUMORISTS have traditionally been identified as the major impulse behind Mark Twain's humor. However, the hallmark of his comedy lies in his egalitarian vision, projected not through the local color elements that characterize the humor of the old southwestern United States as much as through the jokes, ironic inversions, and burlesques of another school of American humor—the literary comedians of the 1850s and the Civil War era. The southwesterners are not respecters of persons as much as they are respecters of social "quality," and a major point of distinction between them and the emerging American middle class can be found in this point. Twain's explosive sarcasm and verbal gags infuse his rambling plots with a thoroughly different and substantially more humane spirit.

Most of the southwestern authors—for example Augustus Baldwin Longstreet, author of *Georgia Scenes*; Johnson J. Hooper, author of *The Adventures of Simon Suggs*; George W. Harris, author of *Sut Lovingood's Yarns*; and Joseph G. Baldwin, author of *Flush Times of Alabama and Mississippi*—belonged to emerging professions in their region, such as law, medicine, or printing. They conceived of themselves not as writing for a general public, but rather as historical reporters describing their unique region at the same time that they scourged vulgar vices. Their humor has consistently been described

2 MARK TWAIN AS A LITERARY COMEDIAN

as undemocratic and unsympathetic to the common man in his irregulated Jacksonian state.[1]

The South itself was a region that remained agrarian while the Northeast industrialized. As W. J. Cash analyzes the southern mind, the simple southern environment produced a lack of complexity. Horses, guns, and dogs remained the preoccupations of even the Tidewater aristocrats. A static literature was called for, and respect for the classics, such as Shakespeare, was superstitious rather than culturally sustained. Urban centers did not compare to those of the North; nor did southern publishers or authors match the achievements of northern counterparts. Conditions were homogeneous, and slavery as a social phenomenon was understood as a constitutional right that safeguarded every social class.[2]

Southwestern humor reflected its environment. Substantial yeomen like the hero of William T. Thompson's *Major Jones' Courtship* are relatively rare, as is a medical man like Madison Tensas, the swamp doctor. Hunters, lubbers, and petty aristocracy are common figures, and they fit easily into William Trotter Porter's *Spirit of the Times*, a sporting magazine that was a center for this genre. The mythical big bear of Arkansas, described by Thomas Bangs Thorpe as both the "creation" bear and the greenhorn who hunts him, is typical in his comic immediacy, vulgarity, and "masculinity" identified with natural backwoods experience. An aristocratic "Native Georgian," like Longstreet's Ned Brace, jibes middle-class travelers and city types, even when his pranks are less comfortable for himself than for the butts of the jokes.

Corporate society is little in evidence in southwestern writings, and its ethical complexities are seldom in view. Business is represented by the horse swap, law by the figure of the sheriff, and religion by the camp meeting and the parson. Harris' Sut Lovingood and Hooper's Simon Suggs are the archetypal figures in the tradition, the former a natural "durn fool," the latter a Jacksonian office-

---

[1] The foremost proponent of this view is Kenneth S. Lynn in *Mark Twain and Southwestern Humor* (Boston: Little, Brown, 1959).

[2] W. J. Cash, *The Mind of the South* (New York: Random House, 1969), 90–102; Ulrich B. Phillips, "The Central Theme of Southern History," reprinted in Kenneth M. Stampp, *The Causes of the Civil War* (Englewood Cliffs, N.J.: Prentice Hall, 1959), 171–72.

seeker whose motto is "It's good to be shifty in a new country." Sut pins lizards to corpses to make them seem alive, feeds people alum, ties woodchucks in a drunkard's pantaloons, and tears his own hide off with an overly starched shirt; his comedy is violent and insensitive. Twain's fiction occasionally shows such traits as verbalized humor but seldom as dramatic incident, with the exception of the "bulls and bees" episode from "Cecily Burns' Wedding," which was purged from at least one manuscript before it was sneaked into *Joan of Arc*.[3] Trapping yokels at camp meetings is merely the "opposition line" to Captain Simon Suggs. Davy Crockett cheats a storekeeper with raffish openness, but Suggs's view of humanity is curdled by his own rapacity. In short narrative after short narrative, violent climax succeeds selfish motive. The tone of the narrator, in contrast, is kept distinct from the vernacular of the corrupted local figure; values are asserted negatively.

There are crucial points in Twain's works that are not explained by reference to southwestern humor. His most significant humor occurs when his pose is most united with his material, contrary to the traits noted here. His response to consciously inflicted pain varies between complicity, as in the Southwest anecdotes, to moral outrage. Perhaps most important, even in humorous episodes, his ironic deadpan commentary builds a democratic social vision opposed to corporate power and social mores. His attitude toward human beings is, at its best, egalitarian, and at his zenith, he finds natural symbols in which he can transmute these values into sustained fiction; his humor asserts positive values.

Walter Blair, in *Native American Humor*, opens the field of American humor to inspection but asserts that Twain was preeminently a product of the Southwest, dependent on its narrative forms. Bernard DeVoto, in *Mark Twain's America*, contends that Twain borrowed no more than a handful of jokes from Artemus Ward and that those were of little significance. More recently Henry Nash Smith has

---

3 Hennig Cohen, "Mark Twain's Sut Lovingood," in B. H. McClary (ed.) *The Lovingood Papers* (Knoxville: University of Tennessee Press, 1962), 19–24; E. N. Long, "Sut Lovingood and Mark Twain's *Joan of Arc*," *Modern Language Notes*, LXIV (January, 1949), 37–39; D. M. McKeithan, "Mark Twain's Story of the Bulls and the Bees," *Tennessee Historical Quarterly*, XI (September, 1952), 246–53.

asserted that the "vernacular" values of the frontier shaped Twain's consciousness.[4] In distinction to these views, an understanding of Twain's sources actually indicates that he borrowed extensively from the tradition of literary humor. Irony, burlesque, and overt borrowings of pose and diction infuse his writings with the social viewpoints of the 1850–1870 era and help him to emphasize the conflict between individuals and corporate power. Literary comedy may not have helped Twain shape his novels, but neither does southwestern humor offer a reliable precedent in this area; but literary comedy does provide a sense of the origin of his ethics and the centrality of his jokes in developing his ethical viewpoints.

Aside from the southwestern school, the British and Irish humorous tradition was a literary force in America in the 1830–1860 period. Dickens and Thackeray are prominent but by no means alone. Virtually every device employed by the literary comedians was first tried out by Laurence Sterne in *Tristram Shandy*, sometimes in a political context close to the American one. Substantial documentation has been offered to suggest that Dickens' early style was widely copied and figured heavily in the offerings of William T. Porter's *The Spirit of the Times* (1831–1861), a magazine that actively fostered American humorous writing in the pre–Civil War period.[5] Sam Weller in *The Pickwick Papers* speaks in a Cockney dialect and acts in the affairs of the Pickwickians with a democratically unsentimental pragmatism that is representative of the lower-class figure seen in America in figures like Seba Smith's Jack Downing. Portions of Dickens' *American Notes*, which Porter's *Spirit of the Times* reprinted, were weighted to show comic American characters, encouraging reader interest, of course, but also helping to develop a literary perception of American materials.

Thackeray, like Dickens, was received with deference by Americans, and, like Dickens, he treated American subjects in his writings.

---

4 Walter Blair, *Native American Humor* (San Francisco: Chandler, 1960 [1937]) 157; Bernard DeVoto, *Mark Twain's America* (Boston: Houghton Mifflin, 1967 [1932]), 165. "But of Ward's manner, his approach, and the content of his humor nothing of Mark's possesses anything at all." Henry Nash Smith, *Mark Twain: The Development of a Writer* (Cambridge: Harvard University Press, 1962).

5 Richard Hauck, "The Dickens Controversy in the *Spirit of the Times*," PMLA, LXXXV (March, 1970), 278–83.

James Fenimore Cooper was caricatured as the author of "The Last of the Mulligans" in *Novels by Eminent Hands* (1847). Cooper's Americans in "The Stars and Stripes," Thackeray's burlesque of his style, are uniformly boorish and vulgar; the chief of the Nose-ring Indians, separated from his companion Leatherlegs, stalks through the royal gardens of France in search of firewater while Dr. Franklin converses with the king in an early version of Pike County dialect. The ranking of Cooper among popular British authors is clearly complimentary. *The Book of Snobs* (1846–1847), with its sophisticated burlesques of fashion, influenced American writers like G. W. Curtis. English reviewers compared Twain's glove-buying episode in Paris, in *The Innocents Abroad*, to Thackeray's book, later. *Lyra Hibernica* and *The Ballads of Policeman X*, in verse, made sarcastic comments in low Irish and Cockney dialects on contemporary events in Great Britain and the continent in 1848. All of this material is consciously literary and addressed to an audience conversant with the belletristic tradition. The author's focus is on social and political currents rather than on local episodes.

Alternative popular sources to the British authors are also important, such as Edward M. Whitty's *The Bohemians of London* and the anonymous *Father Tom and the Pope*. Whitty's wry comments on "smelling salts and Christian consolation" continue the sentimental burlesque mode of Thackeray's *Vanity Fair*. *Father Tom and the Pope*, however, showed a vulgar Irish priest disputing with a burlesque old man (the pope) in the dialect common to such figures as Hugh Henry Brackenridge's Teague O'Regan in *Modern Chivalry*. Published originally in *Blackwood's Magazine* in 1838, it was reprinted in American editions through 1868, probably for its willful confusion of Roman Catholic scholasticism with the drunkenness of low-class characters. The raciness of Father Tom's confrontation with the pope is a product of the low dialect and the depiction of habits clearly at variance with genteel modes of behavior, as the following passage suggests:

> The Pope—and indeed it ill becomes a good Catholic to say anything agin him—no more would I, only that his Riv'rence was in it—but you see the fact ov it is, that the Pope was as envious as ever he could be, at seeing him-

self sacked right and left by Father Tom, and bate out o' the face, the way he was, on every science and subjec' that was started. So, not to be outdone altogether, he says to his Riv'rence, "You're a man that's fond ov the brute crayation, I hear Misther Maguire?"

"I don't deny it," says his Riv'rence, "I've dogs that I'm willing to run agin any man's, ay, or to match them agin any other dogs in the world for genteel edication and polite manners," say he.

"I'll hould you a pound," says the Pope, "that I've a quadhruped in my possession that's a wiser baste nor any dog in your kennel."

"Done," says his Riv'rence, and they staked the money.

"What can this larned quadhruped o' your do?" says his Riv'rence.

"It's my mule," says the Pope.[6]

The dialect could belong to the narrator, or to the characters. The literary effect, however, is to vulgarize the characters' minds without identifying them as vicious in actions. Since their materialism is inconsequential yet inappropriate to their offices, the technique is intellectual. The obviousness of the burlesque diverges from the Dickensian mode, which seldom confuses classes in one voice. For Dickens and Thackeray, the interactions of the classes were comic, but, as here, idealistic values could easily be identified with the lower-class figure. The British humorous tradition thus offered a considerable range of character, dialect, and narrative structure. The English humorists, professional authors, closely identified themselves with the desires of the audience they sought.

Political and social humor characterized still other British humorists in the range of awareness of American writers. Albert Smith, a leading comic lecturer in London in the 1840s, developed the humorous travel narrative as a stage narrative. Several P. T. Barnum experiences appeared in his material, in fact, showing American influence on the British mind. Tom Hood's writings were widely known and admired, and Mark Lemon's *Punch* was ready to lampoon American as well as English subjects—a tendency that grew as the United States became increasingly embroiled in sectional conflict over slav-

---

6 Michael Heffernan [Samuel Ferguson], *Father Tom and the Pope: Or a Night at the Vatican* (New York: Moorhead, Simpson & Bond, 1868), 56–67, with an "Anti-Preface" by Frederick S. Cozzens.

ery. Sydney Smith, who was not related to Albert and was of greater literary stature, established in his writings a tone that seems to have had transatlantic impact. His question "Who reads an American book?" in the *Edinburgh Review* caused Americans to assert a cultural identity in the 1820s and 1830s and was a focal point of concern about a national literature. His political irony, his antagonism toward puns, and his belief that humor was based on incongruity that gave way to higher feelings of tenderness, respect, and compassion seem to have been influential in legitimizing later English and American humorists.[7]

The literary humor of the Northeast consequently had a variety of modes in which to appear. George William Curtis' humorous essays in the 1850s were modeled directly after Thackeray's "Snob" papers. *Potiphar Papers* (1854) and a novel, *Prue and I* (1856), were both published as books after appearing in *Putnam's Magazine*. Potiphar wishes that gilt could be turned into gold, and sugar candy into common sense in his American Vanity Fair society. Religious hypocrisy and national chauvinism are burlesqued. When, after discoursing eloquently on the blood of martyrs as the seed of the church, the Reverend Cream Cheese asks Mrs. Potiphar for a little more breast of chicken, Potiphar has to race, nauseated, from the table. Social snobbery is modified to the American scene as Potiphar resents the "unpatriotic" label attached to anyone who does not follow the "spirit of the time"—to Thackeray "Fashion"—in building large homes in the suburbs.[8] English social burlesque, in other words, proved adaptable to the American experience.

The northeastern humorists benefited from the English in several ways. Washington Irving, although heavily influenced by German romanticism, found ready acceptance by the English for his urbane local tales. Closer to the yankee tradition, Sam Slick, T. C. Haliburton's Down-East clockmaker, was an amalgam of folk heroes of the North and West. Although Jack Downing and Davy Crockett, both

---

7 See [Sydney Smith], *The Wit and Wisdom of Sydney Smith* (New York: G. P. Putman's Sons, n.d.), 303–307.

8 Edward Cary, *George William Curtis* (Boston: Houghton Mifflin, 1894), 95. [George W. Curtis], *The Potiphar Papers* (New York: G. P. Putnam, 1854), 1–10, 52, 97–134.

extremely popular in the 1830s, may both have contributed elements to Haliburton's creation, *The Attaché; Or Sam Slick in England* (1843-1844) extended his yankee adventures across the Atlantic. Nova Scotian Haliburton was thus writing a species of North American humor, cosmopolitan in nature and pointed toward an international as well as a regional framework.

The outstanding political humorists of the pre-Civil War era were almost exlusively northern—Seba Smith and James Russell Lowell being the most evident. Major Jack Downing was invented by Smith in 1830 to criticize the doings of the Maine legislature. Elements in the Downing letters are burlesques of the Crockett type prominent since 1827. In addition, overt comment on the irrational behavior of the legislators could be voiced through the yankee backwoodsman, and Downing also applies his yankee pragmatism to the social mores of Portland. Newspapers, like rum, are accused of making folks see double. Parvenu merchants adopt expensive social habits and fail. Although the cases seem much alike in Smith's Portland, Maine, and Longstreet's Charleston, Smith's satire is abstracted from the local scene-painting of regionalism; instead, general ethics are applied to politics. Social customs rather than local color receive the most attention. Lowell combined literary and political elements with New England traits more expansively than Smith, and he saw himself as more responsible toward national policy. Features of Lowell's letters appear literary; the press notices prefixed to the first edition of *The Biglow Papers* burlesque current publishing practices; the introduction to the second series discusses yankee dialect and "old" versus "new" language, making a case for plain speaking. Sut Lovingood's dialect is close to Lowell's Yankee Speech, but when Lowell names a successor, he is the Reverend Petroleum V. Nasby, and he is named so that political satire will have full justice done it, according to Lowell. In fact, Lowell is interested in yankee vernacular as a tool for criticizing slavery and the Mexican-American war. Even the apolitical "The Courtin'" was connected to this purpose by its inclusion in the introduction to the second series of *The Biglow Papers*. Lowell insisted that "high and even refined sentiment may coexist with the shrewder and more comic elements of the yankee character;"⁹ it is the opposite tendency from the southwestern humorists. Vernacular speech and comic material can directly express ethical and moral positions, even when framing devices parallel to those found in southwestern fiction are employed.

The northeastern experience was diverging rapidly from the southern experience of the 1830–1860 period. In the North, as late as the 1850s, humorous hunting adventures were as popular as J. P. Kennedy's southern sketches were in his own region. Henry William Herbert's *The Warwick Woodlands*, hunting stories by "Frank Forrester" set in Orange County, New Jersey, twenty years earlier, had at least two editions in 1845 and 1851. Two gentlemen, their Yorkshire servant, and a local hostler named Tom Draw, the latter characters speaking in their own dialects, hunt through the Warwick vales for game, indulging in comic repartee at the same time. As a northern writer, Herbert seems to regard his "homeland" with feelings as intense as any southerner's, but he identifies changes unknown in the old Southwest:

It is almost a painful task to read over and revise this chapter. The "twenty years ago" is too keenly visible to the mind's eye in every line. Of the persons mentioned in its pages, more than one have passed away from the world forever; and even the natural features of rock, wood, and river, in other countries so vastly more enduring than their perishable owners, have been so much altered by the march of improvement. Heaven save the mark! That the traveller up the Erie railroad, will certainly not recognize in the description of the vale of Ramapo, the hill-sides all denuded of their leafy honors, the bright streams denuded by unsightly mounds and changed into foul stagnant pools, the snug country tavern deserted for a huge barnlike depot, and all the lovely sights and sweet harmonies of nature defaced and drowned by the deformities consequent on a railroad, by the disgusting roar and screech of the steam-engine.

One word to the wise! Let no man be deluded by the following pages, into the setting forth for Warwick *now* in search of sporting. These things are strictly as they were *twenty years ago*! Mr. Seward, in his zeal for the improvement of Chatauque and Cattaraugus, has certainly destroyed the cock-shooting of Orange county. A sportman's benison to him therefore!¹⁰

---

9 James Russell Lowell, "Introduction [to *The Biglow Papers, Second Series*]" in *The Poetical Works of James Russell Lowell* (Boston: Houghton Mifflin, 1882), 227, 228.
10 [Henry William Herbert,] *The Warwick Woodlands* (Philadelphia: T. B. Peterson, 1850) 16–17.

Although a footnote to Herbert's book, the changes outlined here were the reality for later northern humorists. Their consciousness had to be directed away from the countryside and its local figures, and towards a more generalized urban and literary milieu consistent with the industrial expansion of the North and corresponding political involvements, here identified with Mr. Seward. Violent action and hunting experiences ceased to be major subject matters. Expanding population made social ethics a more pressing matter. Herbert's anger toward the railroad as an agent of geographical change was transferred by later comedians to the railroad as a corporate phenomenon in the social setting.

Social patterns in the North changed rapidly. Ferment was caused by urbanization, industrialization, and changing economic relationships. The middle class, expanding more rapidly than in the South, was keenly interested in labor organizations, public schools, libraries, and a variety of topics relating to the quality of life and social manners. Transportation facilities were expanding. Political parties with ward organizations were increasingly evident in the cities. George P. Morris' "'The Monopoly' and 'The People's Line'" (1839) is an example of the sort of comic story that treats northern subject matter.[11] A yankee and a Dutchman compete for a Long Island stagecoach line. One figure is a Jacksonian upstart; the other represents tradition, loyalty, and quality, however unprogressive. Both cut fares until they finally pay passengers to ride with their respective lines—and go out of business: the railroad replaces them. The story is as comic as any in the southwestern tradition, but differs from that tradition markedly. No joy is taken in conflict, which is mutually destructive. Commercial battle replaces violence. Rather than focusing on a single episode, the story follows a process in time and draws a social point from it, not by inference, but in the literal outcome of the story.

Northern humorists, unlike the southerners, had already discovered a complex urban experience before the Civil War. As early as 1838 Joseph C. Neal's *Charcoal Sketches*, owing a debt to Geoffrey Crayon's Knickerbocker humor, provided a sort of *Georgia Scenes* of

---

[11] The story is reprinted in William E. Burton (ed.), *The Cyclopedia of Wit and Humor* (New York: Appleton, 1875 [1858]), 154–56.

the northern city. The character of a rough urban type, much less polished than Longstreet's "Native Georgian" and much less rambunctious than the bull-roaring flatboatman, appears in "Orson Dabbs, the Hittite": "Instead of stumping an antagonist by launching out his cash (making a bet), Dabbs shakes a portentious fist under his nose, and the affair is settled; the recusant must either knock under or be knocked down, which, according to our hero, is all the same in Dutch."[12] "Rocky Smalt; or, the Dangers of Imitation" is a sort of urban "Georgia Theatrics," and the spoils-seeking political worker makes his appearance in "Peter Brush, the Great Used Up." These Philadelphia "Hard Cases" belong to the city world of politics and political rhetoric. Such concerns emerge even more markedly after the Civil War, but Neal's Peter Brush, sitting on a curb, laments his experiences along lines that anticipate later literary comedians:

A long time ago, my ma used to put on her specks and say "Peter, my son, put not your trust in princes;" and from that day to this I have n't done any thing of the kind, because none on 'em ever wanted to borry nothing of me: and I naver see a prince or a king—but one or two, and they have been rotated out of office—to borry nothing of them. Princes! pooh!—Put not your trust in politicianers—them's my sentiments. You might just as well try to hold an eel by the tail. I do n't care which side they're on, for I've tried both, and I know. Put not your trust in Politicianers, or you'll get a hyst.[13]

Peter's ambivalence about democratic rhetoric, attributed to the unlikely source of his maternal training, is both a burlesque of Peter for his naïveté and a satire on politics, for Peter admits that he changes parties himself for spoils. It shows, however, a much broader milieu than Philadelphia, Pennsylvania. The sketch is literary not only in the nonregionalized vulgar dialect but also in the level of thought. It is concerned not with local politics as such but rather with social precept, personal naïveté, and the generalized worldly corruption that dominates the venality of the speaker. Although the forms of the sketches vary, there is enough consistency to cause the "Editor's Table" of the New York *Knickerbocker Magazine* to reprint most of the "Peter Brush" episode, cited here, as an example of Neal's best

12 Joseph C. Neal, *Charcoal Sketches* (Philadelphia: Carey and A. Hart, 1838), 33–34.
13 Quoted from the New York *Knickerbocker Magazine*, L (August, 1857), 197.

humor—significant "American" humor—in an 1857 article.[14] The ethical themes of the "Peter Brush" piece, in fact, are the major themes of American literary comedy for the next forty or fifty years.

The various humorous traditions before the Civil War era offered a variety of modes and themes. The southwestern emphasized local color and characterization and employed short framed anecdotes. It was philosophically conservative. English humor treated character more broadly, creating unreal situations using realistic diction in characterization. The status of the English writers suggested the possibility of serious literary pretensions for this comic mode. Northeastern humor could be overtly political; political satire was directed at regional and national policies; the local's yankee pragmatism was granted dignity. Appealing to the middle class, authors made subject matter increasingly urban and, especially with the advent of the literary comedians, increasingly egalitarian.

Mark Twain as a literary comedian developed elements from each of these traditions into his own voice. Seeking commercial success and social acceptance in the Northeast, he developed his own egalitarian humor along compatible lines. Southwestern local color and English fancifulness expanded the comic moments of characterization into narrative episodes. Twain's novels mixed these elements in burlesque, in local color, and in melodrama in various proportions. His humor combined with Populist morality to achieve a personalized fictional form, and the form made him famous. The American popular audience bought Twain's novels; the British awarded him academic honors; and American critics came to find him uniquely representative of the American heartland—after they outdistanced the myopia caused by his origins in the popular form. Until now, only the literary comedy that helped express his ethical vision has been denied proper recognition as a vital part of his writing.

---

14 "Editor's Table," *Knickerbocker Magazine*, L (August, 1857), 194–95, relates Neal tangentially to Mrs. Partington, whose English forerunner is identified, in turn, as Mrs. Ramsbottom from the London newspaper *John Bull*.

TWO

Literary Comedy

THROUGH VERBAL HUMOR American literary comedy expressed the ethics of the rising northern and midwestern middle class. The literary comedians were professional literary men, and they sought financial success as writers as well as literary recognition. B. P. Shillaber, editor of the *Carpet-Bag*, a notable humorous weekly of the 1850s, is the father of the movement. Twain gave considerable credit to John Phoenix, George Horatio Derby, as another originator of the mode. The literary comedians of the Civil War era —Artemus Ward, Petroleum V. Nasby, and Orpheus C. Kerr—were the authors who defined the movement for later readers, however, and with whom Twain was in most immediate contact in the formative years of his career. Artemus Ward's commercially successful combination of comic wit, American social ethics, and platform persona was the most significant product of the movement. Ward's synthesis, in its turn, contributed directly to Twain's formation of his own persona.

Some hint of the changes in the northern environment has already been given. No less striking were the attempts to formulate social ethics in the North prior to the Civil War, not only in terms of slavery and emancipation, but in terms of American social experience generally. Horace Mann argued that free education for all children was a matter of political economy and moral responsibility. The human mind was to be the richest resource of the Massachusetts commonwealth. Horace Bushnell declared that children were to be loved from their earliest years, rather than treated as sinners to be converted at maturity. In the 1830s, the Grimke sisters attacked inequities between the sexes, including unequal pay for men and women schoolteachers, and decried the situation of the southern female slave. Increasing emphasis was being placed on the value of the individual and the responsibility of society for his moral status.

Personal ethics and commercial ethics developed in corresponding but not identical ways. As the large cities in the North expanded, village life and family customs were made more problematical. Some students of the culture have found the home and the marketplace to represent opposing values. Competition and materialism conflicted with domestic spiritual ideals. *Reveries of a Batchelor*, by "Ik. Marvel," showed this split in 1850, and resolved it by having Marvel remain a bachelor to avoid home constraints. The same dichotomy was still subject to burlesque in Marietta Holley's *Samantha* series from 1870 through the 1890s. Sam Slick's yankee traits might seem appropriate to this modern experience, but the concept of social Darwinism that finally emerged left little room for neighborly soft soda. Corporate competitiveness was more ruthless than a circuiting yankee trader would find possible. P. T. Barnum's career expanded the role of the sharper so that it included moral dimensions as well as practical ones, and his mixture of commercialism and moral humbug fascinated the American public for decades.[1] The literary comedians represent a response to these developments. The conflicts between institutional and private values ordered their humor and focused their irony. Humanistic practical Christianity conflicted with economic Darwinism, and public rhetoric blended incongruously with simple integrity of purpose.

Benjamin P. Shillaber occupies a central place in the adaptation of American humor to the changing village and urban situation. Both his comic creation, Mrs. Partington, and his short-lived comic paper, the *Carpet-Bag*, give clear evidence of a social and literary

---

[1] William Bridges, "Family Patterns and Social Values," reprinted in Henning Cohen (ed.), *The American Culture*, 254–56; Neal Harris, *Humbug: The Life of P. T. Barnum* (Boston: Little, Brown, 1973).

transition in progress. The Boston *Carpet-Bag* sold weekly to travelers on railroads and steamboats as far as Philadelphia, Cincinnati, St. Louis, and Louisville; clippings appeared in other journals, such as Orion Clemens' Hannibal (Mo.) *Journal*. Franklin Meine, one of the major critics of American comic magazines, identifies the journal as a connecting link between the American humorists of the 1840s and those who followed the Civil War; Shillaber could be mildly satiric in tone whereas Charles G. Halpine, associate editor from the middle of 1852, published relatively harsh burlesques of sentimental literature.[2] Several important comedians of the Civil War era first appeared nationally in the *Carpet-Bag* early in the 1850s. M. Quad, Ethan Spike (John Greenleaf Whittier's brother Matthew), and the sentimental poetess Louise Chandler Moulton supplied varied contributions. Halpine, John G. Saxe, G. H. Derby, Charles F. Browne (Artemus Ward), Samuel L. Clemens (Mark Twain), and others make this comic paper as important to the student of American humor as the more widely studied *Spirit of the Times* managed by Porter. The issue of May 1, 1852, is the landmark issue; in it appear the writers to become famous as John Phoenix, Artemus Ward, and Mark Twain.

Although Shillaber is often classed with the Down East humorists, Mrs. Partington shows elements of transition from localism to the cosmopolitanized urban comedy of the latter half of the century.[3] Her attempts to assimilate the changes in village life are testament to this position. Her whimsy denies the seriousness of the competitive world, and this theme will develop more fully in Phoenix, Ward, and finally, Twain. Yet, despite social complication, she is steadfastly humane and sympathetic; her simplicity subverts a more hypocritical society. Historically, the figure is based on a fictitious character in one of Sydney Smith's speeches to Parliament. She first appeared in the Boston *Post* in the 1840s, and volumes of her sayings were in print from 1854 through the 1890s.

"Partingtonian Philosophy," from the *Life and Sayings of Mrs. Partington*, shows most of the traits of the transitional form of literary

---

[2] Franklin J. Meine, "American Comic Periodicals: No. 1—*The Carpet-Bag*," *Collector's Journal*, IV (October–December, 1933), 411–13.
[3] Walter Blair, *Native American Humor* (San Francisco: Chandler, 1960 [1937]), 38–62.

comedy and even employs Mrs. Partington's own malapropisms less than usual.[4] In the sketch an opening aside criticized the railroads as an agent of change, following in a more homely way H. W. Herbert. The railroad, it seems, has displaced Mrs. Partington from her old homestead, where she used to keep a bountiful Thanksgiving holiday. Nor will she accept the Babylonish invention of Christmas, making Thanksgiving her only festival of the winter season. Thus, Mrs. Partington lives simply, at variance with modernity in changing religious practices and such corporate business interests as the railroad. A socially conservative individualist, she is set to celebrate the holiday in the old and simple way:

One year the gobbler had thus been penned, like a sonnet, with reference to Thanksgiving, and anticipations were indulged of the "good time coming"; but, alas! the brightest hopes must fade. The turkey, when looked for, was not to be found. It had been stolen away! Upon discovering her great loss, Mrs. P. was for a moment overcome with surprise—disconcerted; but the sun of her benevolence soon broke the clouds away, and spread over her features like new butter upon hot biscuit, and with a smile, warm with the feeling of her heart, she said—"*I hope they will find it tender!—I guess we can be thankful on pork and cabbage!*"

"Say, ye severest, what would ye have done" under such circumstances: You would, perhaps, have raved, and stamped, and swore, and made yourself generally ridiculous, besides perilling your soul in the excess of your anger. But Mrs. P. didn't, and there is where you and she differ. She stood calmly and tranquilly—a living lesson of philosophical patience under extreme difficulty. We cite this example that the world may profit by it.

The fashion of italicizing key lines disappeared under the influence of the deadpan monologue practiced by the platform humorists of the 1860s and 1870s. Otherwise, the piece is sophisticated. Common, or even vulgar, subject matter—petty thievery—is presented through an elevated voice that is itself capable of colloquial expression, in this case in the biscuit metaphor. The exaggerated metaphor suggests that the narrator is also a naif in the sense that he, like Mrs. Partington, seems unaware of the conventions that his obvious literary references show him anxious to emulate.

---

4 B. P. Shillaber, "Partingtonian Philosophy," *Life and Sayings of Mrs. Partington* (New York: J. C. Derby, 1854), 97–98.

Significantly, the tendency of the sketch is literary rather than political, and the humor is self-directed rather than satiric. The episode is commonplace and realistic in its setting but is without any sense of local genre painting. The character is integrated into the setting through such metaphoric references as *biscuit, pork*, and *cabbage*, which establish a relatively lower-class level of experience. Mrs. Partington herself is not materialistic and egocentric in her view of events—as suggested by the italicized lines—but is humanistic. She wishes well to all men, even thieves, and is also objective, recognizing that certain surrounding social events affect her basic existence only slightly. Ethics dominate plot action, for no events are actually seen in the piece, only the response of the central figure. It is a radically different perspective on experience from that offered by the southwestern preoccupation with action, as well as in its tendency to moralize events with complex ramifications. The backwoodsman might have urged patience on someone he defeated in a horse swap, but Mrs. Partington's assertion of her positive viewpoint is a passive acceptance of the specific events.

The humor of the Northeast thus combines personal feeling and social ethics in a moderately realistic social milieu. Small town or urban, it features railroads, churches, and other evidence of individual vulnerability to corporate experience. Whereas the narrator's euphemistic apostrophe to the reader is in part a serious injunction, the sketch is based on a "low" rather than an elevated form of experience, paralleled by the class of people who are its visible and invisible participants. The sketch is in a different and more cosmopolitan vein, in its treatment of characters, than are representative sketches of the southwestern humorists, Hooper's "Simon Suggs Attends a Camp Meeting" or Harris' Sut Livingood pieces, perhaps with one or two notable exceptions such as "Sut Lovingood's Sermon" on the "Catfish" tavern.

Shillaber encouraged a variety of literary modes, but maintained a humanistic perspective. He encouraged literary and travel burlesques in the *Carpet-Bag* which show the same antagonism to hypocrisy and social posturing as is credited to westerners like Harte and Twain in the 1860s. In addition to the Partington sayings, his

Blifkins Papers adopted Thackeray's mode, Americanizing the English source. Like other later literary comedians, his primary interest was in asserting an individual standard of achievement that was democratic rather than aristocratic. A commonplace figure like Mrs. Partington was ideal for this purpose. "Man" frequently figures as the touchstone of this ethic, meaning a complex of integrity and individualism. One of the clearest statements of Shillaber's general philosophy, in a poem that applies to Mrs. Partington as well as to the male sex, is the occasional poem "The Mound-Builders" (1871) in which he attacks fashion, quackery, and political greed. Instead, he urges, falling back on the Indian-mound image,

> Stick to your mound persistently and true,
> And dred no failure in the great review,
> When angels, searching for its inner plan,
> Shall say, approvingly, HERE WAS A MAN![5]

To some degree this message figures in most of Shillaber's writings; the didactic tendency is one of the chief points of transition from the southwesterners on one hand and the yankee political satirists on the other to the more universal stance of the literary comedians.

In simple terms, the literary comedians followed the motif. It provided a major concern to their readers, the rising middle class. The opposite pole from this concept of virtue was the subject of burlesque, which figures extensively in the description of social experience by the comedians. Charles D. Warner's *Backlog Studies* (1873) provides a summary of the personal characteristics and social ethics of this opposing type: "There is a man, whom we all know, who built a house that cost a quarter of a million dollars, and furnished it for another like sum, who does not know anything more about architecture, or painting, or books, or history, than he cares for the rights of those who have not so much money as he has. I heard him once, in a foreign gallery, say to his wife, as they stood in front of a famous picture by Reubens: 'That is the Rape of the Sardines!'"[6] Mark Twain's "Vandal Abroad" lecture concentrated on the same type. The come-

---

5 B. P. Shillaber, *Lines in Pleasant Places* (Chelsea: By the Author, 1874), 25.
6 Charles Dudley Warner, *Backlog Studies* (Boston: James R. Osgood, 1873), 16.

dians approved of the self-made man only when his lack of aristocratic graces was matched by a corresponding egalitarian sympathy and humility. In the Warner passage, the equation is explicit; in almost all literary comedy it is implicit in one way or another.

Twain occasionally called George Horatio Derby the father of American humor. Derby combined the sensitivity of the moral humorist with the literary persona that resembled Thackeray's characters and was consequently popular in the 1850s. He followed Shillaber in technique, using a burlesque elevation of tone to describe the commonplace experiences of a figure who is frequently the naïve victim of his social surroundings. Derby himself vanished into Phoenix. As "John Phoenix," Derby was the first American humorist to be associated with the Far West, and his exaggerated imitations and burlesque slapstick comedy have been seen by critics as an identifying factor for the whole of western American humor. As George R. Stewart points out, identifying Phoenix's manner as more flamboyant than that of easterners does not mean that his humor was crude or directed at bumpkins; his San Francisco audience was sophisticated and highly literate, and his writings appeared frequently in the New York *Knickerbocker* as well.[7] *Phoenixiana* (1856) treats astronomy, California cities, grammar, and newspaper editing—subjects appealing to a rising middle and even upper middle class—in its own characteristic combination of exaggerated anecdotes, burlesque diction, and naïvely shrewd posing. Phoenix seems to have been, for this audience, the first of the literary comedians who combined actual and fictive personalities.

Phoenix the character appears inept at dealing with the ordinary problems of social intercourse. Sailing to California by way of the Isthmus, his international travels place him in social circles that his

---

7 Louis Budd, "Mark Twain Talks Mostly about Humor and Humorists," *Studies in American Humor*, I (April, 1974), 15. Bret Harte states this premise emphatically in "Artemus Ward" and then modifies it in his later essay "American Humor" in Charles M. Kozlay (ed.), *Stories and Poems and Other Uncollected Writings* (Boston: Houghton Mifflin, 1914), 126–28, 225–31; Most English critics have agreed with this definition. Mody C. Boatright, *Folk Laughter on the American Frontier* (New York: MacMillan, 1949), 87–88, has qualified his point, however, by noting that the manner of the exaggeration is really more significant than the mere inflation of terms—a significant point in understanding not only western humor but the literary comedians as well. George R. Stewart, Jr., *John Phoenix, Esq.: The Veritable Squibob* (New York: Henry Holt, 1937), 198.

innocence unfits him to enter. In the *Squibob Papers* (1865), he appears in the role of cosmopolitan innocent; humble himself, he cannot keep pace with parvenus who lack his modesty. Presumably he belongs to the world rather than to any specific locality, but he still holds the manner of the naif: "The officers were all there, moreover, radiant in brass coats and blue buttons—I mean blue buttons and brass coats—and looked divinely. One of them accidentally trod on my toe, but before I could utter the exclamation of anguish that I was about to give vent to, he said so sweetly, 'Don't apologise', that the pain left me in a moment."[8] Most of the elements which appear in Shillaber's "Partingtonian Philosophy" reappear here—a sophisticated tone is coupled with the simplicity of the central character. The central character is a victim rather than a victimizer; the scene is not motivated by the author's romantic desire to show local peculiarities but rather by his generalizing interest in social interactions. The passage is an advance over the Partington pieces in that it is a burlesque of the author himself as traveler; the narrative is unified. Through dramatic irony, based on words such as *divinely, radiant,* and *sweetly* applied to Phoenix's antagonist, the author indicates the naif's inability to account for his personal discomfort in the situation. Despite his reputation as a rogue, P. T. Barnum, the yankee showman, portrayed himself similarly in his *Life* (1855). Artemus Ward's description of a quadrille in his *Works* is a close analogue to the scene from Phoenix, and other parallels can be found in later humorists.

The comic journalists of the Civil War, each in their own idiosyncratic manner, brought the nascent middle class ethics of the Shillaber-Phoenix pose to bear on the national experience as understood by the North and West. Lincoln's rise to prominence allows an identification of the sources of their appeal.[9] Although the old party alignments were breaking down in the 1850s, particularly in the case of the traditional Whig party, the changing social conditions were masked by political compromises and obscured by rhetorical

---

[8] John Phoenix [George H. Derby], *The Squibob Papers* (New York: Carleton, 1865), 125.
[9] I am indebted to James F. Cox for this suggestion.

generalities. Both Lincoln and the literary comedians represented the new forces at work, declaring the rise of the democratic middle-class citizen to a position of social responsibility. The Civil War became the national focal point of the resulting issues.

Lincoln himself was a moderate. His reputation in Illinois prior to 1854 rested on his integrity and his rise from common roots. "Honest Abe" was a lawyer who would refuse cases that, though they could be won in law, were not based on the grounds of justice and equity. Evidence of his common origins was obvious in his history as a laborer, his skill as a log-splitter, and his fame as a humorous storyteller. In political life, the latter reputation was both asset and liability. It was a liability because it allowed him to be branded as vulgar and common; it was an asset because the irony and witty implication of the literary comedians was a useful part of his oratorical pose. His stories burlesqued hypocrisy, and his speeches inflated opponents' twisted logic and absurdity.

Jokes on honesty and ugliness, duty, and death contributed to Lincoln's fund of humor. Walking out on a case after discovering his client to be a fraud, Lincoln said, "Tell the judge that my hands are dirty and I've gone to wash them."[10] Challenged to a duel, he suggested cow dung for weapons. His politics as well as his pragmatism were illuminated by this humor. One example of his anecdotal affirmation of his faith in himself and the nation is noteworthy because it is cast in terms already used here. Shortly after he took office as president, he wrote to a friend using a metaphor based on Maelzel's chess player:

That reminds me of a man who prided himself greatly on his game of chess, having rarely been beaten. He heard of a machine called "The Automation Chess Player" which was beating everyone who played against it. So he went to try his skill with the machine. He lost the first game, so with a second and a third. Then, rising in astonishment from his seat, he walked around the machine and looked at it a few minutes. Then, stopping and pointing at it, he exclaimed, "There is a man in there."
Tell my friends there is a man in here.[11]

10 Keith W. Jennison, *The Humorous Mr. Lincoln* (New York: Bonanza Books, 1965), 23.
11 *Ibid.*, 87.

Shillaber and Ward used the same reference point, "a man," to distinguish the beliefs they valued, and Lincoln undoubtedly subscribed to the same popular sentiment that they expressed. For Lincoln as president, the application of such a principle meant cheap lands for farmers to earn an independent livelihood, tariffs to protect American workers from foreign competition, and belief in the Union as a political entity embodying democratic laws and Christian principles.

The literary comedians espoused the same values in their humor that Lincoln expressed in politics. It is small wonder that Lincoln himself found their humor so amusing. They described situations in which violent suffering, such as Sut Lovingood inflicted, offered no solution to the problem at hand. Life held moral objectives and was lived within social boundaries. In newspapers throughout the North and Midwest, and in the same typefaces, literary comedy appeared in columns beside the political and commercial news of the day. Almost every literary comedian wrote an interview taking place between Lincoln and himself, and in some cases, as with C. G. Halpine's "Miles O'Reilly," the anecdotes they fabricated for Lincoln took on a life of their own.[12] Since the literary comedians wrote for a popular audience at a time when moral issues were fully intertwined with national politics, the uniformity between Lincoln's beliefs, and even his rhetorical materials, and their own is not surprising.

The literary comedians, of course, viewed their creations from a literary rather than a political viewpoint, although they frequently took on pressing issues. C. G. Leland identified himself with the abolitionist movement. Nasby and Kerr are notable primarily as Civil War comedians, but both attempted to develop careers beyond that identity. Only Ward and Twain found a way of uniting universals with specific events, and they did this through their cosmopolitanism. Prior to the war, most of the humorists identified themselves with the Democratic rather than the Republican party, as did many of their moderate readers in the North, but they strongly supported the threatened Union. Josh Billings was the most general of the moralists. He affirmed middle-class conservative virtues flatly: "Dutys

12 William Hanchett, *Irish: Charles G. Halpine in Civil War America* (Syracuse: Syracuse University Press, 1970), 91.

are privileges" and "Liberty iz a just mixture ov freedom, restraint, and protektion."[13] His anecdotes commented bemusedly on contemporary experience; animal fables were moralized upon; a series of comic Allminax provided his only sustained literary format, but his sales and popularity were both enormous in the late 1860s and early 1870s, and he clearly writes in the homiletic mode.

P. V. Nasby was created as a direct result of the agitation surrounding the abolition movement and the counterattacks by the proslavery forces in Ohio and Kansas. Once his originator, David Ross Locke, felt the issue to be "squeezed out" by Reconstruction, the *raison* of the figure was dissipated. Although one of his best recent biographers separates him entirely from the literary comedians on the grounds that he is a political satirist, his generalized caricatures identify him as a literary comedian, as in his tableau of Confedrit X-roads:[14] "I am at home, and glad am I that I am at home. Here in Kentucky, surrounded by Dimicrats, immersed a part of the time in my offishel dooties, and the balance uv the time in whiskey. With the privilege uv wallopin niggers, and the more inestimable and soothing privilege uv assisten in mobbin uv Northern Ablishnists, who are not yet all out uv the State, time passes pleasantly, and leaves no vain regrets. I alluz go to bed nites, feeling that the day hez not bin wasted." "Realism" is not at issue; the viewpoint is purposefully burlesque localism. "A Vision of the World," a framed dream-vision like some of Twain's work, offered an explanation of Locke's ethical viewpoint in the devil's explanation of Copperheads and southern politicians: "It takes a modritly smart man to be vishus enuff to come to me; he hez to hev sense enuff to distinguish between good and evil, cussidnis enuff to deliberately choose the latter, and brains enuff to do suthin startlin in that line."[15] In the Civil War, this description fitted what northerners felt about the South; in broader outlines, it is an inquiry into how a man stands as a man, just as Ward and Lin-

---

13 [Henry W. Shaw], *The Complete Works of Josh Billings* (New York: G. W. Dillingham, 1876), 270.

14 John M. Harrison, *The Man Who Made Nasby: David Ross Locke* (Chapel Hill: University of North Carolina Press, 1969), 4–5, 101–109.

15 Petroleum V. Nasby [David Ross Locke], *"Swingin Round the Cirkle"* (Boston: Lee and Shepard, 1867), 214.

coln proposed. Notably, the irony is connected to free will and choice in action, democratic principles.

On the lecture platform, Nasby spent part of his time personifying the southern fire-eater and the remainder explaining the evil in that viewpoint. The complete split in ethical pose represented a literary problem. As an author, he mused in interviews that although Billings was the worst speller, his own spelling was based on phonetic principles "much in advance of the civilization of the age"; he joked that of the books he started with, the Shakespeare was worn out but the Testament was as good as new.[16] But the literary pose could not be blended with the powerful Union and antislavery sentiments in the Nasby persona. Later, in his travel narrative, *Nasby in Exile*, his prose is bitter and sarcastic, burdened with newspaper factuality where Ward and Twain created semifictional adventure.

Orpheus C. Kerr was a more elevated and detached satirist than Nasby. A member of the New York bohemian circle of the period, Kerr was married to Adah Menken, whom Twain burlesqued for her pretentiously artistic near-nude scenes in "Mazeppa." He took a literary tone in burlesquing Union inaction and inefficiency. The army, it appeared, was composed of drunken poetasters; government agencies slept amidst cobwebs and dust—natural curiosities like mummies in neglected pyramids.[17] Kerr's "Letters" were the most whimsical and consciously literary of the comedians' products. The skeptic's viewpoint is mirrored in the vulgarized diction; action is even less believable than in Nasby; the interest is shifted toward the aesthetic and away from the ethical or national. Kerr thus represents one pole of the literary comedians' spectrum.

After the Civil War, Kerr, like the others, tried to write sustained fiction. The handful of novels he produced were only modestly successful; the last of them, which appeared in *Lippincott's Magazine* in 1884, is almost without trace of any literary humor. Kerr had articu-

---

16 Newark (N.J.) *Courier* quoted in Frederic Hudson, *Journalism in the United States, from 1690 to 1872* (New York: Harper & Brothers, 1873), 692–94; Harrison, *Nasby*, 104. According to A. B. Paine, *Mark Twain: A Biography* (New York: Harper & Brothers, 1912), 426, Jack Van Nostrand wrote to Twain that he saw two books in a cabin in Colorado, *The Bible* and *The Innocents Abroad*, "the former in good repair." Perhaps the influence flowed through Twain.

17 [Robert H. Newell], *The Orpheus C. Kerr Papers* (New York: Carleton, 1866), 254.

lated the problem in sustaining his type of literary humor as early as 1867, posed in terms of *Lothair* in Kerr's introductory essay to *The Cloven Foot*. Although Kerr saw his audience as corresponding to Disreali's, he recognized that an American readership suited to the "high" style was a much narrower public. He was consequently reduced to throwing blame on the physical, social, and artistic crudity of the country for the lack of a higher order of imaginative fiction, the sort he wished to produce himself. Without a "permanent romantic background" in America, the novelist of high society could only be a didactic social essayist or a satirist of shopkeeper parvenus. The Old South might have offered a background, he conceded, but he would rather treat the discontinuities of wealth and poverty in the great cities.[18] He could not exploit this outlet, and a decade passed before any other writers attempted to. Also, the temperance writers and other do-gooders had preempted much of the territory for their tract literature and the potential audience must have been a small one.

Artemus Ward was the outstanding literary comedian of the 1860s, and his reputation lasted well beyond his death in 1867. Nasby's political power and Kerr's literary consciousness were fused in his expressions of middle-class northern sentiment. He was pragmatic, humorously vulgar, intolerant of radical fringe groups only insofar as they were harmful extremists; he was concerned with maintaining his own income; he saw the Constitution as superior to the issue of abolition on either side, a stance very close to Lincoln's. He was moderate, and his humor endorsed moderation and personal integrity just as Shillaber had in the patient Mrs. Partington. In pose, too, he attained flexibility which Nasby merely breached and Kerr never attempted. Although he disavowed outright didacticism, he took humor to be moral and serious, consistent with the qualities of a "man" as previously defined; he wanted his voice to be meaningful.

Most of Ward's letters have an ethical dimension. Public figures should have enlightened concern; his showman, a transparent fraud to a skeptical public, is nonetheless capable of detecting other falsi-

---

18 Orpheus C. Kerr, "Apology," *The Cloven Foot* (New York: Carleton, 1870), 10–15.

fications by virtue of his own skepticism. So he interviews Brigham Young on polygamy and burlesques the free lovers, Shakers, and other enthusiasts. His comment on the Shakers is characteristic: "Shakers was all goin kerslap to the Promist Land, and nobody want goin to stand at the gate to bar 'em out, if they did they'd git run over" (43). Ward responds to their physical denial by advising that their daughters marry manly young suitors—a practical and conventional suggestion that stresses natural intimacy between individuals.

As Walter Blair notes, in *Horse Sense in American Humor*, the practical showman who appears so eager to gain patrons actually drives the free lovers at Oberlin away with a sermon, and Ward elsewhere delivers moralistic rebukes to spiritualists, women's rights fanatics, and the spoilsmen surrounding Lincoln; he forthrightly advises the Prince of Wales and Prince Napoleon and stands uncompromisingly by the threatened flag, both in Dixie and in Baldinsville: "The country may go to the devil, but I won't!" (67).[19] Lincoln loved Ward's humor for this reason. Lincoln too had to reject extremist political and moral issues in attempting to sustain the Constitution, as he rejected Horace Greeley's demands for abolition in 1862. Lincoln and Ward are united in their political idealism; and when Ward depicted his visit to Lincoln, his most prominent statement is "I have no politics." Ward does not come to collect political debts. An outsider to political spoils, he attacks the officeseekers who, in the burlesque, are even sliding down on Old Abe through the chimney (109–13). Much of Ward's humor is maintained within this ideological framework; if "refined" northeasterners missed the ideology, Confederates and their Bill Arp bitterly recognized it.

Ward's comments are really universal, going beyond the Civil War in philosophy if not in subject matter. The naïve materialist is a moralist who confronts high-principled neighbors with low-principled humanity: "Sez Perfesser Peck, 'Mister Ward, I don't know 'bout this bizness. What air your sentiments?' Siz I, 'I hain't got any.'" Ward adds: "The pint is, can I hav your Hall by payin a fair price? You air

---

19 Artemus Ward [Charles F. Browne], *The Complete Works of Artemus Ward* (London: Chatto & Windus, 1922). All references are to this edition unless otherwise noted and are included in the text.

full of sentiments. That's your lay, while I'm a exhibiter of startlin curiosities" (59-60). The cacography works innocently and perfectly ("air full" of sentiments), while the polarity between worldly work and moral rigidity is only superficially negative, since a higher order of liberalism is involved and "fair" is the point of negotiation.

Ward's interview with the Prince of Wales was an instant national success. Appearing in September, 1860, just before he moved to New York to work for *Vanity Fair*, it made Ward nationally known. William Dean Howells, the arbiter of American literary realism in the later nineteenth century, remembered the "universal joy" with which the piece was greeted.[20] Although using contemporary news as its subject matter, the burlesque was directed at formal conventions in international politics:

We sot & tawked there sum time abowt matters & things, & bimeby I axed him how he liked bein Prince as fur as he'd got.
"To speak plain, Mister Ward," he sed, "I don't much like it. I'm sick of all this bowin & scrapin & crawlin & hurrain over a boy like me. I would rather go through the country quietly & enjoy myself in my own way, with the other boys, & not be made a Show of to be garped at by everybody. When the *people* cheer me I feel pleased, fur I know they mean it, but if these one-horse offishuls cood know how I see threw all their moves & understan exackly what they air after, & knowd how I larft at 'em in private, theyd stop kissin my hands & fawnin over me as they now do." (98)

In answer to the Prince's democratic spirit, with its emphasis on "the *people*," Ward makes a burlesque affirmation of the Prince's humanity which corresponds to the idea of manliness characteristic of the literary comedians: "Albert Edard, I must go, but previs to doin so I will obsarve that you soot me. Yure a good feller, Albert Edard, & tho I'm agin Princes as a gineral thing, I must say I like the cut of your Gib. When you git to be King try and be as good a man as yure muther has bin! Be just & be Jenerus, espeshully to showmen." (99). Several analogues come to mind for this brief exchange. The Prince's conversation with Ward suggests the plot that Twain was to develop in *The Prince and the Pauper*, an appealingly democratic viewpoint

---

20 William Dean Howells, "Introduction" to *Artemus Ward's Best Stories* (New York: Harper & Brothers, 1912), ix.

28 MARK TWAIN AS A LITERARY COMEDIAN

toward commonplace experience. The showman's response re-echoes Dickens' showman Sleery in *Hard Times*, and Ward digresses even further as that figure would have.[21] Most important, however, is the continued emphasis, in burlesque, on "being a man," and the sketch makes clear that Ward understands and admires this trait and that he will even accept a monarch who has it. Both the Prince and Ward hold "objective" viewpoints, a fictional equivalent of the deadpan; they are "good fellers" distinguished from a procession of "noosenses" trying to start a religious war and from the venal politicians already described. The sentiment is northern; although it may be "conservative," it is genteelly idealistic; it is democratic: a social viewpoint is dramatized in a partly real but mostly fictional format.

Reality and the detachment from reality form the major component of Ward's comic vision, separating him from the ferociously attached Nasby and the ironically aloof Kerr. Describing the war fever in Baldinsville, he declared, "If I'm drafted I shall resign . . . everywheres I've bin inrold" (157). The naif withdraws himself from enthusiasm, as with moderates everywhere, but without withdrawing himself from his basic ethical position. His promoral but seemingly antiwar statements are thus as consistent with his pro-Union sentiments as Lincoln's pro-Union and antislavery beliefs proved to be during the course of the Civil War. The excesses of the opposition provide the antagonist to the objective humanitarian. Ward depicted them in burlesque as nuisances; Twain was later to melodramatize them as the political and religious fomenters of atrocities.

---

21 Sleery, in Dickens' *Hard Times* (1954), is representative of the characteristics that attached themselves to the showman as a literary type. Kindly and sympathetic to the requirements of human nature, he is also penny-wise and disregardful of conventions of middle-class manners. Boasting that he is "known all over England, and alwayth paythe ith way" (page 36 in the New York: Holt, Rinehart and Winston, 1963, edition), Sleery pleads to Sissy Jupe, "But if, when you're grown up and married and well-off, you come upon any horthe-riding ever, don't be hard upon it, don't be crothe with it, give it a Bethpeak if you can, and think you might do wurth. People must be amuthed, Thquire, thomehow . . . they can't be alwayth a working, nor yet they can't be alwayth a learning. Make the beth of uth; not the wurtht" (38). Sleery's asthmatic "th" sound foreshadows Ward's cacography, as well, although any direct relationship is speculative.

THREE

Artemus Ward as Pioneer Funnyman

ARTEMUS WARD was the preeminent literary comedian in America prior to Mark Twain's emergence as a serious humorist during the 1870s and 1880s. His career established the possibility of a writer of literary comedy enjoying the acceptance of the genteel and the economic satisfaction of general popularity. Because of Charles F. Browne's own aspirations to literary achievement, the figure of "Artemus Ward" was a double figure in a state of constant change until Browne's death in 1867, and it offered significant potential for further refinement as a literary persona. The figure developed through a literary character who embodied the ethics of his creator—sometimes directly and sometimes in a burlesque of opposing attitudes—in a "vulgar" or popular and slangy voice. Browne the platform lecturer was considerably more cosmopolitan than his literary persona, and he was accepted into the circles of the New England literati early in his career in this guise. Finally, Ward actively encouraged other literary comedians and was the focal point of national and even international interest beyond anything accorded an American humorous writer with the exception of Washington Irving.

Charles Farrar Brown[e] was born in Waterford, Maine, on April 26, 1834. His boyhood was spent in typical Yankee Congregationalist surroundings. Schools met the year round, and Browne could not have gone untouched by formal education even though his schoolmates remembered him as a prankster who never cared greatly for schoolwork. Although Browne himself commented that he had only "about enough education for a signboard,"[1] his apprenticeship as a printer compensated. And it came early, for his father died when he was thirteen and his close relationship with his mother had to give way to the work of a typesetter.

Like Mark Twain and William Dean Howells, Browne's newspaper apprenticeship gave him considerable experience in the journalism of the late 1840s and early 1850s. He set type for five papers and, as was generally the case, had opportunities to write paragraphs. One of these already evidences the cosmopolitan tone of later writings; burlesquing the rivalry between the Norway and Paris, Maine, newspapers, he exalts, "A large improvement has been made in our office. We have bored a hole in the bottom of our sink and set a sloppail under it. What will the hell hounds over to Paris think now."[2]

Browne moved to Boston in 1851, becoming an office boy for B. P. Shillaber's comic magazine the *Carpet-Bag*. He first appeared in the *Carpet Bag* as "Lieut. Chubb" on December 27, 1851, and made nine more contributions in 1852. Browne's "Oil vs. Vinegar; or the Rantankerous Lecturer"[3] and Clemens' "The Dandy Frightening the Squatter" belong to the same genre. Browne's scene is set in B–, Maine, and the central character is a yankee, "Uncle Thad," rather than a raw-boned Mississippian, but the vernacular characterization is very similar: a vulgar countryman gets the better of a "sophisticated" poser, and naturalness is shown as superior to social manners. There is no evidence of political satire, but the artificial quality of some 1850s humor like *The Fudge Papers* is avoided through direct sentences and relatively plain words.

Between 1853 and 1857, Browne traveled through New York State and into Ohio working as a journeyman printer. His first reputation

1 Don C. Seitz, *Artemus Ward: A Biography and Bibliography* (New York: Harper & Brothers, 1919), 230–36. Dates in this chapter are taken from Seitz unless there is reason for dispute. The *e* on Browne was added in 1861. All references to Ward's writings are given as page numbers in the text for *The Complete Works of Artemus Ward* (London: Chatto & Windus, 1922). Other references are footnoted individually. Clifton Johnson, "Recollections of Artemus Ward," *Overland Monthly*, 2nd Ser., LXVII (January, 1916), 31.
2 Johnson, "Recollections," 32.
3 Identified by James C. Austin, *Artemus Ward* (New York: Twayne, 1964), 24, 26, 28, who concluded that their short, clear sentences made them attractive to Shillaber.

was established at Toledo as a local reporter; he began working at the Cleveland (Ohio) *Daily Plain Dealer* in November, 1857, and rapidly established a reputation for caustic wit. The *Plain Dealer*, owned and edited by twenty-four-year-old Joseph W. Gray, was the major Democratic newspaper in the West, comparable to Horace Greeley's Republican New York *Tribune*; it was claiming a circulation of 65,000 by 1860. Rambunctious and outspoken, it carried lurid local crimes, humorous columns, and commercial news mixed together. *Mots* such as Browne's comment that a rival paper's reporter was so ugly that he had to get up at night in order to rest his face were read and clipped throughout the West.[4]

By the winter of 1857–1858, Browne was well established in Cleveland, had identified himself with the theatrical culture of the city, and was producing gleeful literary hoaxes for the pages of the *Plain Dealer*. Ward's hoaxes had the grotesque flavor and exaggerated tone associated with western journalism. One of them concerns the escape of a dangerous man-eating hyena in Paulding County, Ohio. The hyena, Ward claimed, killed a German named Paffenberg, injured several others, and "disinterred two newly buried bodies and mostly devoured them." Later in the article, Browne began correcting details, one at a time, until every fact had been retracted, but he avoided acknowledging that the story was a lie.[5]

Artemus Ward, the old showman, was born by combining literary hoaxes like the Paffenberg story with newspaper commonplaces, the puff, the letter to the editor, and a new element. The personality of P. T. Barnum, who had popularized himself as the purveyor of "moral" tent shows throughout the East, Midwest, and South to supplement his American museum, provided the vulgarly hypocritical showman of the Artemus Ward pieces. By the middle 1850s almost every American and most Englishmen were aware of P. T. Barnum's career. Barnum was actively creating his own legend in this period, and *The Life of P. T. Barnum, Written by Himself* was pub-

4 *Ibid.*, 32, from J. W. Gray's comments in the *Plain Dealer*, October 15, 1860; C. C. Ruthrauff, "Artemus Ward in Cleveland," *Scribner's Monthly*, XVI (October, 1878), 787.
5 Frank Luther Mott, "The Beginnings of Artemus Ward," *Journalism Quarterly*, XVIII (June, 1941), 146.

lished in 1855. It chronicled his rise from humble yankee origins to acknowledged mastery in humbug, fraud, and chicanery. He also outlined his many successful campaigns, including Jenny Lind's tour of America, the exhibition of Washington's nursemaid Joice Heth (an admitted fraud), and General Tom Thumb's successful tour of the British Isles. His exposure of the devices and tricks he had used to arouse public interest—with great financial success to himself—infuriated reviewers of his book, but broadened sales to half a million copies.[6] Ward the old showman mentions Barnum's American museum a number of times in his letters, connecting himself with the myth as a lesser offspring of Barnum's entrepreneurial spirit.

Barnum's *Life* was a presentation of the showman's career revealing the element of hokum and humbug lying behind his successful exploitations of Joice Heth, the Feejee Mermaid, Tom Thumb, and even to some extent Jenny Lind. Beginning with anecdotes about yankee sharpers which disgusted most serious reviewers, Barnum gradually enlarges the scope of his autobiography to take in his moral and political aspirations, including his claim that even his fraudulent exhibits were justified by the elevating and instructive material for which they served as a drawing card:

The moral drama is now, and has been for several years, the principal feature of the Lecture Room of the American Museum.

Apart from the merit and interest of the performances, and apart from every thing connected with the stage, my permanent collection of curiosities is, without doubt, abundantly worth the uniform charge of admission to all the entertainment of the establishment, and I can there afford to be accused to "humbug" when I add such transient novelties as increase its attractions. If I have exhibited a questionable dead mermaid in my Museum, it should not be overlooked that I have also exhibited cameleopards, a rhinoceros, grisly bears, orang-outangs, great serpents, etc., about which there could be no mistake because they were alive; and I should hope that a little "clap-trap" occasionally, in the way of transparencies, flags, exaggerated pictures, and puffing advertisements, might find an offset in the wilderness of wonderful, instructive, and amusing realities.[7]

---

6 M. R. Werner, *Barnum* (New York: Harcourt, Brace, 1923), 212–15.
7 [P. T. Barnum], *The Life of P. T. Barnum, Written by Himself* (New York: Redfield, 1855), 225.

In a number of cases, Artemus Ward echoed Barnum's pretensions, explaining, "As I'm into the moral show bizniss myself, I ginrally go to Barnum's moral Museum" (80). He describes the attractions of his own show in the same terms as Barnum: "My Show is ekalled by few and exceld by none, embracin as it does a wonderful colleckshun of livin wild Beests of Pray, snaix in grate profushun, a endliss variety of life-size wax figgers & the only traned kangaroo in Americky—the most amoozin little cuss ever introjuced to a discriminatin public" (63). The vulgarization of Barnum's prose is only partly a rejection of Barnum, particularly aimed at his commercialization and vulgarization of knowledge—the business side of the figure. Barnum's hostility toward slavery is never burlesqued, even though Ward was negative on the emancipation issue before the war broke out. When Ward has a Britisher confront the old showman with the claim, "Sir, you air not a human bein—you hav no existents —yure a Myth!" (97), he is actually paying tribute to the yankee Barnum's refusal to be cowed by British manners, and in this case by British royalty, as well as to the stature of Barnum's reputation.

There are also precedents in Barnum's life for a marked Americanism and an enthusiasm for democratic institutions. Barnum recounts with pride his first visit to the national Capitol, and later tells of the meeting between Jenny Lind and President Fillmore, as well as dwelling on calls paid her by Webster, Clay, Cass, and Benton. Barnum lectured on the temperance movement while traveling with his shows, thoroughly establishing the character of a showman as a social lecturer. He also lectured on "The Philosophy of Humbug," delivering such rules as "Let your pledged word ever be sacred." Even though reviewers persisted in calling him a rogue and a sharper,[8] the strict moralisms set a precedent for the outspoken morality of Artumus Ward and perhaps of Mark Twain's Barnumesque yankee, Hank Morgan, as well.

The range of possible adaptations of the Barnum figure, either seriously or in burlesque, is broad enough that specific Barnum anecdotes can be traced into English and American literature from the

---

8 [Barnum], *Life*, 162, 322, 362–64, 374, 394; "Revelations of a Showman," *Blackwood's Magazine*, XLVII (February, 1855), 187–201.

1840s through the 1890s. Albert Smith combined a Barnum story with his panorama of Mont Blanc and lectured at London's Egyptian Hall in 1844; Ward brought his comic Mormon panorama to this same spot in 1866.[9] Smith's "Phineas Cutecraft" is the yankee myth of Barnum and Ward:

[Smith] introduced Phineas in the Cologne church, and made him say at the end of the sexton's story about the virgin's bones: "Old fellow, what will you take for that hull lot of bones, I want them for my museum in America."
When the question had been interpreted to the old German, he exclaimed in horror, according to Albert Smith:
"Mine Gott! it is impossible! We will never sell the virgin's bones!"
"Never mind," replied Phineas Cutecraft, "I'll send another lot of bones to my museum, swear mine are the real bones of the Virgin of Cologne, and burst up your show!"

Barnum tells this story in his *Life* as occurring at Warwick Castle in 1844; it serves as the basis of jokes by Ward in his Canadian travels and Twain in *The Innocents Abroad*.

Perhaps most important of all Barnum's characteristics was his degree of self-awareness and his conscious exploitation of his audience. To a large extent, the literary comedians adapted this pose, claiming in preface after preface that their books were written merely for money, never to serve a political or social motive although they more persistently dealt with social and political issues than any other form of American literature with the exception of the newspaper editorial itself. Barnum was also able to indulge in sophisticated self-parody, without ever abandoning his serious pretensions, as when he appeared on the stage before the opening of Dickens' *Great Expectations* in his theater in the fall of 1864:

> "That Prince of Humbugs, Barnum," so it appears
> Some folks have designated me for several years.
> Well, I don't murmur; indeed, when they embellish it,
> To tell the truth, my friends, I rather relish it.
> Since your true humbug's he, who as a host,
> For the least money entertains you most....
> The bearded lady with her (h)airs and graces,

---

9 Joel Benton, *Life of Hon. Phineas T. Barnum* (N.p.: Edgewood, 1891), 355–57.

> The Astec children with their normal faces,
> The twins of Siam—rarest of dualities—
> Two ever separate, ne'er apart realities? . . .
> The Happy Family—cats, rats, doves, hawks, harmonious!
> Their voices blend in tones euphonious.[10]

A witty and sophisticated vulgarian, Barnum *in propria persona* developed his own fund of images. When Ward developed as a comic presence, he made use of all the self-contradictory aspects of the figure. Smith as an anecdotalist or Barnum as a reciter of verse was far more witty than vulgar. Browne as a platform humorist dressed as a dandy and concentrated on whimsy and literary burlesque despite Artemus Ward the showman's rough personality.

Frank Luther Mott portrays the combination of traits in Artemus Ward as a systematic development through 1857 and 1858, but it more probably began as early as the *Carpet-Bag*, when Charles Halpine came as editor after managing Barnum. Comments by Browne and E. P. Hingston, his manager in the 1860s, make it clear that the actual literary persona was a matter of chance. The Artemus Ward letters "were not the result of any preconcerted and well-matured plan of writing a series of amusing articles. The first one was written on the spur of the moment, merely to supply 'copy' for the paper when the writer had nothing better with which to fill up the column."[11] This chance combination and the ambiguities inherent in Barnum himself (a conniver with morality and sophistication as well as shrewdness) helps to account for the radical disparities between a literary showman who was supposed to be fat and vulgar and a lyceum lecturer—Charles Browne—who was lean and cosmopolitan. Ward's initial letter to the *Plain Dealer* clearly shows the lineage of the Ward figure through Barnum and the "Hard Cases" of Joseph Neal, linking him with the literary comedy of the North rather than with the Southwest:

To the Editor of the—(*Plain Dealer*)
Sir,—I'm movin along—slowly along—down tords your place. I want you should rite me a letter, saying how is the show bizniss in your place. My

---
10 *Ibid.*, 486–89.
11 Edward P. Hingston, *The Genial Showman* (New York: Harper & Brothers, 1870), 37.

show at present consists of three moral Bares, a Kangaroo (a amoozin little Raskal—t'would make you larf yerself to deth to see the little cuss jump up and squeal), wax figgers of G. Washington Gen. Tayler John Bunyan Capt. Kidd and Dr. Webster in the act of killin Dr. Parkman, besides several miscellanyus moral wax statoots of celebrated piruts and murderers &c., ekalled by few & exceld by none. Now Mr Editor, scratch orf a few lines sayin how is the show bizniss down to your place. I shall hav my hanbills dun at your office. Depend upon it. I want you should git my hanbills up in flamin stile. Also git up a tremenjus excitemunt in yr. paper 'bowt my unparaleld Show. We must fetch the public sumhow. We must wurk on their feelins. Cum the moral on 'em strong. If it's a temprance community tell 'em I sined the pledge fifteen minits arter Ise born, but on the contery ef your peple take their tods, say Mister Ward is as Jenial a feller as we ever met, full of conwiviality, & the life an Sole of the Soshul Bored. Take, don't you? If you say anythin abowt my show say my snaiks is as harmliss as the new born Babe. What a interestin study it is to see a zewological animil like a snaik under perfeck subjecshun! My kangaroo is the most larfable little cuss I ever saw. All for 15 cents. I am anxyus to skewer your infloounce. I repeet in regard to them hanbills that I shall git 'em struck orf up to your printin office. My perliteral sentiments agree with yourn exackly. I know thay do, becawz I never saw a man whoos didn't.—Respectively yures,

A. WARD

P.S.—You scratch my back & Ile scratch your back. (37–38)

The listing of pirates and Founding Fathers together is consistent with the heritage of the Civil War era, without being directly committed to current events, and when current events like the Parkman murder figure, they actually are used to symbolize the profiteering instinct of the "moral" showman. Typographical tricks reinforce the writer's vulgarity, as in "skewer" for "secure," and serve a function, unlike Josh Billings' misspellings; they also masquerade as dialect. As with Shillaber's Mrs. Partington, the primary interest is in the characterization of the central character, and there is not much in the way of dramatic plot. The speech of the figure carries much of the burden; although it is concrete, it is attuned to the philosophy of the Barnum myth. The ethical implications of the personality make it fascinating.

Over a period of two or three years, Artemus Ward became a major national figure through his varied responses to the American experience. Fred L. Pattee sees an uneasy merging in the voices of Browne the author and Ward the persona, and this is certainly the result of the persona's origins. In Ward's reforming indignation against the Shakers, free lovers, spiritualists, and women's rights fanatics, Professor Pattee hears the voice of Charles F. Browne, moral showman from New England, rather than the opinions of a frontier roughneck.[12] But this is to miss the changing nature of the North, as revealed in Forrester or Shillaber and Neal. Ward was actually developing one of the first comic voices in American literature, which was flexible enough to encompass Boston, New York, Salt Lake City, the Isthmus of Nicaragua, Washington, and backwoods Indiana. The pose matches the changing composition of America as it emerged in the modern world.

The Ward letters were well managed as a business proposition. By 1860 Ward was producing two Ward letters a month and began sending them to the comic weekly *Vanity Fair* in New York in the fall of that year. Browne wanted to publish simultaneously in Cleveland and New York—one of the first suggestions of syndicated humor—but could not get Gray at the *Plain Dealer* to agree. In October, 1860, Ward also appeared for the first time on the platform, in Toledo, Ohio, lecturing as a well-dressed dandy. None of this work encouraged longer productions in the novel genre. He gained experience as an advance agent on the road and arrived in New York City to become assistant editor on *Vanity Fair* on January 2, 1861.[13] In May, 1861, Browne became *Vanity Fair*'s editor-in-chief when Charles G. Leland, the editor, left to edit an abolitionist magazine.

Vanity Fair provided a congenial atmosphere for Ward's writing. He appeared alongside burlesque novels and war reports by "McArone," George W. Arnold, the leading writer of burlesques prior to the emergence of the San Francisco bohemians in the second half of the decade. There was also material from Ethan Spike, Hans Breitmann (Charles G. Leland, the editor), Thomas Bailey Aldrich, Wil-

---

12 Fred Lewis Pattee, *A History of American Literature Since 1870* (New York: Century, 1915), 36–37.
13 Seitz, *Artemus Ward*, 62–63. Ward worked as an advance agent for Ossian E. Dodge, a comic singer who gained notoriety from P. T. Barnum's Jenny Lind promotion by purchasing the first ticket for her concert in Boston for $625.

liam Dean Howells, R. H. Stoddard, John G. Saxe—many of them members of the bohemian circle of Pfaff's Cellar. "Essentially mild and genteel," *Vanity Fair* was pleasant in its satire and caricature. The outlook was national and political and cultural; there was little of the narrative detail, character description, and violence of the southwestern school of humor. Ward interviewed in burlesque not only Abe Lincoln, but also Brigham Young and international figures such as the "Prince Napoleon." The real strong point of the magazine, however, was the burlesque, which *Vanity Fair* developed in political and literary areas following Thackeray's *Novels by Eminent Hands* and *The Book of Snobs*, foreshadowing Bret Harte's *Condensed Novels* and Charles H. Webb's stories. Bearing titles like "Moses, the Sassy; or the Disguised Duke," or "Washy-Boshy; or, the Prestidigitating Squaw of the Snakeheads," Ward burlesques blew up the heavily mannered novel of sentiment or placed it in the context of the popular theater of the era. Irish dialect and the commercial attitude of the urban laborer are juxtaposed with romantic scenery; star-crossed lovers, with unsentimental practicality, recognize their lack of money and social position and return to the world of shopgirls and clerks. At the core of this skepticism is the egalitarian practicality which underlies the philosophy of the other literary comedians, and frequently enough the Fourth of July or American sailors are brought into the action for a further national dimension.

Artemus Ward: His Book, a collection of *Vanity Fair* burlesques, old showman letters, and mock interviews of famous people by the showman, was published by G. W. Carleton in May, 1862, to national acclaim. Forty thousand copies were sold outright, which Don Seitz and Walter Blair identify as a tremendous success for the publishing field of that period.[14] Dion Boucicault's "The Octoroon" was burlesqued in a letter showing Ward victimized by a pretty swindler who claimed to suffer the agony of miscegenation. Baldinsville, Indiana, Ward's fictive hometown, is described in grotesque detail. "The Soliloquy of a Low Thief" made use of a naïve petty crook as its narrative persona in place of the old showman. The crook's story at-

---

14 *Ibid.*, 120; Blair, *Native American Humor*, 111.

tacks wealthy corporate heads who appear to be educated thieves different from the "low" narrator only in their political connections. The thief, Jim Griggins, is a notable forerunner of the Populist viewpoint later in the century. "In Canada" even took the old showman outside the United States. As traveling showman, Ward exceeded Barnum in attacking religious sectarianism, political venality, "big" business in the form of railroads, banks, and the government; the humor is more pointed than the comedies of manners of the Fudges, Potiphars, and Sparrowgrasses before the Civil War.

Although the war occupied several of Ward's sketches, it did not dominate the character of the showman. "Thrilling Scenes in Dixie" and two accompanying pieces describe the showman's adventures and demonstrate middle-of-the-road politics but uncompromising patriotism. Ward says "let 'em secesh," at first, but comes around to Union sentiments: "But J. Davis, the minit you fire a gun at the piece of dry-goods called the Star-Spangled Banner, the North gits up and rises en massy, in defence of that banner. Not agin you as individooals—not agin the South even—but to save the flag." For these sentiments, the old showman is mobbed repeatedly in the Confederacy. The position, of course, is Lincoln's position that the Civil War was for the defense of and continuation of the Union, not against slavery per se, a position that northern abolitionists resented, but that Lincoln felt necessary to retain general support for the government. Lincoln read a piece from this volume, "High-Handed Outrage at Utica," which does not treat the war directly, before reading the Emancipation Proclamation to his cabinet. In this item, a jury brings a verdict which is unrelated to the event—arson for the smashing of Ward's Judas Iscariot waxwork by a local resident. Lincoln then read an emancipation proclamation which freed no slaves, but did improve the North's philosophical position. Ward's best hit appeared in his second book, *Among the Mormons*, in 1865; it was a vicarious sacrifice: "I have already given two cousins to the war, & I stand reddy to sacrifiss my wife's brother ruther'n not see the rebelyin krusht" (290). Twain adapted this attitude to describe the Sandwich Islander's sense of Christian atonement, and it is really a generalized burlesque of human values, not merely a war joke.

Ward's career as a lecturer allowed him some freedom in persona. Ward had begun lecturing in the fall of 1860, and he continued to give comic lectures in 1861 after joining *Vanity Fair*. It is as a lecturer that Artemus Ward contributed the most significant kind of flexibility of persona and philosophical statement to the American comic mode. E. P. Hingston, who managed his western and English tours, makes the clearest connection between Ward and the more sophisticated literary comedians in relation to his stage presence:

> A statement had appeared in some of the American papers, to the effect that "Mrs. Partington" was the model which Charles Browne used for the creation of that peculiar display of humor which characterizes the writings of "Artemus Ward:" but I have the authority of the author's own statement to me for recording that the humorous writings of Seba Smith were his own models, so far as humor thoroughly *sui generis* can be said to have had any model whatever. It is true, as one Transatlantic writer has suggested, that the satirical vein in which Mr. Saxe writes of the commonplaces of society, and the sarcasm with which Mr. Halpine treats political topics, may have influenced the mind of the young humorist from Maine, and contributed to form the characteristics of his style; but John Phoenix was an author of whom Artemus Ward was accustomed to speak in terms of admiring familiarity, more than of either of the above-named contributors to the comic literature of America.[15]

The Downing letters would have been models of the written letters of the old showman in the vulgar persona and employing the pretentiousness of character of the showman. The whimsy of Shillaber and Saxe are related, however, to the platform figure. Likewise, Phoenix' writings, which include the text of at least one burlesque Fourth of July oration, were in a literary voice which was colloquial on occasion but was also sophisticated and intellectual in diction and in the interplay of cultural and personal concepts. Many of Ward's auditors had a sense of newness about his spoken productions which probably derives from his development of a literary form into a comic spoken medium for the first time in America.

Ward's lectures were more complicated and more sophisticated

---

15 Hingston, *The Genial Showman*, 81.

than his letters. All stressed digression, as in his earliest lecture, "The Babes in the Wood," where posters proclaimed that Ward would "touch on many topics, tell many thrilling anecdotes; attempt a few pleasant jokes and make an occasional allusion to his subject." One critic wrote, "Everything that came under his notice, all in their turn, became pegs, as it were, on which to hang some witticism."[16] Burlesquing the serious lyceum speaker, Ward played with the expectations of an audience seeking "moral" instruction. In "Sixty Minutes in Africa," he referred to the continent only in beginning and ending. His "Lecture on the Mormons" used a burlesque panorama to provide visual subjects for a continuing string of digressions. On the picture of a Salt Lake City temperance hotel, he commented, "I prefer temperance hotels—altho' they sell worse liquor than any other kind of hotels" (372). The Overland Mail Coach was uncomfortable in a way that included the audience: "Those of you who have been in Newgate—and stayed there any length of time—as visitors—can realize how I felt" (373). The implication that the audience is criminal (the Newgate reference was used in Britain) adds social irony to the "moral" reversal of the nonsense lecture. Notably, the lecture form, like the comic newspaper letter, was a limited rather than a sustained genre, and it encouraged one-liners and intellectualized humor.

One critic commented that Ward "was not ever affected by local coloring or prejudice, nor was his speech marked by a single provincialism. He was a cosmopolitan gentleman in every relation of life. And this is what was the beginning of the power he had over his audiences, that . . . he was not to attempt to amuse them by antics, but by quietly saying things worth saying." Ward burlesqued old saws and sentiment, romance and warfare, all as related to his audience and the United States. The serious intention was a phenomenon of major significance for American humor. When he spoke in Boston on December 6, 1861, he was breakfasted the next morning at the home of publisher James T. Fields, editor of the *Atlantic Monthly*

---

16 Quoted from the *Daily Union Vidette* (February 5, 1864), in Paul Fatout, "Artemus Ward Among the Mormons," *Western Humanities Review*, XIV (Spring, 1960), 196; George J. H. Northcroft, "Artemus Ward, the Baldinsville Showman," *Littell's Living Age*, CLXXVII (May 5, 1888), 302. Reprinted from London *Times*.

Magazine. Annie Fields recorded Oliver Wendell Holmes's compliments to Ward over the teacups. In response to Holmes's recognition, "Artemus twinkled all over, but said little after the Professor arrived. He was evidently immensely impressed by him."[17] The significance of such recognition from "Dr. Holmes' Boston," as Van Wyck Brooks has called it, cannot be overestimated in its suggestion that American literary comedy could be taken seriously. In 1862–1863 Ward lectured as far south as Tennessee. In 1863–1864 he went west to San Francisco, returning to the East through Mormon country. His lectures were greeted with enthusiasm everywhere. By the 1865–1866 season he was earning from $300 to $600 per night, proving that comedy and comic lecturing could easily be a sustaining occupation.

A stenographic copy of Ward's lecture on "Robinson Crusoe" was taken in St. Louis, Missouri, and published in the *Missouri Republican* on March 27, 1864. Ward had been in Virginia City, Nevada, with Mark Twain only three months before, and this text is probably close to what Twain heard. The speaker deals freely with the steamship journey and overland travels across the Isthmus—establishing a comic format much like Twain uses in his works. The speech is digressive, but Ward maintains one or two themes throughout dealing with vanity and hypocrisy. He poses as a lyceum lecturer who could not decide on a topic, maintaining a literate tone in conjunction with the naïve pose. Such a persona could achieve a variety of effects through burlesques, anecdotes, and jokes per se, and all three forms of humor are blended together in the recorded speech.

The Mormon trip produced both a lecture on the Mormons and a book. The lecture featured a burlesque panorama, projecting pictures of the West; illustrations of such places as San Francisco might center around a small dog pulling on the pigtail of a Chinese while the speaker continued in deadpan description. The book, *Travels Among the Mormons*, was published in 1865 and contained the work identified in the title and a second part, "Perlite Literatoor," which brought together more Ward letters, including the one on the Prince

---

17 Enoch Knight, "The Real Artemus Ward," *Overland Monthly*, 2nd ser., XVIII (July, 1891), 56; Seitz, *Artemus Ward*, 104.

of Wales, and various burlesques of novels and stage plays which appeared in *Vanity Fair*. The discussion of the Mormons was an attempt to rise above comedy, which enraged such critics as Arthur George Sedgwick, who wrote in the *North American Review* that the book was low, impudent, and purposeless.[18] Even a hostile review from this quarter, however, indicates the extent to which Ward's work demanded serious attention.

The final stage of Ward's career was an English tour, begun in June, 1866, which continued the assault of American comedy on the bastions of literary respectability. Like Barnum and Twain, later, Ward approached English landmarks with enthusiasm and reverence, even in humor. Although dying of consumption, he received in London "a welcome greater than any the British ever accorded to a travelling American"[19] and began an arduous round of writing, lecturing, and club dinners. By January, 1867, he had suspended his lectures, and he died on March 6.

His letters to *Punch*, at the invitation of Mark Lemon, represent a high-water mark, prior to Twain's successes, in the British enthusiasm for American humor. From September through November of 1866, Ward the old showman appeared in *Punch* as an American traveler, innocent but shrewd, a social critic who could be bamboozled by sharpers but who viewed historical sham with a jaundiced eye. History, symbolized in the Tower of London, spiritualists and sectarians, and commercial fraud were burlesqued in Britain as they had been in America; the figure was still Ward the old showman, but the cacography was sharper in undercutting pretentiousness, the internationalism was more obvious, and some of the vulgarity was given to a foil character, a London bartender who held the same attitudes as a "vernacular" American backwoodsman, and inquired of the ghost of Cromwell, "Is he dead?"

Ward wrote that the opportunity to appear in *Punch* was the "proudest moment of my life," but the general success of his literary and lecturing pose is suggested by Melville D. Landon's correspon-

---

18 "Artemus Ward's Travels," *North American Review*, CII (April, 1866), 586–92.
19 Jennette Tandy, *Crackerbox Philosophers in American Humor and Satire* (New York: Columbia University Press, 1925), 141.

dent, who said that the idea of this ruthless yankee poking among the revered antiquities of Britain even tickled the beef-eating Britons themselves. Most of his reviewers paid attention to his humor as being "of the true transatlantic type" in one way or another.[20] Thus, Ward's "At the Tomb of Shakespeare" and "The Tower of London" brought a new viewpoint to history and culture as perceived by his audience. Ward's letters exploited the travel narrative format to its fullest, using the barkeeper foil, playing American against European perspectives, and fictionalizing the cultural experience. They showed how far P. T. Barnum's stance could be broadened and reinterpreted to provide humorous social commentary. The British were not scandalized by the comedian's views. Institutions rather than individuals are burlesqued, and Ward, like Dickens' Sam Weller, expresses through his pragmatism the power of the individual. It is this stance that seems most to foreshadow Mark Twain's works.

Ward's career develops so naturally up to the time of his death that it is tempting to view it as a rounded whole. However, Ward intended to go on a tour of the world, carrying the outlook of American literary comedy into Australia and China, as Twain eventually did in *Following the Equator*. Furthermore, the early success of the old showman persona restricted Ward as Twain's more slowly emerging persona did not restrict him, and Ward was actively seeking a more flexible voice. Ward may be said to have developed the archetypal figure of the literary comedian. Throughout his career, other comedians were aware of his model, including such writers as Nasby, Eli Perkins, and Twain, and they all show a similar interaction between their own narrative figures and the social surroundings. His financial success demonstrated the possibility of a career as a humorous writer, and his death left a void in the field of American literary comedy that demanded a successor to fill it. Yet he had not attempted sustained fiction in any form, and the possibilities of American humor in that area remained untapped until the successes of Mark Twain.

---

20 Seitz, *Artemus Ward*, 190; Melville D. Landon, *Eli Perkins: Thirty Years of Wit, and Reminiscences of Witty, Wise, and Eloquent Men* (New York: Cassell, 1891), 181–82; Knight, "The Real Artemus Ward," 58.

FOUR

The Social Ethics of a Comedian

THE SOCIAL ETHICS expressed through the mode of literary comedy are often overlooked. Whereas cacography, persona, and exaggeration have been analyzed, and the nihilism of the comedian's irony has been noted, almost no attention has been paid to the beliefs that their writings express. In fact, Artemus Ward expresses through his humor a complex democratic ethic which is consistent with the origins of literary comedy. His viewpoint is pragmatic and egalitarian, preeminently; vanity, sham, and social position are consequently subject to his irony. With a kind of early populism, the comedians registered suspicion of government, church, and political organizations. Institutions were seen as corporate antagonists to individuals. Even if the individual is only a small-time crook, he is still allowed more tolerance than organizations. Finally, the detachment and naïveté of the Ward figure is a statement for immediate human relationships and against social convention. These elements compose a fairly consistent social doctrine which Ward attempted to elaborate in humor. He struggled to adapt his platform voice to a cosmopolitan presentation of this stance in his Mormons lecture and book, but remained most successful in the Ward persona and similar dramatic figures, such as the low thief Jim Griggins to be introduced in this chapter.

Even in the simple device of cacography—misspelling for effect—Ward's attitude toward popular projects is clear when the celebration of the Atlantic cable produces incongruities like "the sellerbrashun and illumernashun ware commensin," and "Trooth smashed to erth shall rize agin—YOU CAN'T STOP HER" (46). Bill Arp, Ward's southern counterpart, wrote even more forcefully ironic lines, as on Lincoln's emancipation policies: "When Niggerdom ar to feel the power of your proklamation . . . what a galorious day that ar to be! What a sublime ery in history! What a proud kulmination and konsumation and koruskation of your politikul hoaps." As Richard Bridgman points out, there were two competing rhetorical traditions in America at this time; the comedians used the implied simplicity of the more commonplace to undercut the bombast of the more highly turned style. Potent though the device appears in undercutting political and social pretension, it was attacked by established literary critics as a *grotesquerie*, a "habit of trying to make letters do the grinning," caught from Negro minstrelsy without any legitimate relationship to yankee dialect. Even Bret Harte accepted it only as a mechanical trick from the printer's background.[1] Yet, when used carefully, it is a significant thematic tool; Huck Finn's "sivilization" represents the identical impulse raised to the level of symbol.

Cacography was joined with comic social observations to portray the "low" character's view of society, critical of many of its political and religious pretensions. Ward the showman said, "I'll jine the Meetin House in Baldinsville, jest as soon as I can scrape money enuff together so I can 'ford to be piuss in good stile, like my welthy nabers" (118). Vanity, religion, and wealth are brought into equation through the low viewpoint. The southwesterners described commonalities of lower class origin; Holmes was in a slightly more elevated vein; the comedians looked at the social circumstances of the emerging towns from a lower middle-class viewpoint and yearned to rise. Nor were political ideologies limited by devices; "Southern Conthieveracy" is as bad as not having "any American Egil to onchain" (117, 260, respectively). Even the audience at popular lectures is due to accept criticism in burlesque for their social preten-

---

[1] Bill Arp's third letter to Lincoln on the Emancipation Proclamation, dated December 2, 1862, reprinted in Tandy, *Crackerbox Philosophers*, 108–109. Richard Bridgman, *The Colloquial Style in America* (New York: Oxford University Press, 1966), 8; "Yankee Humor," *Quarterly Review* (London), CXXII (January and April, 1867), 226; Harte, "Artemus Ward," 127.

sion, "9 out of 10 of um don't have no moore idee of what the lecturer sed than my kangaroo has of the sevunth speer of hevun" (83). Turn of phrase and spelling helped project skepticism; the only notable limitation is the persona of the showman, and Ward made many attempts to modify that.

Ward's humor develops a specific viewpoint toward politics that might be most simply characterized as distrustful. His description of a senator who makes money on lobbying through contracts while private individuals lose money on the Atlantic cable is antagonistic: "The Hon. Oracular M. Matterson becomes able to withstand any quantity of late nights and bad brandy, is elected to Congress, and lobbies" (478). Politics easily expands into history—an important precedent for Mark Twain—in the description of the Puritans in Ward's "Fourth of July Oration": "People which hung idiotic old wimin for witches . . . may have bin very nice folks in their way, but I must confess I don't admire their stile" (124). It is the individual who is respected and the users of political and religious power who are viewed unfavorably.

The beginnings of the Gilded Age lie in the Civil War era, and Congress is a significant representative of the growth of established institutions. Characteristically, individuals are generalized as the butts of the comedy for failing in their institutional roles: "At a special Congressional 'lection in my district the other day I delib'ritly voted for Henry Clay. I admit that Henry is dead, but inasmuch as we don't seem to have a live statesman in our national Congress, let us by all means have a first-class corpse" (258). The tenor of this passage is different from that found in the yankee correspondents who used political satire to attack specific legislative events. The humor is historical rather than contemporaneous. This is literary humor using Henry Clay symbolically as much as factually.

When Ward combines his attitude toward government with comic criminality and vulgarity, he approaches the sort of fictional effects that create sustained literature. The showman growled, "These western bankers air a sweet and luvly set of men. I wish I owned as good a house as some of 'em would break into!" (53). The fully developed sentiment, with politics added in, is Ward's best burlesque of a vulgar type, "Soliloquy of a Low Thief." The piece is an extremely important foreshadowing of the relation of Twain's heroes to society —government, wealth, law, and criminality are united with the "objectivity" of an outsider's viewpoint. The speaker is a low character who hopes for office and political protection and even architectural splendor as the wealth earned by a distorted virtue. Thus, Jim Griggins:

> I growed up in the street . . . and took to vice because I had nothing else to take to, and because nobody had never given me a sight at virtue.
> . . . .
> I shall always blame my parients for not eddycatin' me. Had I been liberally eddycated I could, with my brilliant native talents, have bin a big thief —I b'leeve they call 'em defaulters . . . . I could have plundered princely sums—thousands and hundreds of thousands of dollars—and that old humbug, the Law, wouldn't have harmed a hair of my head! For, you see, I should be smart enough to get elected State Treasurer, or have something to do with Banks or Railroads, and perhaps a little of both. Then, you see, I could ride in my carriage, live in a big house with a free stun frunt, drive a fast team, and drink as much gin and sugar as I wanted. A inwestigation might be made, and some of the noosepapers might come down on me heavy, but what the d-l would I care about that, havin' previously taken precious good care of the stolen money? Besides, my "party" would swear stout that I was as innersunt as the new-born babe, and a great many people would wink very pleasant, and say, "Well, Griggins understands what he's about, HE does." (150)

The emphasis finally rests on a sort of rudimentary system of corporate corruption tied in with politics and appearance. The comedians who wrote primarily about social manners lacked this political dimension. Furthermore, the emphasis is on the magnitude of a crime as the surest guarantee of social respect. The rich defaulters, from Griggins' cell, are "too big game for the Law to shoot at. It's as much as the Law can do to take care of us ignorant thieves" (151). The law is already a circus show—a humbug. This is also a populist viewpoint in embryo, consistent with attitudes in the 1890s and directly at variance with the optimistic social Darwinists. Jim Griggins is a fictional character, ready to be placed in a longer work to represent his viewpoint; he foreshadows some of the most significant innovations of the writers of the decades following the Civil War.[2]

Ward as a travel narrator, in his showman persona, revealed much of the Griggins attitude, but cosmopolitanizes his vulgar pragmatism by visiting a variety of places. As a travel narrator, Ward discloses how commercial exploitation obscures the value of history—as a would-be member of the genteel class might feel it, in this case, in Montreal: "On the Plains of Abraham there was once some tall fitin, and ever since then there has been a great demand for the bones of the slew'd on that there occassion. But the real ginooine bones was long ago carried off, and now the boys make a hansum thing by cartin the bones of hosses and sheep out there, and sellin 'em to intelligent American towerists. Takin a perfessional view of this dodge, I must say that it betrays genius of a lorfty character" (262–63). Materialism and fraud here parallel Ward's patriotic and moral falsity in describing his own show. Ward's "perfessional view" pretends to be the objective, businesslike attitude of a big thief. Later, in Nevada, another piece is even more sophisticated, the story of the man of "Boston dressin'," and exhibits the style that Mark Twain transformed into his major travel narratives.

The dodge on the Plains of Abraham looks both back to Barnum and forward to Twain, reemphasizing Ward's importance in transmitting a mode of comedy and ideology. In 1855 Barnum, in a paragraph that is probably the source of Ward's anecdote, discussed the manufacture of fraudulent relics for tourists: "Several months subsequent to our visit to Waterloo, I was in Birmingham, and there made the acquaintance of a firm who manufactured to order, and sent to Waterloo, barrels of 'relics' every year. At Waterloo these 'relics' are planted, and in due time dug up, and sold at large prices as precious remembrances of the great battle. Our Waterloo purchases looked rather cheap after this discovery."[3]

---

[2] Nor is he without precedent in Ward's experience, not only in Neal's *Charcoal Sketches*, but even in burlesques of Neal in the *Carpet-Bag*, I (January 7, 1851), 7, "Hardcoal Sketch, No. 2": "It seems mighty strange to me that in this city, where they have so many benevolent institutions, that some great charitable mind has not conceived the stupendous idea of providing relief, in some form, for deplorable cases like mine . . . and yet I am still permitted to sit here hankering arter a drink."

[3] [Barnum], 273.

Although Mark Twain was not a buyer of relics in *The Innocents Abroad*, he commented on Blucher's retrieval of animal jawbones from the battle of Sarajevo and complained generally of "this relic matter": "We had seen St. John's ashes before, in another church. We could not bring ourselves to think St. John had two sets of ashes. ... We find a piece of the true cross in every old church we go into ... as for bones of St. Denis, I feel certain we have seen enough of them to duplicate him, if necessary."⁴ The consistency of comment by the three writers indicates the extent of their shared values regarding history, despite the potential difference between burlesque showman, real showman, and "western" traveler. They form a sort of "school" in which their earnestness is hidden in burlesque or comic anecdotes. The chief advance by Twain is in fictionalizing more than the others, as in the extended dramatization around Blucher.

Ward's "In Canada," from which the dodge was taken, is a digressive piece that actually molds such practical insights into a rudimentary plot. After noting this dodge, he describes his own dodge in Maine, trying to palm off a wax figure as a child murderer by claiming the "figger has growd"; this is the innocent at work. He continues, musing on politics, "I wouldn't mind comin over here to live in the capacity of a Duke, provided a vacancy occurs." Every bit of humor reasserts the democrat's individuality. Titles are as interchangeable as bones; any crook can claim a noble job. He concludes that he hasn't skedaddled to avoid the draft, turning to duty; we should "have the Union restored as it was, if we can; but if we can't, *I'm in favor of the Union as it wasn't*. But the Union anyhow" (264). He is finally a Union man and a patriot. His idealistic inversion uses burlesque to bring forth, finally, a positive statement in which there is a realist's recognition of present failings in conjunction with the political sentiment.

All of the themes under discussion here were further elaborated in an urbane persona in *Among the Mormons*. Ward's statements on royalty and the standing of a man were well known; in the persona of the platform humorists—a role in which Dr. Holmes had taken

---

4 Mark Twain [Samuel Langhorne Clemens], *The Innocents Abroad* (New York: Harper & Brothers, 1917), I, 162–63.

him seriously enough—he could expect to show the same social fraud at work in a voice that allowed more variation on the themes of innocence and honesty. Business can be venal and also cause embarrassment to the genteel traveler in other ways. Burlesquing his own statements on morality,[5] Ward writes: "I have my boots repaired here by an artist who informs me that he studied in the penitentiary" (199). In fact, the traveler becomes the real center of interest rather than his travels. If such a pose could be extended and developed into a dramatic character, longer works of fiction could be created.

Throughout the letters, the innocent tries to overcome his own fears, but pretentiousness bears heavily on him. Phoenix' world in the 1850s was much like this. In trying to survive encounters, the passive naif sees through social manners to class and class values: "We have a quadrille, in which an English person slips up and jams his massive brow against my stomach. He apologises, and I say, 'All right, my lord.' I subsequently ascertained that he superintended the shipping of coals for the British steamers, and owned fighting cocks" (193). So, Ward is his own victim; he has not measured the man, but appearances. To reassess the man in terms of fighting cocks seems clearly to indicate the genteel basis of this ethic, which appears to equate quality with refinement, and certainly many of the comic writers—Aldrich, Howells, Warner—seem to have done this in Victorian America. The Yankee naif becomes cosmopolitan and meets the modern entrepreneur on the international scene; the persona could belong to almost any decade of the later nineteenth century.

In *Among the Mormons*, Ward's conversational voice is more modern than the old showman's idiom.[6] Perhaps even more significant, however, the social order, which Ward describes again, manifests the split between individual and corporate needs. Ward offers a few

---

[5] Ward wrote: "So with actors ... we must still acknowledge the star's genius, and applaud it. Hence we conclude that the chronic weaknesses of actors no more affect the question of the propriety of patronizing theatrical representations, than the profligacy of journeyman shoemakers affects the question of the propriety of wearing boots. All of which is respectfully submitted." Artemus Ward, "Morality and Genius," *Artemus Ward in London and Other Papers* (New York: G. W. Carleton, 1867), 108–10.

[6] It is for this reason that Walter Blair places the Mormon's writings after Ward's letter to show stylistic progression in *Native American Humor*, 407–408.

brief episodes where Twain created an expanded narrative in *Roughing It*. Nevertheless, the westerners provide a background against which civilized values can be measured. Ward's introduction to frontier ethics comes when he meets a driver for the California Stage Company whose loyalty to the company would cause him to kill off the injured passengers in the event of a wreck because "dead folks don't sue. They ain't on it" (202). Not only is the driver like Jim Griggins in his practicality, since "juries is agin us on principle," but he is a cool professional, intending to "keerfully examine" the victims and only finish "them as is mutilated" (202). The narrator is a potential victim; the values of the company employee foreshadow those of the Darwinist corporations of the Gilded Age.

The most striking episode that indicates the conflict of values between the genteel individual and the stage driver appears in the chapter "I am Here"[7]:

"A good thing happened down here the other day," said a miner from New Hampshire to me. "A man of Boston dressin' went through there, and at one of the stations there wasn't any mules. Says the man who was fixed out to kill in his Boston dressin', 'Where's them mules?' Says the driver, 'Them mules is into the sage-brush. You go catch 'em—that's wot you do.' Says the man of Boston dressin', 'Oh no!' Says the driver, 'Oh yes!' and he took his long coach whip and licked the man of Boston dressin' till he went and caught them mules. How that strike you as a joke?" (217–18).

Ward comments: "It didn't strike me as much of a joke to pay a hundred and seventy-five dollars in gold fare, and then be horse-whipped by stage-drivers, for declining to chase mules" (218). Vernacular clues in Ward's voice are absent; *horse*, for example, appears rather than the vernacular *hoss*. Unlike the usual dandy, moreover, the man of Boston dressin' is guilty of little save his clothes; this is also a joke between *easterners* of varying vulgarity and refinement; it is class humor, not regionalism. The sketch illustrates a prevailing attitude among literary comedians as described by one commentator in the early 1880s: "If an aspiring and nice young American of Ward's

---

[7] *Genteel* is assumed here, but other comments in the text make the mind-set clear. For example, Ward notes that a driver who can do his job without swearing at his mules is "distinguished all over the plains" (230). Twain uses this same trait to distinguish the working professional type from the culturally elevated.

class feels a friendly equality with stage-drivers, he also has a great respect for the genteel classes, and a desire to be genteel."[8] Remembering the showman's notice of the substituted bones on the Plains of Abraham, readers ought to note that a comparable sense of *values* is present in both sketches. This is a far more significant precedent in the Ward canon for Mark Twain's writing than is any specific borrowing.

Ward's canon should not be distorted by the appearance of the consistency that it gains in critical analysis. Like Twain, later, Ward wrestled with style. Attempting the reportorial, he can forget how he is handling persona and speak of passengers' trunks as "their" and "our" in the same sentence. He seeks a sophisticated voice, but the vulgar showman's style was a useful anchor. He also switches jokes from one person to another. In the book, a young naval officer carries saltpork and molasses to seasick passengers, but in his "Robinson Crusoe" lecture, his own friend becomes seasick and *I* "did all I could for him. I carried him raw pork, swimming with molasses."[9] He followed, in the lecture, with a literary burlesque about runaway lovers:

> Ellen—"No, dearest Henry, you have thrown up far more than I have. Your commission in the army . . .
> Young man—"Don't, my dearest Ellen, talk so much about throwing up."

Undistinguished though such burlesque may be, Ward is experimenting with voices and viewpoints, trying to combine travel material and antisentimentalist viewpoint. In "Pyrotechny," such a burlesque combines form and theme to attack unreflective patriotism brilliantly; in this case, the success is, at best, modest, but Bill Nye, in "John Adam's Diary" in *Bill Nye's Remarks*, was redoing the same joke on Irish maids: "It was a close fight between Tootie and the

---

[8] I am following Richard Bridgman's analysis of *hoss* in *Colloquial Style in America*, 47. Nadel, "Artemus Ward" 126.

[9] From Ward's *Works*, 190: "Her decks are crowded with excited passengers, who insanely undertake to 'look after' their trunks and things; and what with our smashing against each other, and the yells of the porters, and the wails over lost baggage, and the crash of boxes, and the roar of the boilers, we are for the time-being about as unhappy a lot of maniacs as were ever thrown together. I am one of them. I am rushing round with a glaring eye in search of a box." St. Louis *Missouri Republican*, March 27, 1864, n.p.

Ocean, but when they quit, the heaving billows were one heave ahead by the log."[10] Involving a new generation of immigrant-urban characters, the comedian tests voices. Burlesque, narrative, and posed persona seem to be about equivalent as potential modes and occur side by side.

The London letters of 1866-1867, just prior to Ward's death, summarize most of the themes of historical corruption and egalitarian naïveté that characterize Ward's canon. They are not regional, but cosmopolitan. Unlike Kerr and Nasby, they are middle class and urban, mixing vulgarity and sophistication. Their ethics are presented through humor: the pen is "more mightier than the sword, but which, I'm afraid, would stand a rayther slim chance beside the needle gun" (427). Ward is reporter, historian, and vulgar moralist, with his focal point in the showmanship surrounding British history. His showman persona is appropriate, although limiting.

Had Ward mastered the problem of voice, he might have been able to fashion a far more modern-seeming statement than the old showman's letters. Joking in his own voice, he had written to his manager about crossing the "big ditch," "See the Prince of Wales, and ask him to let me have a room for my show in St. James's Palace. Any room will do. I can run round and board with the Royal Family. Their dinner-hour will suit me. I am not particular."[11] Even the timing of the lines suggests Twain, but it is also the yankee Barnum, whose autobiography had played on the same line, "It had been my intention to proceed directly to London and begin operations at 'head-quarters'—that is, at the Palace, if possible. But I learned the royal family was in mourning."[12] The viewpoint is "irreverent" in its egalitarianism; at the same time that its incongruity with facts makes this thinking comic, the idea is village democracy in an open vein; the voice is cosmopolitan.

Jokes may as easily be Ward's as Barnum's, and later Twain's, for the viewpoint is consistent. All three notice the beggars and the guides. Ward and Barnum are both duped by veteran beggars;

---

10 [Edgar W. Nye], *Bill Nye's Remarks* (Chicago: F. T. Neeley, 1887 [?]), 252.
11 Hingston, 154.
12 [Barnum], 253.

Ward's comments on the use of royal patronage mirror Barnum's surprise at the commercialization of Shakespeare's name; burlesquing Barnum's near-successful bid for Shakespeare's home, Ward noted that he couldn't buy the place on the Avon where the bard had once fallen down on the ice. The element of yankee myth is equaled by the element of yankee reverence concealed in the format. Twain's "Vandal" is also Ward's when a tourist complains that St. Paul's should be "a older edifiss,"[13] "I decline to hold myself responsible for the conduck of this idyit simply because he's my countryman. I spose every civ'lized land is endowed with its full share of gibberin idyits, and it can't be helpt" (416). The same principle holds when applied to the foreign scene, especially where a genteel American might have elevated expectations, as when Ward is faced with rows of pots labeled "uncertain date" in the British Museum: "I can cry like a child over a jug one thousand years of age, especially if it is a Roman jug; but a jug of a uncertain date doesn't overwhelm me with emotions" (444). This disappointment is followed by another more personal when he discovers that his lunch is also "of a uncertain age." Twain in Constantinople less than a year later offered the same disappointment in an extended anecdote covering the anticipated glories of a Turkish lunch. The pragmatic American traveler tries to romanticize experience, but the actual institutions he finds betray his expectations. His discoveries suggest that, if foreign institutions are so much worse than expected, maybe America is better than it is taken for. It is uniformly true of the writers in this tradition that they are patriotic about much that is "American."

Ward's London letters also give examples of an attempt to distribute his viewpoint among minor characters, a nascent move toward sustained fiction. English figures are localized in conception; a cockney's mother sees her son after a thrashing by Ward and offers a vernacular soliloquy, "My son, I see how it is distinctually. You've been foolin round a Thrashin Masheen. You went in at the place where they put the grain in, cum out with the straw, and you got up into

---

13 Samuel S. Cox, *Why We Laugh* (New York: Harper & Brothers, 1880), 24, gives this joke an Irish origin: "'Where,' exclaimed a Hibernian, 'will you find a modern building which has lasted as long as the ancient ones?'" This derivation supplies further evidence of the universal literary currency of "American" humor.

the thingamyjig, and let the horses tred on you, didn't you, my son?" (415). American "vernacular" traits (as identified by Henry Nash Smith in Twain) are thus extended to include the British by this cosmopolitanized vulgarian narrator.[14] Characterization, even as early as the 1860s, is thus partly detached from a regional setting, as Twain was later to do with some of his medieval novels.

In "The Green Lion and Oliver Cromwell" Ward used a comic landlord to voice a skeptical viewpoint. Ward plays a younger character, close to his platform persona, whereas the landlord is the plain-dealing old hand. At a spiritualist's seance, Ward tells the landlord that the spiritualist will speak with Oliver Cromwell. The proprietor of the Green Lion responds, "And this Mr. Cromwell—is he dead?" (420). Learning that he is, the landlord flatly declares the man a humbug. The landlord continues in his aggressive ignorance about Cromwell and focuses on the payment of the spiritualist's hotel bill. Huck Finn, who didn't take stock in dead people, is cut from the same mold.

In other pieces, Ward also spreads out vulgar traits through a range of characters. Spoon stealing, as seen in a low figure like Jim Griggins, is attached to Ward's uncle, causing Ward to complain that there is something wrong in our "social sistim" (410). Values are expressed in a social context. Ward has good reason to expand such characterizations—through humor or description—but did not.

Finally, "The Tower of London," reprinted in Walter Blair's *Native American Humor*, fully elaborates the tráveling showman's social opinions. As in Twain's *A Tramp Abroad*, Ward finds his European adventures bring him back to comment on the American West and compare medieval weapons to the arrows of American Indians. The narrator confirms his pragmatic attitude by asking what is the value of the queen's crown, concluding to send his wife a watch instead. Shown torture instruments in the Tower, a little girl traveling in Ward's group of visitors remarks that it was "rich" to talk about Spanish tortures when they were in the Tower where heads had been cut off. Political history conceals cruelty, as Twain was to bring out in his medieval novels. The context of Ward's remarks on political

---

14 Henry Nash Smith, *Mark Twain: The Development of a Writer* (Cambridge: Harvard University Press, 1962), 8–9.

definitions are in this vein and bear a clear American reference in the last line (to which Twain also alluded in his travel letters):

> A Warder now took us in charge, and showed us the Trater's Gate, the armers, and things. The Trater's Gate is wide enuff to admit about twenty traters abrest, I should jedge; but beyond this, I couldn't see that it was superior to gates in gen'ral.
> Traters, I will here remark, are a onfornit class of peple. If they wasn't, they wouldn't be traters. They conspire to bust up a country—they fail, and they're traters. They bust her, and they become statesmen and heroes.
> Take the case of Gloster, afterwards Old Dick the Three, who may be seen at the Tower on horseback, in a heavy tin overcoat—take Mr. Gloster's case. Mr. G. was a conspirator of the basist dye, and if he'd failed, he would have been hung on a sour apple tree. (433)

The showman approaches conventional views of monarchy with the skepticism of an American democrat to whom titles are assumed as easily as any other nickname. His viewpoint is egalitarian, as it was with the Prince Napoleon, Prince Albert Edward, and other political figures of the times; the only difference here is in the historical perspective. Twain, Adeler, and other comedians elaborated this perspective in the 1880s.

The concept of social ethics is a relatively recent invention, although social Darwinists certainly recognized that their economic doctrines must have social consequences. The egalitarian viewpoint, however, is opposite to that of the Darwinists. It emphasizes the individual and his personal standing. A figure like Jim Griggins as a low thief outside the protection of larger corporate thievery is a significant statement of the concerns of the egalitarians, and as an egalitarian comic statement, its burlesque format cannot be said to detract from its point. American "western" attitudes are really variations from this source and many "genteel" values are prominent within western motifs; there is not a polar dichotomy in Ward's humor. Both England and America seem to provide a corporate social aspect that leaves the detached outsider in a skeptical or overtly antagonistic position. This was Ward's legacy to Twain, which, assimilated into his more inclusive comic vision, produced Twain's major novels of the later nineteenth century.

FIVE

Mark Twain
The Development of a Literary Comedian

MARK TWAIN'S DEVELOPMENT as a literary comedian was shaped by his attitude toward apprenticeship and his persistence in viewing political authority in ethical terms. There are hints from early in his life that he wanted to become a serious writer, and many of his decisions regarding his career were directed to this goal. By the 1860s he had developed a flexible persona that was far more sophisticated than Ward's old showman, but he remained uncertain of how to use this voice during the middle of the decade. Offered a chance to go east with Ward and benefit from his reputation as a comedian, Twain refused, continuing to balance reporting, editing, and literary comedy until 1871, when the profits from his humorous writings and lectures seemed to assure success.

Samuel Clemens' childhood was centered in the Mississippi River town of Hannibal, Missouri, and assessments of Twain's early background give the town a crucial place in his writing.[1] The "Matter of Hannibal" represented a realistic fund of material which the author could presumably draw on more than was common among other literary comedians. Certainly specific experiences in his background, such as Tom Blankenship's aid to a runaway slave—the basis of Huck Finn, were recast into meaningful literature. Certainly color-

---

[1] Dixon Wecter, *Sam Clemens of Hannibal* (Boston: Houghton Mifflin, 1952), and "Mark Twain" in *LHUS* (New York: Macmillan, 1968), 917–39, offer useful background. DeVoto, *Mark Twain's America*, although melodramatic, is also notable.

ful scenery and character types were inescapable; the potential for adapting such materials to local color narratives was immense. The only further things to be discovered in his growth as a writer are thus a motive for writing, a literary heritage to draw on, and a specific form of genius.

Minnie Brashear concludes that Jane Clemens, Sam's mother, was partly responsible, through her hatred of cruelty, for shaping his character,[2] and since the earliest materials such as the Snodgrass letters point in the same direction, there may be a meaningful literary influence. Most of the available information comes from Twain's *Autobiography*. In one elaborate story, Twain describes his mother as tricked by conspirators testing her Presbyterianism against her sympathy with the underdog: she was backed into defending Satan as the one sinner who most needed the prayers of Christendom.[3] Her "strong interest in the whole world and everything and everybody in it," and in everything beyond it, as well, must have influenced Twain in matters of the spirit just as it left its mark on the patterns of language he used and his persistent biblical references. Twain also reminisced about her defending a girl from her reckless father, upbraiding the man "in tones not audible to the middle of the street but audible to the man's conscience and dormant manhood." In still another anecdote, Twain described his mother seizing a drayman's whip and convincing him never to beat his horse again—an extorted promise which Twain the mature pessimist expected that he would never be able to keep. In fact, the attribution of these stories is significant in itself, indicating that Twain ascribed a strong ethical force to his early background. Like the other literary comedians, he was oriented toward social questions early.

Twain's father died in 1847, and he began work as a printer's apprentice in the newspaper office of Joseph Ament, owner of the Hannibal *Courier*. He later worked for his brother Orion at the Hannibal *Journal*. His first identifiable work in print, "The Dandy Frightening the Squatter," appeared in the *Carpet-Bag* in 1852. A vulgar Missis-

---

2 Minnie M. Brashear, *Mark Twain: Son of Missouri* (New York: Russell & Russell, 1964), 83.
3 *The Autobiography of Mark Twain*, ed. Charles Neider (New York: Washington Square Press, 1961), 28–30, contains the anecdotes treated here.

sippian bests a vain dandy; the reversal of vanity foreshadows later works and a southwestern milieu is obvious, but, as Edgar Branch has noted, it is typical of its period, using the formal diction of Longstreet's *Georgia Scenes*, a style which lacks the homespun quality of its subject.[4] Nevertheless, Clemens was only seventeen when this piece appeared, and his submission of his work to a nationally circulated comic paper indicates a measurable degree of literary ambition.

One distinction can be drawn between the "Dandy" story and the other *Carpet-Bag* offerings. Most of the material, by writers as diverse as Charles Halpine, Shillaber, or Phoenix, was in the form of the literary burlesque. Although Clemens' story is in a conventional form of earlier southwestern humor, it is nevertheless individualized in its study of the impregnable irony of the woodsman assured of his identity in the world. Henry Nash Smith has noticed the same trait in Huck Finn's Pap, calling it an almost medieval detachment in regard to his own position in the fixed "natural-social reality."[5] Rather than being burlesque or social satire, the story tends toward the dramatic. In other respects, the story is stilted and compares unfavorably with the *Carpet-Bag*'s burlesque novels and travel pieces, which were frequently as pointed as the later burlesques by Harte or Thackeray.

The experience of apprenticeship itself seems to have been a second important shaping influence on the values that Twain later expressed in his writing. At least he continued to hold high expectations of newspapers and reporters. Comparing those of "thirty or forty years ago" with the papers of 1873, he asserted that "in those days the average newspaper was the champion of rights and morals, and it dealt conscientiously with the truth." The writer-lecturer of 1873 identified himself with an ethical responsibility, in other words, and found it in his early profession. He continued to stress the values of apprenticeship in such a system, raging in the *Galaxy* against novices who hadn't acquired skills through unpaid apprenticeship.

---

4 Edgar M. Branch, *The Literary Apprenticeship of Mark Twain* (Urbana: University of Illinois Press, 1950), 9–20.

5 Smith, *Mark Twain: The Development of a Writer*, 126.

Thirty years later he documented the same point in *McClure's Magazine* with six case studies.[6] Twain's sense of individualism coincided with this moral system, it appears, and the play of the tenderfoot against the old hand in his travel narratives expresses the philosophy in another guise.

In addition to the influences of family and apprenticeship, Clemens was undoubtedly reading extensively during this period, as he later did on the river. Dickens and Thackeray, Paine and Poe were available to him, cited frequently in the journals for which he set type. Although Dixon Wecter describes Hannibal as literate but not literary, Clemens was both. George Lippard's *Legends of Washington and His Generals* is referred to in a letter as sanctifying Pennsylvania locations to him. He threatened to write funnier books than contemporary humorists were producing.[7] He knew John Phoenix' work, Mitchell's *Reveries of a Bachelor*, Curtis' *The Potiphar Papers*, Cozzins' *The Sparrowgrass Papers*, Widow Bedott, and Mrs. Partington; many of them were favorably reviewed in the *Southern Literary Messenger*, for example. Ward and Breitmann pieces are preserved in an early Clemens family scrapbook. Twain also knew the southwestern humorists, and in the area of American humor he had clearly covered the ground.

Clemens' writing throughout the period from 1853 through 1857 probably was limited to filler items which fell to most apprentices and journeymen. Edgar Branch has commented that contemporary journalism seems to be the shaping force on those writings that have been traced. Clemens' diction is more colloquial in Orion's Hannibal *Journal* than in the "Dandy," and his penchant for local satire was indulged. As a journeyman, he sent occasional letters, scarcely more than six from November, 1853, to March, 1855, to Orion's Muscatine (Iowa) *Journal*. Formal and conventional, they labor after sublimity

---

6 "License of the Press," in Albert Bigelow Paine (ed.), *Mark Twain's Speeches* (New York: Harper & Brothers, 1923), 47. *Contributions to "The Galaxy," 1868–1871, by Mark Twain*, ed. Bruce R. McElderry (Gainesville, Fla.: Scholar's Facsimiles and Reprints, 1961), 96–98; Robert Barr, "Samuel L. Clemens, 'Mark Twain' (A Character Sketch)," *McClure's Magazine*, X (January, 1898), 248–51.

7 Paine, *Mark Twain: A Biography*, 100, 106–107. Both Hannibal acquaintances and friends from his piloting days report that he was extremely bookish, frequently appearing with a volume under his arm. References to his reading in later letters confirm this trait.

in descriptions of Philadelphia, Washington, and New York. Similar letters are on record in 1856 and 1857, signed Thomas Jefferson Snodgrass. These letters are closer to conventional literary burlesque, with misspelled quotations from Shakespeare and humorously vulgarized dialect. Walter Blair, in comparing one of Clemens' letters to one of Ward's, has concluded that even though the Clemens letter is earlier (April 10, 1857, versus May 25, 1858), both follow established traditions of literary comedy and are substantially the same.[8] Twain's sense of social outrage at civic indifference and his preoccupation with physical comfort are evident: in one Snodgrass letter, particularly, he attacks the complicated procedure involved in a poor Irish woman getting cheap coal from the city government of Cincinnati, a concern inconsistent with the letter's roughneck tone. Twain was thus encountering some of the same problems of voice and persona that troubled Ward's mixture of vulgar voice and cosmopolitan viewpoint.

From April, 1857, to July, 1861, Clemens' career as a writer diverged radically from that of other literary comedians. While they were active in refining and freezing the personae that became famous through early commentary on the Civil War, Twain dropped out of the printing trade altogether to undertake a new apprenticeship as a pilot on the Mississippi River. While he learned the river and published an occasional item, such as the burlesque of Captain Isaiah Sellers in the New Orleans *Daily Crescent* in May, 1859, Ward became established in Cleveland and rose from local to national celebrity. About the time Ward became editor of *Vanity Fair*, Twain left piloting for the West. The delay gave time for reading and experience, and it ordered his career so that his development as a writer occurred outside the context of the Civil War.

Delancey Ferguson has written that whatever Hannibal had failed to exhibit, the schooling on the river supplied.[9] Twain's attitude toward apprenticeship was strengthened by the care invested in training a young pilot. The knowledge and skill required in piloting were extensive, and, if stories like the "Lightning Pilot" episode in "Old

---

8 Blair, *Native American Humor*, 147–50.
9 Delancey Ferguson, *Mark Twain: Man and Legend* (Indianapolis: Bobbs-Merrill, 1943), 66.

Times on the Mississippi" are creditable, the sense of community and responsibility must have influenced Clemens' sense of social order. John Hay's poem "Jim Bludso" in the *Pike County Ballads* expresses the identical sentiments about the pilot's responsibility for the safety of his passengers and his selflessness in his trade.

Although Twain wrote later in his life that he knew human nature because he had met almost every type of character on the river, he had met many of them in his reading. As early as 1853 he wrote home from New York to say that he was spending every evening in the New York Public Library. On the river, Horace Bixby taught him the crossings, but another pilot, George Ealer, with whom Twain sailed, was a fanatical devotee of Shakespeare. A letter to Orion in 1858 expresses enthusiasm over Satan's energy as described in *Paradise Lost*. Despite his complaint to Orion that learning the river did not permit time for newspaper correspondence, he was reading Hood, Goldsmith, Cervantes, Sterne, Smollett, Tom Hood's "Frank Somerville" travels *Up the Rhine*, and *The Spectator*.[10] No wonder other pilots on the Mississippi regarded him as a great reader. If Cervantes, as O. H. Moore suggests, provided Twain with a position from which he could express both a romantic and realistic viewpoint, then he must have read *Don Quixote* during this same period. His letters from the West, even including letters to the Keokuk (Iowa) *Gate City* in 1861, show this interplay, which does not appear in the earlier Snodgrass letters to an appreciable extent.[11] J. Ross Browne's travelogues and Horace Greeley's *Overland Journey* added less literary fare, one guesses. There was an extensive literary background to the maturation of Twain's imagination during the river years.

When the Civil War ended trade on the Mississippi, the appointment of his brother Orion as secretary of the Territory of Nevada took Twain west. This break from his second, and promising, career turned him once again to writing. The prospecting he did served only as an interlude, for almost from the beginning of his travels Clemens had been a correspondent. The *Gate City* published several

---

10 Cited in E. Hudson Long, *Mark Twain Handbook* (New York: Hendricks House, 1957), 113*n*.
11 O. H. Moore, "Mark Twain and Don Quixote," *PMLA*, XXXVII (June, 1922), 324–46.

letters by Sam and Orion Clemens in 1861 and 1862. These letters contain much that is representative of Twain's pose as a novice literary comedian. In reprinting the letters, Franklin Rogers observes how Mark Twain sets the skeptical reporter against the sentimentally romantic "Ma." Twain's sense of irony causes him to play poker advice against morality, counseling his mother that four aces is the best hand: "Make a note of that on the fly-leaf of your Whole Duty of Man, for future reference."[12] James Fenimore Cooper's portrait of the Indian is compared to the lousy type of "this corner of Paradise Lost." Even while the voice is vernacular or colloquial, such references indicate the humor to be partly literary and intellectual. Twain's later habit of larding out subscription books with long excerpts from other works may be related to this tendency, for the references are not as yet fully blended with his own voice.

The literary humor is more mature at one or two points of social comment. In describing a western town: "Now, although we are *surrounded* by sand, the greater part of the town is built upon what was once a very pretty grassy spot; and the streams of pure water that used to poke about it in rural sloth and solitude, now pass through our dusty streets and gladden the hearts of men by reminding them that there is at least something here that hath its prototype among the homes they left behind them." The mock pastoral voice contributes to the irony of transforming streams into sewers. The passage relates progress to waste in an interesting way, and a somewhat different but similar interplay seems to appear at the beginning of *Roughing It*. Since Twain was writing to a mixed audience, no cacography is present, but there are biblical allusions in the *Gate City* letters and the colloquial diction allows for the characteristic "constant switching from the fool way of talking to the wise way of seeing and putting things" that Walter Blair has noted.[13]

In August, 1862, Twain took a job as a reporter with the Virginia City (Nevada) *Territorial Enterprise*; the experience was crucial for

12 Franklin R. Rogers, *The Pattern of Mark Twain's Roughing It* (Berkeley: University of California Press, 1961), "English Studies: 23," p. 40.
13 *Ibid.*, 24; Walter Blair, *Horse Sense in American Humor* (Chicago: University of Chicago Press, 1942), 197–98.

him in his own development as a writer, bringing him into contact with Dan DeQuille (William F. Wright) and Artemus Ward. He refined the developing style of the *Gate City* letters into a sophisticated voice; he added, from his experience of the Nevada legislature during this period, a sense of governmental jargon—outside of the specific context of the Civil War—which complemented his mock biblical rhetoric. He also gained practical experience as a lobbyist, a side of Twain that remained apparent in his public literary life in relation to the international copyright law. Throughout the period from 1862 to 1864 his reputation as a western humorist grew steadily on the Coast.

The *Enterprise* offered an atmosphere of freedom that must have been beneficial to Twain's development. DeQuille noted that there was a "constant rush of startling events" and that Twain was an "earnest and enthusiastic" reporter in matters that interested him. This point might be applied to his pieces on the territorial legislature. Henry Nash Smith says that Twain's political reporting shows a greater quantity of serious work than Twain has traditionally been credited with. Twain's *Autobiography* describes how he got the legislature to pass a law requiring that all corporate charters within the territory be recorded. Such activity not only exposed corporate fraud; it furnished work for Orion.[14]

Twain's "The Bloody Massacre at Dutch Nick's" was a particularly outrageous hoax that illustrates the support that Twain got at the *Enterprise*. The story appeared in the fall of 1863 and was a harsh indictment of the San Francisco newspapers for failing to expose stock frauds. The piece was reprinted in California as literal truth rather than the grotesque fabrication that Twain created. As a storm of criticism mounted over the deception in California, Goodman refused, according to Paine's biography, to accept Twain's resignation, and DeQuille stood firm: "Mark, never mind this bit of a gale, it will soon blow itself out. This item of yours will be remembered and talked about when all your other work is forgotten. The murder at

14 Paine, *Mark Twain: A Biography*, 230–31.

Dutch Nick's will be quoted years from now as the big sell of these times."[15] This support was offered to Twain as a moralist-humorist, not simply to a funny man, and it compares very favorably indeed with the cold comfort offered Twain by Howells after his gaffe at the Whittier dinner a decade later. With this encouragement, Twain continued on the offensive with a piece combining burlesque biblical allusions with a falsely naïve statement of purpose—not unlike the over-obvious slyness of Artemus Ward's first letter. This piece, "Another Bloody Massacre," has not been reprinted, but it gives a significant indication of Twain's maturation as a serious literary humorist:

LETTER FROM MARK TWAIN

Carson, November 15, 1863

Editors Enterprise:—"Compiled by our own reporter!" Thus the Virginia Union of this morning gobbles up the labors of another man. That "Homographic Record of its Constitutional Convention" was complied by Mr. Gillespie, Secretary of the Convention, at odd moments snatched from the incessant duties of his position, and unassisted by "our own reporter" or anybody else. Now this isn't fair, you know. Give the devil his due—by which metaphor I refer to Gillespie, but in an entirely inoffensive manner, I trust; and do not go and give the credit of his work to one who is not entitled to it. I copied that chart myself, and sent it to you yesterday, and I don't see why you couldn't have come out and done the complimentary thing, by claiming its paternity for me. In that case, I should not have mentioned this matter at all. But the main object of the present letter is to furnish you with the revolting details of—

ANOTHER BLOODY MASSACRE!

A massacre, in which no less than a thousand human beings were deprived of life without a moment's warning of the terrible fate that was in store for them. This ghastly tragedy was the work of a single individual—a man whose character was gifted with many strong points, among which were great benevolence and generosity, and a kindness of heart which rendered him susceptible of being persuaded to do things which were really, at times, injurious to himself, and which noble trait in his nature made him a very slave to those whom he loved—a man whose disposition was a model of

---

[15] Dan DeQuille [William F. Wright], "Reporting with Mark Twain," *California Illustrated Magazine*, IV (July, 1893), 170–78; Henry Nash Smith (ed.), *Mark Twain of the Enterprise: Newspaper Articles and Other Documents*, (Berkeley: University of California Press, 1957), 7.

mildness until a fancied wrong drove him mad and impelled him to the commission of this monstrous crime—this wholesale offering of blood to the angry spirit of revenge which rankled in his bosom. It is said that some of his victims were so gashed, and torn, and mutilated, that they scarcely retained a semblance of human shape. As nearly as I can get at the facts in this case—and I have taken unusual pains in collecting them—the dire misfortune occurred about as follows: It seems that certain enemies ill-treated this man, and in revenge he burned a large amount of property belonging to them. They arrested him, and bound him hand and foot and brought him down to Lehi, the county seat, for trial. And the Spirit of the Lord came mightily upon him, and the cords that were upon his arms became as flax that was burnt with fire, and his bands loosed from off his hands. And he found a new jaw-bone of an ass, and put forth his hand and took it, and slew a thousand men therewith. When he had finished his terrible tragedy, the desperado, criminal (Whose name is Samson), deliberately wiped his bloody weapon upon the leg of his pantaloons, and then turned its edge upon his thumb, as a barber would a razor, simply remarking, "With the jaw-bone of an ass, heaps upon heaps, with the jaw of an ass have I slain a thousand men." He even seemed to reflect with satisfaction upon what he had done, and to derive great comfort from it—as he would say, "ONLY a mere thousand—Oh, no I ain't on it, I reckon."

I am sorry that it was necessary for me to furnish you with a narrative of this nature, because my efforts in this line have lately been received with some degree of suspicion; yet it is my inexorable duty to keep your readers posted, and I will not be recreant to the trust, even though the very people whom I try to serve, upbraid me.

MARK TWAIN.

P.S.—Now keep dark, will you? I am hatching a deep plot. I am "Laying," as it were, for the editor of that San Francisco Evening Journal. The massacre I have related above is all true, but it occurred a good while ago. Do you see my drift? I shall catch that fool. He will look carefully through his Gold Hill and Virginia exchanges, and when he finds nothing in them about Samson killing a thousand men, he will think it is another hoax, and come out on me again, in his feeble way, as he did before. I shall have him foul, then, and I will never let up on him in the world, (as we say in Virginia). I expect it will worry him some, to find out at last, that one Samson actually did kill a thousand men with the jawbone of one of his ancestors, and he never heard of it before.

MARK.[16]

16 "Letter from Mark Twain/Another Bloody Massacre!" *Territorial Enterprise* (dated November 18, 1863), in Scrapbook One, p. 71, in Mark Twain Papers, University of California, Berkeley.

The most important feature of Twain's reportorial format is its flexibility. Artemus Ward at this point in his career was limited to a vulgarized pose that militated against burlesque elevations of tone, although Ward compensated through cacography. Twain, however, is able to move away from his own diction into that of the King James Bible. In fact, his diction does not *copy* the King James version; several sentences are taken directly from Judges (15:14–16). In other words, where Ward developed satire around a vulgarization of Barnum, Twain applies a fixed point of Christian culture and develops his irony by returning to local diction and establishing comic conditions in the frame of the story.

The pretended shrewdness of the final paragraph in "Another Bloody Massacre" is comparable to the effect of Ward's first "old showman" letter. The audience is intended to see through the pretense. The satire in Twain's letter, however, is directed outward rather than toward his own persona—it is the editor who is the relative of an ass, specifically, and is made to appear as the unconscious dullard. The letter thus has a social—or "political"—motive. Yet it remains literary, "Lehi, the county seat," is an obvious anachronism burlesquing the localism of the present rather than the past (Ward sought such effects in calling Shakespeare a "boss poit"). Twain's own pose is not frozen into a vulgar dramatization, but is closer to something like John Phoenix' with a more serious interest. Although the piece is the result of a newspaper controversy, it still retains a literary effect and narrative interest. Part of the secret of Twain's development of the pose of the literary comedians into a permanent stance may lie in this delicate balancing of materials; and even though the attack seems crude, the balancing is delicate. Nor is the piece an accident, for other comparable pieces exist. In "Doings in Nevada" dated January 4, 1864, he commented on the Territorial Constitution as something other than an "immaculate conception," reechoing the flavor of his biblical diction, and continued from there to burlesque the state seal and offer a comic advertisement selling the state's officers—the last portion was reprinted in New York under its subheading "For Sale or Rent."[17]

---

[17] "Doings in Nevada," *Territorial Enterprise* (dated January 4, 1864), *ibid*.

How Dan DeQuille fitted into this development of style is not fully clear. As Edgar Branch describes his work, it was something of a transitional medium between the comedy of manners of the 1850s and the western humor of Phoenix and Twain. DeQuille is certainly more flatly reportorial in diction, and Twain's writing is closer to Ward's showman diction in its freedom of word choice. Twain and DeQuille worked at the same desk in the offices of the *Territorial Enterprise*, at any rate, and split the various items of news according to their own preferences. The four thousand words a day remained his preferred pace into the 1870s. Hints of self-consciousness about style appear in some of the legislative burlesques: "Even Judge Brosman's stately eloquence, adorned with beautiful imagery and embellished with classic quotations, hath been reported by us thus tersely: "Mr. Brosman opposed the motion."[18] The diction of the line is its own illustration, transmitted in the nature of the narrator's voice itself. Whatever DeQuille's influence, Twain's comic voice was ripening during the time when they worked together.

The controversy surrounding Twain's piece on the bloody massacre at Dutch Nick's was gaining him considerable notice on the West Coast when Artemus Ward and E. P. Hingston came through Virginia City in December, 1863, with the idea of meeting the young humorist. E. P. Hingston may have encountered him in the *Enterprise* office with his feet up on the desk, or it may have been Ward, armed with letters of introduction from the literati of San Francisco who came to meet the "moral phenomenon" of the West Coast. It is reasonably certain, however, that Ward spent much of his visit in the editorial rooms of the *Enterprise* and more time touring the mines and other interesting Virginia sights with Twain. Ward probably arrived on the nineteenth or twentieth of December, 1863, and left on the morning of the twenty eighth for Austin, two hundred miles east by stage, writing back to Twain from there on January 1, 1864. While in Virginia, Ward lectured on at least four nights and gave

---

18 Branch, *Literary Apprenticeship*, 108–109; DeQuille, 171; Smith (ed.), *Mark Twain of the Enterprise*, 17, 93. In Frederick Anderson, William Gibson, and Henry Nash Smith (eds.), *Selected Mark Twain-Howells Letters* (New York: Athenaeum, 1968), 43, Twain boasts that Howells' visit inspired him to a very good working day, basing his statement on the same figure of four thousand words (March 16, 1875).

impromptu speeches, one of which, recounted by Albert Bigelow Paine, clearly remained fresh in Twain's memories. Ward commented, "I never was in a city where I was treated so *well*—nor so *often*—."[19]

A meeting with Ward at this time was an important event for Mark Twain. Ward was the doyen of American literary comedians. Twain had experimented with something like the old showman's persona in "Snodgrass Dines with Old Abe," borrowing one of Ward's comic interviews, in the New Orleans *Daily Crescent* in 1861. Eli Perkins [Melville D. Landon] had been named by Ward, and Josh Billings had been given an introduction to the Pfaff's Celler bohemians (although he complained that Ward offered him no more help at that time, 1864). Ward was eager to talk about his craft. He told Dan De-Quille that he was thinking of altering his peculiar spellings, except in the Ward letters themselves, and was thinking of turning his literary persona into a stage figure surrounded by his family and local characters from his hometown. Twain no doubt discussed such things and saw, as others had, that Ward "was not even affected by local coloring or prejudice, nor was his speech marked by a single provincialism. He was a cosmopolitan gentleman in every relation of life. And this is what was the beginning of the power he had over his audiences, that . . . he was not to attempt to amuse them by antics, but by quietly saying things worth saying."[20] This shoptalk and increasingly sophisticated comic lecture technique broadened Twain's horizons.

Ward's influence, according to several scholars, came in the area of the oral tale. His burlesque of the lyceum speaker was refined in its presentation, material and pose coinciding. Phoenix had pretended to this blending in a written lecture, but Ward was the pioneer who actually developed the spoken comic lecture as practiced

---

19 E. P. Hingston, "Introduction," *The Innocents Abroad* (London: J. C. Hotten, 1872), 3–8. Twain recounted their first meeting in "A Reminiscence of Artemus Ward," New York *Sunday Mercury* (July 7, 1867), reprinted in *Sketches, New and Old* (New York: Harper & Brothers, 1917), 334–38. Paine, *Mark Twain: A Biography*, 238–44; Sir Charles W. Dilke, *Greater Britain* (London: Macmillan, 1885), 140.

20 Recounted in "Gath's" letter to the Philadelphia *Free Press*, dated January 31 [1878], "An interview with 'Josh Billings,'" in Scrapbook Twenty-Six, pp. 100–106, Mark Twain Papers, University of California, Berkeley. Dan DeQuille [William Wright], "Artemus Ward in Nevada," *California Illustrated Magazine*, IV (August, 1893), 406; Knight, "The Real Artemus Ward," 56.

by Twain, Nasby, Billings, and Nye. The traveler-commentator aspects of the old showman remained, the social bias and tendency toward rhetoric became substantially more literary, mixing a cosmopolitan blend of experience, backwoods innocence, and foolish-seeming naïveté. The pose militates against the incongruities of dialect spelling and cacography, as Richard Bridgman notes, throwing emphasis on mood changes, understatement, and anticlimax. Thus, the platform pose brings out relatively more thematic areas of the author-narrator's pose, the areas most likely to appeal to Twain. It was *managed* humor using vernacular, local, and lower class themes. Not only did Twain see an innocent who provided a model for his own persona in Ward's manner, as Paul Fatout has thoroughly documented; he also saw the visible evidence that an informal style, even one including social criticism and literary burlesque, could gain public acceptance. The fruit of this observation in the "Jumping Frog" story of 1865 has caused Edgar Branch, discussing the background of the story, to conclude that "Ward, the lecturer and writer, was alive in Clemens' literary imagination when he finally wrote the tale."[21]

Twain continued his own development as a writer independently of Ward. He declined an invitation to accompany Ward back to New York, though the invitation itself was a significant recognition. Ward wrote back to Twain, as well, that Twain was wasting himself amid the sagebrush and offered to get him printed in the New York *Sunday Mercury*; "For Sale or Rent" appeared in the *Mercury* on February 7, 1864, and "Those Blasted Children" appeared two weeks later.[22] He was soon to move from Nevada to California and a wider and more refined audience.

II

Twain's activity in the 1860s was not without an underlying order. His reporting, his early lectures, and his first publications in the

---

21 Paul Fatout, *Mark Twain on the Lecture Circuit* (Bloomington: Indiana University Press, 1960), 29, 41, 47, 51, *et passim*. Edgar M. Branch, "'My Voice is Still for Setchell': A Background Study of 'Jim Smiley and His Jumping Frog,'" *PMLA*, LXXXII (December, 1967), 597.

22 Paul Fatout, *Mark Twain in Virginia City* (Bloomington: Indiana University Press, 1964), 131, concludes that these pieces and the "Jumping Frog" introduced Twain to eastern editors before he reached New York in 1867, an important point in terms of Twain's overall design for his career.

East were all part of his intention to establish himself as a serious writer. In 1885 he was still reiterating his ideas on apprenticeship, that writing was a trade that had to be learned not in a year or five years but through a long course of personal experience.[23] Clearly, in 1864 he had not yet gone through what he took to be his apprenticeship. He worked for the San Francisco *Call* from June 7, 1864, to October 11, apparently leaving because his social comments were repressed. More imaginative items were also appearing in the San Francisco *Golden Era*, and when Bret Harte began editing the *Californian* in September he contributed a sketch a week for fifty dollars a month. Working on the *Call*, the *Golden Era*, and the *Californian* provided a chance to practice his "voice" and gain exposure. His later travels to the Sandwich Islands and later to the Holy Land gave him external observations to combine with the diction and pose already apparent in the early 1860s. He also broadened his experience through public lectures, thereby increasing his income markedly, as had Ward, while filling out his public presence as a literary comedian.

Ward's interest in Twain continued, evident by his request to Twain at the end of 1864 for a written version of "The Notorious Jumping Frog of Calaveras County" for his book of Mormon travels. Twain wanted to be identified with this book, Ward's second and based on Twain's adopted region, but he returned the sketch too late. Although he was initially upset at missing the chance, he later claimed to regret the story. It was published in Henry Clapp's New York *Saturday Press* on November 18, 1865, and made a tremendous success, being widely recopied in newspapers throughout the East. When Charles H. Webb tried to get Twain to publish a volume of sketches grouped around the frog story in 1867, Twain felt that any reputation based on it must have been of a "very attenuated sort." Other skeptical comments are also on record. Although he wrote his mother that Ward's book was a poor one and it would have been no credit to appear in it, he complained about the success of the story and the possible consequences to his reputation of a "villainous back-

---

23 Dixon Wecter (ed.), *The Love Letters of Mark Twain* (New York: Harper & Brothers, 1949), 227–28.

woods sketch." Clearly looking ahead, he referred at the same time to writing a book about the Mississippi River and also to potential collaborations with Bret Harte and opportunities to write for New York newspapers.[24] The potential for confusing the moral showman (Ward) and the moralist of the Main (Twain) and the wild humorist of the Pacific slope (Twain) with the wild humorist of the Plains (Ward) was large, as Twain found out to his dismay when he lectured on Ward in 1871–1872; he was better off pursuing his own course.

Twain and Ward nevertheless had much in common. Ward was making decisive innovations in American humor, not only in the voice of the skeptical traveling showman—which appears more subtly in Twain's reportorial tone—but also in the lecture pose. Franklin Walker has pointed out that the writers of San Francisco were deeply impressed with Ward because "he was producing something indigenous" in his championing of American humor.[25] Twain undoubtedly shared this belief that American character and American humor had unique potential and that formal demands would be rejected; Ward's works were more democratic in treating lower social types and offered a mode for literary comedians to develop.

In March, 1866, Twain sailed for the Sandwich Islands to report on the sugar interests there for the Sacramento *Union*, his first major travel reporting assignment. These letters, although they expanded his reputation on the Coast, are less sophisticated in their humor than his Nevada writings. Rather than casting himself as a humorist, he tends to speak in Horace Greeley's manner about the commercial possibilities of the various Sandwich Island trades. This material was not well synthesized with his literary comedy. What Franklin Rogers, in *Mark Twain's Burlesque Patterns*, describes as the Twain-Brown character axis, for example, is a retrogression in style in which Twain splits aspects of his persona into two speakers in the manner of Cervantes' treatment of Sancho and the Don. One is the overly forthright and vulgar Brown, the other a more reticent and genteelly pretentious Twain; both are more rigid and inflexible in outlook

---

24 *Autobiography*, 166. In a letter to his mother dated January 20, 1865 [1866], in Mark Twain Papers, Berkeley.

25 Franklin Walker, *San Francisco's Literary Frontier* (New York: Alfred A. Knopf, 1939), 162–63.

than the unified Twain voice. Brown's throwing up, inspired by seasickness and sentimental poetry, is a revamping of Ward's "Robinson Crusoe" lecture from Nevada and the midwestern tour of 1864. Furthermore—perhaps even more important—the Twain persona preempts the Brown character's tone when he attacks Sandwich Island dignitaries. Finally, when his political sense overtakes the author, Clemens makes a forceful statement in his *own* idiom, ignoring discriminations of voice and approaching the final voice.

At points in the letters where Twain is most himself, he is most successful in literary terms. The material on the "Equestrian Excursion" and the horse Oahu, which appears prominently in *Roughing It*, is a notable blending of the humor of 1863 with the style of the traveler's observations to come in the *Quaker City* letters. A framework of real experience is distorted through tone and burlesqued through subtle exaggeration, dramatizing the psychology of the narrator in a sort of semifiction. Ward had experimented with such a voice in describing the Isthmus crossing in the *Mormons* book. Twain elaborates on such brief letter-style anecdotes, as in the following passage which parallels Ward's one-liner about sacrificing a relative to the draft. Taking a broader subject—religion—and including the southwesterner's indifference to violence with his mother's religious sympathy and his own sense of social irony, Twain's platform voice is evident:

Near by is an interesting ruin—the meager remains of an ancient heathen temple—a place where human sacrifices were offered up in those old bygone days when the simple child of nature, yielding momentarily to sin when sorely tempted, acknowledged his error when calm reflection had shown it to him, and came forward with noble frankness and offered up his grandmother as an atoning sacrifice—in those old days when the luckless sinner could keep on cleansing his conscience and achieving periodical happiness as long as his relations held out; long, long before the missionaries braved a thousand privations to come and make them permanently miserable by telling them how beautiful and how blissful a place heaven is, and how nearly impossible it is to get there; and showed the poor native how dreary a place perdition is and what unnecessarily liberal facilities there are for going to it; showed him how, in his ignorance, he had gone and fooled away all his kinfolks to no purpose; showed him what rapture it is to work all day long for fifty cents to buy food for next day with, as compared with fishing for pastime and lolling in the shade through eternal Summer, and eating of the bounty that nobody labored to provide but Nature. How sad it is to think of the multitudes who have gone to their graves in this beautiful island and never knew there was a hell! And it inclines right thinking man to weep rather than to laugh when he reflects how surprised they must have been when they got there. This ancient temple was built of rough blocks of lava, and was simply a roofless inclosure a hundred and thirty feet long and seventy wide—nothing but naked walls, very thick, but not much higher than a man's head. They will last for ages, no doubt, if left unmolested. Its three altars and other sacred appurtanences have crumbled and passed away years ago.[26]

The paragraph continues into a sublime statement ("If these stones could speak") of sentimental romantic attitudes toward the Hawaiian past. The immense variety of material in the passage makes it especially interesting here. Ironic diction, a borrowed joke developed into a sequence on "relations," criticism of the concept of missionary work, social criticism on conditions for native labor, romantic naturalism, historical detail, and sublime reflections are all subsumed in the single reportorial voice of Mark Twain. In theme the piece shows Twain's preference for the underdog against social institutions. In form, the elaboration of Ward's one-line joke from "The Draft in Baldinsville" into a commentary on religion and selfishness, still controlled by the attitude of the literary comedian, alters the tone of a "jokist" into that of a reflective narrator. Thus the passage ceases to be the sort of literary comedy that was so closely associated with the Civil War and becomes subordinated to the viewpoint of the observer. This is the departure which distinguishes all of Twain's work from that of his predecessors.

Notably, Twain viewed the Sandwich Island letters in terms of their business potential. He did not foreclose plans on a Sandwich Islands book until June 7, 1867, when he wrote to his mother that the current state of the book trade did not justify a book.[27] Twain made a journalistic scoop at that time in reporting, with the help of

---

26 "Scenes in Honolulu—No. 6," Sacramento *Daily Union* (April 21, 1866), in Scrapbook Six, p. 112, in the Mark Twain Papers, Berkeley. The whole series of letters is reprinted in A. Grove Day (ed.), *Mark Twain's Letters from Hawaii* (New York: Appleton-Century, 1966).
27 Albert Bigelow Paine (ed.), *Mark Twain's Letters* (New York: Harper & Brothers, 1917), 127.

Ambassador to China Anson Burlingame, the burning of the *Hornet* and the survival of her crew for forty-three days in open boats. Knowing that the report would be republished all over the world, he rushed the story to the *Union* and later capitalized on the diary of one of the participants in an article for *Harper's New Monthly Magazine*. Unfortunately, "Forty-Three Days in an Open Boat" was published over the name "Mark Swain." In fact, Swain's first appearance in a major eastern periodical in December, 1866, shows a degree of insecurity; the *Union* report had only two or three intrusions in Twain's comic voice, the *Harper's* piece had none. Twain's negative attitude toward "The Jumping Frog" might be understood in this context; he was not yet certain of how much of the literary comedian's voice and attitude could be adapted to the role of the serious writer.

Lecturing may have helped Twain to recognize that the voice he used in his newspaper humor was capable of employment in serious and mock serious platform presentations. He undertook his first public lectures in San Francisco and based them on the Sandwich Islands experiences. On October 2, 1866, he gave his first lecture and was reviewed favorably. Later reporters were to praise him as superior to Ward both in ease of humor and value of content. He toured California and Nevada successfully, building the public recognition that justified his assignment by the *Alta California* to write humorous travel letters from the East and the Holy Land. The lecturer's style relaxed and complemented the reporter's style of the *Union* letters.

Twain's letters to the *Alta*, which began when he left San Francisco in December, 1866, again employed Brown and were similar to the Sandwich Island letters. His traveling bore other fruits, however. Some of his most interesting burlesques of governmental rhetoric, forestudies for "Cannibalism in the Cars," which have never been reprinted, appeared in the St. Louis *Republican* in March, 1867. Other material had been appearing in the New York *Saturday Press* and *Weekly Review* throughout 1866. From March, 1867, his sketches also started appearing on the humor page of the New York *Sunday Mercury*, which carried all the leading humorists of the era; "Jim

Wolfe and the Tom-Cats" and "A Reminiscence of Artemus Ward" appeared there. These offerings show more characteristics of Twain's mind than did the *Hornet* account. In fact, when Howells praised *Sketches, New and Old* in 1875 as showing Twain's increasing seriousness, he was reviewing many of these same sketches written from 1864 through 1867. The *Alta* letters treated the same things in America that were the staple of the Holy Land letters: Russian baths, food, ostentatious religiosity and commercialism in churches, and social mores—all described more factually than they had been by earlier comic reporters.

Twain was immersed in American popular culture. His sketches dealt with woman's suffrage, P. T. Barnum's bid for a congressional seat, and the declining political ethics noticeable in New York and Washington. He also continued to be closely identified with other literary comedians *by choice*. Handbills for his lectures relied on Ward's style of listing a long series of humorous topics. He burlesqued the catch phrases of advertisements for Barnum's "Moral Show" by listing Barnum's exhibits as *not* being present at his own lectures. Further evidence of his association with other literary comedians exists. On May 14, 1867, he wrote to a popular Brooklyn newspaper humorist and lecturer, Corry O'Lanus (Joseph Howard), requesting that Corry O'Lanus introduce his Brooklyn lecture on the stage, a request which Howard apparently accepted.[28] Twain mentioned in a letter to the *Alta*'s New York agent that he had dined with Miles O'Reilly (Charles Graham Halpine), Ward's friend and a *Vanity Fair* contributor. He also sought out the New York comic writer Doesticks (Mortimer Thomson) and formed a friendship with him that involved advice about Twain's literary plans for the *Quaker City* letters, for Thomson reminded Twain later, "I believe, you told me you were going to go off in the Quaking City.—You stated that if there was any book matter in the journey, the ship, the people, or the heathen lands and the inhabitants thereof, you proposed to extract the same

---

28 Although the introduction was never delivered, Twain's letters were preserved. Twain wrote on May 20 to thank Howard but noted that he had decided not to do the lecture since he had eighteen letters and a magazine piece to do before sailing on the *Quaker City* eighteen days later.

and build a book."²⁹ So this period was a time for Twain to develop further professional contacts while planning future literary ventures.

By 1867 Twain's career as a humorist was clearly laid out. *The Celebrated Jumping Frog of Calaveras County*, rejected by the leading humorous publisher Carleton without a glance, was published by C. H. Webb, a California friend, in May, 1867, coincidentally with Twain's first lecture in New York. E. P. Hingston later wrote that the story was known in Australia and India, as well as having been praised by Tom Hood in the English magazine *Fun*. The *Quaker City* voyage lasted from June 8, 1867, through November 9, 1867, and added a new factor to Twain's final development; he began reading letters to a circle on shipboard and altered tone and even tore up and rewrote a letter under the guidance of "Ma" Fairbanks, an adopted literary counselor. In addition to corresponding with the *Alta*, laying the groundwork for the book he had suggested to Doesticks, Twain was sending two letters a month to the New York *Tribune*. Anxious about the success of his work, he wrote to his mother from Constantinople detailing the correspondence and asking how much of it had appeared in print, for European postal problems had been extreme. By December 2, 1867, he had offered the letters from his trip to Elisha Bliss of the American Publishing Company, weeded of their "chief faults of construction and inelegancies of expression."³⁰ In addition to the *Alta* and *Tribune* letters, he was writing for the New York *Herald* and the California *Enterprise* and had been contacted by the Chicago *Tribune*; an article (which he described as "stupid") was placed in the *Galaxy* magazine for January 1868 as well.

In 1868 the process continued. He took his clippings back from his mother in January to begin work on his book and began lecturing in New York and Washington. "The Frozen Truth," based on the *Quaker City* voyage, was successful, and favorable comparisons were again made between Twain and Ward. Unable to settle down in Washington and write political columns, he traveled to San Fran-

---

29 Letter dated June 8, 1867, reprinted in New Haven (Conn.) *Register* (November 29, 1964); Fred W. Lorch, "'Doesticks' and *Innocents Abroad*," *American Literature*, XX (January, 1949), 446–49.

30 Hingston, "Introduction," *The Innocents Abroad*, 7; Dixon Wecter (ed.), *Mark Twain to Mrs. Fairbanks* (San Marino, Calif.: Huntington Library, 1949), xxiii–xxiv; Paine (ed.), *Letters*, 141.

cisco in May, attracting houses for his lectures of sixteen-hundred-dollars top. True to the artistic form of the literary comedians, he was reworking his material orally as "The American Vandal," a lecture which followed Nasby's format to an extent. Prior to submerging in the persona in mid-lecture, Twain offered his ethical premises directly to the audience in opening and closing statements.[31] He described the vandal as a "free-and-easy character of that class of Americans who are *not* elaborately educated, cultivated, and refined, and gilded and filigreed with the ineffable graces of the first society." An incorrigible relic gatherer, the vandal and his like were said to collect enough stones from Columbus' house to build one fourteen thousand feet long. After galloping across Europe, he "finally brings up" in Italy and identifies "The Last Supper" with a critical eye, saying "its a perfect old nightmare of a picture and he wouldn't give forty dollars for a million like it (and I endorse his opinion)." Until the parenthesis, Twain is consistent with Ward's humor, but then he ceases suffering from his countryman's vulgarity and makes a cosmopolitan vision enhanced by his comic irony:

If there is a moral in this lecture it is an injunction to all Vandals to *travel*. I am glad the American Vandal *goes* abroad. It does him good. It makes a better man of him. It rubs out a multitude of his old unworthy biases and prejudices. It aids his religion, for it enlarges his charity and his benevolence, it broadens his views of men and things.... It *liberalizes* the Vandal to travel. You never saw a bigoted, opinionated, stubborn, narrow-minded, self-centered, *almighty mean man* in your life but he had stuck in one place ever since he was born and thought God made the world and dyspepsia and bile for *his* especial comfort and satisfaction. So I say, *by all means* let the American Vandal go on travelling, and let no man discourage him.

The framing stance is educational and tolerant, closer to Mrs. Partington or Artemus the oral humorist than to familiar southwestern figures. As a literary comedian, Twain defines the world in jokes, as his comment on the mean man, and he is clearly addressing the socially rising American middle class that Shillaber, Phoenix, and the

---

31 Washington *Evening Star* (January 10, 1868) said that "as in the case of the well-remembered 'discursive' lecture of the lamented 'Artemus Ward' upon 'The Babes in the Wood,'" Twain referred to his subject only once. The reviewer pointed out that Twain reminded him of Ward in a "certain grotesque fanciful humor" and that the sultan's wives story was in the same vein as Ward's Brigham Young piece without being imitative. "The American Vandal," *Mark Twain's Speeches*, 21–30.

other northern literary comedians found as central to the American experience. The broadly liberal vision announced here is consistent with the diction and psychology of Twain's persona. It is perfectly fitted to the role of a traveler, allowing humor over the range of travelers and travel sites without limiting the viewpoint. Since the sublime elements of *Innocents* were important in establishing a positive viewpoint toward real beauty to play against false historicity, this flexibility is important.

Both lectures and the book *The Innocents Abroad* were well received. Local material directed to the San Francisco audience was trimmed out of the book and sublime passages added or enhanced. Pushing Bliss for early publication, he had written that his "bread and butter" reputation was at stake. As sales mounted in September, 1869, he mused, rather ambivalently, "The irreverence of the volume appears to be a tip-top feature of it, (financially) diplomatically speaking, though I wish with all my heart there wasn't an irreverent passage in it."[32] Literary comedy superficially clashed with his interests as an ethicist, as it did with other comedians, and the problem was not ever to be fully resolved.

There were many favorable comments on the *Innocents* volume. Oliver Wendell Holmes wrote from Boston, with considerably more caution than Emerson had exercised in acknowledging Whitman's *Leaves of Grass*, that he appreciated Twain's *Yankee* attitude toward things that were either intellectualized into unintelligibility or sentimentalized into absurdity by other travelers. As if echoing Twain's sentiments, William Dean Howells wrote in *The Atlantic Monthly*: "Yet the man who can be honest enough to let himself see the realities of human life everywhere, or who has only seen Americans as they are abroad, has not travelled in vain and is far from a useless guide."[33] Howells' sympathy with Twain and with the literary tra-

---

[32] Hamlin Hill (ed.), *Mark Twain's Letters to His Publishers, 1867–1894* (Berkeley: University of California Press, 1967), 24.

[33] Quoted in Paine (ed.), *Letters*, 166–67. In the *Atlantic Monthly*, XXIV (December, 1869), 764–66, Howells consistently wrote "Clements" as the author's name. This was probably due to Bliss's use of forged autographs on presentation copies rather than to carelessness on Howells' part. Doesticks returned one such autograph to Twain according to the letters reprinted by Lorch, "'Doesticks' and *Innocents Abroad*."

dition that he was coming to dominate established a lifelong friendship. Only Bret Harte's unsigned review in the *Overland Monthly* treated Twain as a western writer, and his description of the persona was shrewd in comparing Twain and Ward:

> Most of the criticism is just in spirit, although extravagent, and often too positive in style. But it should be remembered that the style itself is a professional exaggeration, and that the irascible pilgrim, "Mark Twain," is a very eccentric creation of Mr. Clemens'. We can, perhaps, no more fairly hold Mr. Clemens responsible for "Mark Twain's" irreverence than we could have held the late Charles F. Browne to account for "Artemus Ward's" meanness and humbuggery. There may be a question of taste in Mr. Clemens permitting such a man as "Mark Twain" to go to the Holy Land at all; but we contend that such a traveler would be more likely to report its external aspect truthfully than a man of larger reverence.[34]

The *Atheneum*, in London, indicated how really literary the Mark Twain figure is by comparing it to the Thackeray persona in *The Book of Snobs*. Finally though, as Holmes implies, the impression of the book is close to *Sam Slick* without the regional limitation.

Entering the 1870s, Twain was throwing rays of energy into every corner penetrated by the literary comedians. *Innocents* was bringing in fourteen hundred dollars a month. Twain was offered a partnership by Nasby in the Toledo *Blade* in April, 1869, and Charles Dudley Warner tried to get him a partnership in the Hartford *Courant*; he briefly settled in as editor on the Buffalo *Express*, with the help of Jervis Langdon, and took on a comic column, "Memoranda," for the *Galaxy Magazine* from March, 1870, through April, 1871. Nasby turned down Twain's offer of a joint lecture tour because the Fourteenth Amendment had sapped the point of his "Cussed be Canaan." Lecturing in New England, Twain evidenced his own ambivalence about the comic platform in requesting Redpath not to advertise his appearances.[35] In the summer of 1870 he was thinking

---

34 [Bret Harte,] "Current Literature," *Overland Monthly*, IV (January, 1870), 100–101. The reviews cited here can also be found in Frederick Anderson (ed.), *Mark Twain: The Critical Heritage* (New York: Barnes & Noble, 1971), with others.

35 Wecter (ed.) *Love Letters of Mark Twain*, 85. Nasby's letter was preserved and is in the Mark Twain Papers at Berkeley. Fatout, *Mark Twain on the Lecture Circuit*, 122–23.

about a Western book and wrote his brother Orion for his notebooks on the journey West; in mid-May, 1871, with the help of Joe Goodman from Virginia City, he had finished four hundred pages.

A letter in the Mark Twain papers indicates the forces that haunted even the successful literary comedian in the rapidly changing literary atmosphere of America in the 1840-1880 period. B. P. Shillaber wrote to Twain on New Year's Day, 1871, on the nature of the phenomenon that Twain, inheriting Ward's mantle, seemed to represent. Thanking Twain for a contribution to his paper and requesting a copy of the recently published *Burlesque Autobiography*, Shillaber went on to say that he was out of a job and looking for something to turn up:

I am glad to see such evidence of your popularity, that augurs prosperity. The papers are full of you, from East to West and all delight in the genial Mark. You seem inexhaustible—the young juices not having all been exhausted in the stalk is a promise given of ripe growth. Well, bless you my dear fellow! Make your hay while your sun shines—advice that I can give from my own experience as I have thrown away several fortunes through my cussed foolishness in neglecting to do what I now advise.[36]

Shillaber had published Sam Clemens' first offering in the *Carpet-Bag* in 1852 and had fostered Phoenix, Ward, and Halpine. He had written a poetic "Congratulatory" on February 7, 1870, on the occasion of Twain's marriage to Olivia Langdon, praising Twain's success there as well.[37] The conjunction of praise and warning must have been a grim New Year's greeting to Twain, emphasizing the prevailing ephemerality of the medium in which he worked. Yet his career was full and successful. Lecturing, newspaper work, and, with *Roughing It* in 1872, four books testified to his energy. "Cannibalism in the Cars" had been published in England (where his works were being actively pirated) in Routledge's *Broadway Magazine*. In 1872 he sailed for England as the preeminent American humorist.

After 1871 Twain's career changes in tone. Where he had sought connections with literary comedians in the 1860s, later comedians

---

36 Shillaber's Letter, dated January 1, 1870 [1871], is in the Mark Twain Papers at Berkeley and is quoted by permission.
37 B. P. Shillaber, *Lines in Pleasant Places*, 157-58.

sought connection with him. Letters from Bill Nye, James Whitcomb Riley, Robert Burdette, and others are extant. Howells moved from favorable reviews to publication of short pieces in the *Atlantic*, and from 1874 on through the decade, Twain pieces appear in every volume save one. P. T. Barnum pursued Twain to advertise his show, and the two became close friends—Barnum sending Twain batches of newspaper clippings about odd items on more than one occasion. Twain accepted such friendships, and in Barnum's case drew on Barnum-related materials to begin his best later novels, *A Connecticut Yankee* and *Pudd'nhead Wilson*. J. W. DeForest, the realist writer who anticipated *The Gilded Age* with "An Inspired Lobbyist" and *Honest John Vane*, wrote to Twain in 1874 about the possibility of publishing a joint volume of short stories. Both Charles Dudley Warner and Bret Harte, the latter applauded on two continents for his verse and short stories, were glad to coauthor works with Twain. At his fiftieth birthday, the *Critic* celebrated his half-century in one issue in 1885 with poems by O. W. Holmes and testimonials from other popular regionalists. Grateful for his advancing reputation, Twain could write to Howells that he approached the *Atlantic* cheerfully because he did not have to paint himself striped and stand on his head. Still, he continued to write as a literary comedian. And it is the saturation of his fiction with the elements of literary comedy that expresses Twain's ethics as they have been discussed in this chapter, and as they were to appear in his novels.

SIX

Toward the Novel

TWAIN'S VOICE—the persona—focuses the literary comedy. The 1860s was a time for experimentation with this voice in a variety of subjects—burlesques, travel narratives, semiserious reporting—and he never really stopped developing, as his travel narratives show. Twain advanced literary comedy significantly by using the flexibility of his voice to blend plot and author, playing humor against the dramatization of events. The literary comedian thus came to occupy a place inside the novel by virtue of his characteristic attitude toward social and political events. The recording of Pap's "call this a gov'ment" speech in Huck's voice is a natural outgrowth of this management of tone, the technique which originates in the burlesques of the 1860 period. Twain's letters to the *Alta California* and a series of letters for the *Missouri Democrat* in 1866 and 1867 give particularly clear revelations of Twain's experiments in such forms. The resolution which he achieved shapes his novels.

The literary interests of the San Francisco bohemians probably encouraged Twain to attempt an increasingly elevated tone in his writing, and Ward had attempted to refine his voice similarly in the course of his development. Twain's writing, aside from the jumping frog story which he sent east to Ward, included reviews, city news, burlesques of plays as well as of the local government, miscellaneous items on the spiritualists, fashions, and local amusements, and, of course, travel letters. Edgar Branch notes the entrance into the San

Francisco writing of a sense of Twain's own past, enriching descriptions with a more broadly implicative consciousness, as in the case of a mural at a local establishment which is described with mock piety as being as gorgeous "as a Presbyterian picture of hell." His letters from Hawaii are in a Twainian voice, but with a perspective that reverses later views; in order that San Francisco get more whaling business, he suggests that the city "cripple your facilities for 'pulling' sea captains on every pretense that sailors can trump."[1] His later egalitarian ethics solidified on his trip from San Francisco to New York.

Where Ward's national popularity was based on contemporary events, religious sects, and local events like the visit of Albert Edward, Twain's reputation was based on more literary-seeming material, the frog story and travel letters which were identified for their representation of the narrator's American egalitarian viewpoint. His pose was not burdened with any visual limitation such as the cacography that Ward, and following him Josh Billings, labored under. The transition from reportorial commentator to lyceum lecturer was consequently more natural, and corresponded comfortably to the establishment of the lyceum agency, which brought such lectures to predetermined audiences. As Twain's audience became sophisticated culturally, politically, and economically, his stance as a comedian was flexible enough to permit him to speak to them. Where Ward was aware of contemporary literature and employed the burlesque freely, Twain was not only literary but also religious in his exact biblical references and cosmopolitan in his mixture of colloquial and sublime diction and attitudes to build comic statements into longer narrative formats.

Experimenting in humorous modes, Twain recast columns of reportorial comedy into dramatic pieces. His burlesques began to capture the political and moral overtones of the democracy. A series of paralleling newspaper items exist from the 1860s which show Twain presenting material in reportorial format and then reworking the same material into dramatic pieces. He touched on marriage and

---

[1] Branch, *Literary Apprenticeship of Mark Twain*, 130; Day (ed.), *Mark Twain's Letters from Hawaii*, 94–95.

morality, Barnum's candidacy for Congress, and the woman's suffrage question, exploring the possibilities of comic writing in the dual formats. A vulgar persona like Barnum or Captain Ned Wakeman could sometimes demonstrate a point through burlesque; at other times Twain the semiserious reporter could speak. The moralist of the main was finding a dramatic voice.

Twain's treatment of Barnum's American Museum in conjunction with his bid for Congress is well beyond Ward's showman even though both are burlesques of the same figure as an American type. Dated March 2, 1867, Twain's report on Barnum's museum to the *Alta California* was published on April 9, 1867, under the title "How Are the Mighty Fallen!"; "Barnum's First Speech in Congress," a variant of this article, appeared in the New York *Evening Express* on March 5, 1867.[2] In "How Are the Might Fallen!" Mark Twain the reporter visits Barnum's museum in New York because Barnum's running for Congress imbues everything connected to him with a new interest. He notices the stairs running from floor to floor, the crowds, and the general seediness of the museum. The eight-foot-high woman merely sits, for "there was no one to stir her up and make her show her points," a phrase reminiscent of the frog story. The giant, too, merely sits, making Twain declare that if he was impresario of that "menagerie," he would "make that couple prance around some, or dock their rations." Two dwarfs, a speckled Negro, and a Circassian girl "complete the list of human curiosities." Otherwise, Twain comments that Barnum's museum is "one vast peanut stand now."

The reporter is commenting on the same things that would preoccupy him in Europe. Experiences held out to be elevating turn out to be vulgar or fraudulent; this is more obviously the case with Barnum and such exhibits as the "Happy Family." The lions and other beasts that make up the show sleep all the time, and Twain notes the spiritless bear, mangy puppies, and meek tomcats—all "bossed

---

2 "How are the Mighty Fallen!" is reprinted in Franklin Walker and G. Ezra Dane (eds.), *Mark Twain's Travels with Mr. Brown* (New York: Alfred A. Knopf, 1940), 116–19, as part of Letter XI. "Barnum's First Speech in Congress" has been made available to me by Professor Louis Budd. This selection from the New York *Express* matches a portion of the letter reprinted in *Brown*, 286, as being from the New York *Telegram* and subsequently the *Alta*.

and bullied" by a monkey who cuffs the rabbits and raccoons and chases all the other animals away from the feed tub. Twain remarks that "the world is full of families as happy as that," but the monkey who lost his tail to the boss monkey will have to find his solace in philosophy. The reporter Twain also describes the dust-covered Venus and the leering drunken waxwork representing Queen Victoria. These displays and the moral drama called the "Christian Martyr" compose the attraction of Barnum's show, and Twain concludes that "if he has no better show to get to Congress, he ought to draw out of the canvass." This is acerbic Twain, both expository *and* narrative with the description of the "Happy Family" approaching burlesque.

The parallel item to "How Are the Mighty Fallen!" is a dramatized speech to Congress by Barnum, delivered to Twain out of the future by "spiritual telegraph." The introduction which frames Barnum's speech is a considerable advance over the formal style of Twain's youthful writing, for it is cast in the relatively modern reportorial style of the 1860s rather than in the formal diction of Longstreet. Twain observes that it would be a "genuine pity" if Barnum could not find a way of dovetailing business and patriotism "to the mutual benefit of himself and the Great Republic." Barnum's burlesque speech begins crassly: "Mr. Speaker—What do we do with a diseased curiosity? Sell him!" This mood is developed as Barnum takes the opportunity of the speech to praise his animals, Jenny Lind, his low admission price—reminiscent of Artemus Ward's claims for his show —and the numerous peanut stands, "two peanut stands to each natural curiosity," recapturing an idea stressed in the narrative article. Stating that his numerous curiosities are no excuse for him to become complacent, Barnum describes his spotted Negro, camels, "Sacred Cattle from the sacred hills of New Jersey," and "two plaster of Paris Venuses and a varnished mud-turtle." The last line doubles the number of Venuses from Twain's account—exaggeration—and adds the mud turtle to undercut the speech through anticlimax. The narrative account is consequently expanded through comic devices when it is placed in the voice of a character. This is a chief reason why the narrators of Twain's novels embody many of his important social ironies in their own deadpan comic presentations, and it is a controlling factor in the texture of Twain's major works.

As Barnum's speech continues, the same exhibits that Twain the reporter noticed appear as part of the boast of the burlesque congressman. Twain's line that he would dock the rations of the giant is transformed into a consistent strain of materialism in Barnum. The objective irony becomes part of the dramatization of the character. Artemus Ward's only such fully dramatized creation, besides the showman himself, was Jim Griggins. Barnum, however, like the congressmen in *The Gilded Age*, is a self-burlesquing dramatic entity: "Shall I bask in mine own bliss and be mute in the season of my people's peril? No! Because I possess the smallest dwarfs in the world, and the Nova Scotian giantess, who weighs a ton and eats her weight every forty-eight hours; and Herr Phelim O'Flannigan the Norwegian Giant, who feeds on the dwarfs and ruins business; and the lovely Circassian girl; and the celebrated Happy Family." Ward's style of comic rhetoric is almost reversed in this passage. Instead of using moral and political sentiments as a means of describing his show, Barnum in Twain's hands is made to employ the mentality of a showman to decide the course of the nation. In similar cases, Ward's sentiments were expressed as an incongruously idealistic projection of his professional experience, not as a part of the fabric of his commercial enterprise. By connecting the showman with this sort of submerged venality, Twain is attacking a double corruption, first of Congress, and second of the real role of businessmen. Significantly, Twain's dramatization carries an implied rejection of the likelihood of a moral truth coming from a "vulgar" person.

As Barnum continues speaking, more of the facets of his museum are drawn into the texture of his supposed world view, even including the arrangement of stairs to direct attention of displays. His mind, in fact, begins to run his show and the Congress together, as he appeals to "every true heart in this august menagerie" to save the nation from demagogues who beard the starry-robed woman in her citadel while "to you the bearded woman looks for succor." The conflict between the executive and the legislative branches of government over the Fourteenth Amendment is breaking up the happy family of the Union. Barnum further complains that the poor Negro is only white in spots like his Leopard Boy, and has gained universal suffering rather than universal suffrage. By the close of the speech, Twain has completely submerged Barnum's radical Republicanism in the museum curiosities dominating the burlesque rhetoric. Irony has become literary characterization as the materialistic mind is discredited through its incapacity to sever its selfishness from the concerns of government:

> The country is fallen! The boss monkey sits in the feed-tub, and the tomcats, the raccoons and the gentle rabbits of the once happy family stand helpless and afar off, and behold him gobble the provender in the pride of his strength! Woe is me!
> Ah, gentlemen, our beloved Columbia, with these corroding distresses upon her, must soon succumb! The high spirit will depart from her eye, the bloom from her cheek, the majesty from her step, and she will stand before us gaunt and worn, like my beautiful giantess when my dwarfs and Circassians prey upon her rations! Soon we shall see the glory of the realm pass away as did the grandeur of the Museum amid the consuming fires, and the wonders the world admires shall give place to trivialities, even as in the proud Museum the wonders that once amazed have given place to cheap stuffed reptiles and peanut stands! Woe is me!
> O, spirit of Washington! forgotten in these evil times, thou art banished to the dusty corridors of memory, a staring effigy of wax, and none could recognize thee but for the label pinned upon thy legs! . . . Woe is me!
> Rouse ye, my people, rouse ye! rouse ye! rouse ye! Shake off the fatal stupor that is upon ye, and hurl the usurping tyrant from his Throne! Impeach! impeach! impeach!—Down with the dread boss monkey! O, snake the seditious miscreant out of the national feed-tub and reconstruct the Happy Family!
> Such is the speech imparted to me in advance from the spirit land. Mark Twain.

The happy family, the inactive giantess, the museum fire of 1865, and the wax figures that annoyed the reporter Twain all become parts of Barnum's mental apparatus. The speaker's attack on Andrew Johnson, made obvious by the references to the Fourteenth Amendment and Negro suffrage, as well as to the "Executive," is discredited by the ridiculous boss-monkey metaphor; Barnum's rhetorical "woe is me!" suggests a repetitious posturing that also casts doubt on his argument. Twain's restraint in the final sentence, which frames the story without any comment, is an ironic contrast.[3]

"Barnum's First Speech in Congress," like Twain's other experiments in this political idiom in 1867 and 1868, is a partial reflection of the influence of Ward's success in the old showman persona. Twain rejected the mind of Barnum as he understood it at that time but employed the comic representation of legislators and legislative jargon, much as Ward used the showman figure and contemporary social events. Another piece of social commentary handled similarly was based around Captain Wakeman's marriage of two runaway lovers on the trip from San Francisco to the Isthmus, recorded in *Mark Twain's Travels with Mr. Brown*.[4] Conventional morality is thrown into colloquial dialect as Wakeman advises the lovers to "splice and make the most of it," an ironic proposal since the couple placed no value on marriage, according to Twain. The dominant feeling imparted by Twain is genteel skepticism, and the bride's father is given an imaginary line—"You miserable, heartless dog, you have stolen away my child!"—which melodramatizes the incident; reporting is approaching fiction increasingly in such a piece.

Twain's newspaper burlesques on the woman's suffrage question show an even wider range of techniques in imaginative fiction than the other items from the 1867 period. They burlesqued the newspaper letter, reportorial prose, and legislative debates. "Cannibalism in the Cars," which represents a finished application of political burlesque to fiction writing, belongs to the final stage of this development. Taken together, the materials indicate a unity in Twain's newspaper writing in the late 1860s and foreshadow the political sections of *The Gilded Age*.

The suffrage items are as clearly transitional as anything Twain had previously done. In the first item, Twain creates a list of pseudo-government positions, such as "State Crinoline Directress" at $10,000

---

[3] There is a paradigm for Twain's depiction of Barnum in "Artemus Ward in Washington" in which the showman employs the terminology of national politics in conjunction with his private interests: "I'm reconstructing my show. I've Bo't a collection of life-size wax figgers of our prominent Revolutionary forefathers. I bo't 'em at auction, and got 'em cheap. They stand me about two dollars and fifty cents (2 dols. 50 cents) per Revolutionary forefather. Ever as always yours, A. Ward."

[4] Walker and Dane (eds.), *Travels with Mr. Brown*, 13–15, 18–19, 23–25.

salary per year, to be filled by greedy female officeseekers. Lists of offices, as in *The Gilded Age*, are mixed with echoes of the coal oil lamp era of political canvassing seen in Ward's Baldinsville. "Mr. Twain" concludes, as a "family" man, which he was not, that his wife will leave him to such chores as wet nursing. He was following Billings in this irony; Billings said he would rather a woman beat him at nursing a baby than at a stump speech or a lecture on veterinary practice. Twain's second item uses the letter convention to present burlesque attacks on him as an opponent of female suffrage. The first two letters are closely parallel diatribes by Mrs. Mark Twain and Mrs. Zeb Leavenworth.[5] Both spend a paragraph berating Twain and threatening him with violence; they conclude with pious hopes that their arguments may have benefited the cause, enabling the two to die "happy and content." The fullness of the repetition projects the suffragists as uniformly bloody-minded harridans. More importantly, Twain's characteristic diction and exaggeration flow into his characterizations; the way was being paved toward fiction.

Twain's third letter on the suffrage issue was written in response to a real letter to the *Democrat* and was written in yet another reportorial voice. In stating his serious premises before turning to burlesque, he reveals that he, like Ward, was genteel and idealistic: "I never want to see women voting, gabbling about politics, and electioneering. There is something revolting in the thought. It would shock me inexpressibly for an angel to come down from above and ask me to take a drink with him (although I should doubtless consent); but it would shock me still more to see one of our blessed earthly angels peddling election tickets among a mob of shabby scoundrels she never saw before." The reactionary sentiment—like Ward, showing a dislike for the ignorant and loathsome with the

---

5 Mark Twain, "Female Suffrage/Views of Mark Twain," St. Louis *Missouri Democrat*, March 12, 13, 1866; "Female Eddikashun," *Josh Billings: His Sayings* (New York: Carleton, 1866), 26–27. As a tangential point, the use of "Mrs. Zeb Leavenworth," offers evidence of the continuity of Twain's mind in holding comic formulations. In 1864, three years earlier, he signed the name "Zeb Leavenworth," a pilot friend from his Mississippi days, to a burlesque letter in "Those Blasted Children" which also uses strong language treating Twain as an advice-giver, while mentioning loss of hair, here, Mrs. Leavenworth threatens to "snatch hair out of his head till he is as bald as a phrenological bust." The phrase and joke were retained together with their context and later recast to suit current needs. This ability bears on the relation between Twain and previous literary comedians.

vote[6]—is blended with the parenthetical pose of the loose-moraled reporter—an almost all-inclusive pose.

Twain describes suffragette women as interested in abolishing tobacco, alcohol, late evenings out for men, and little else. He complains that women will even want to go to war. The piece is drifting, however, toward a better stance as the irony broadens: "We will let you teach school as much as you want to, and we will pay you half wages for it, too, but beware! We don't want you to crowd us too much!" Humorous devices—the comic aside, the termagant type, legislative burlesque—are being turned to the uses of social criticism. As Louis Budd points out, the mixture of attitudes is unsatisfying in its failure to coalesce into a single unified statement.[7] Yet Ward, without the variable persona, had struggled with similar topics in similar ways. The flexibility of Twain's newspaper voice is an advance that brings him near to the first-person narratives of the travel books and novels. He is ready to offer multiple viewpoints, and his sense of ethics and justice is beginning to form his material and infuse his voice.

The next suffrage piece, "Petticoat Government," is a dramatic burlesque along the lines of Barnum's burlesque speech to Congress.[8] The women betray their personal preoccupations—with gored dresses and waterfall hair styles—to the exclusion of any legislative business other than antidrinking and antitobacco laws. The speeches and asides are recorded as formal oratory, while interspersed among the digressions on fashion are a few harried male attempts to invoke parliamentary rules; the men's chief concern—and here Twain's consciousness is again clearly at work—is the granting of five million dollars for the relief of the Great Pacific Railroad. Beginning the report he had remarked that if women entered government "there would occur almost as disgraceful scenes as have lately blurred the record of Congressional proceedings," and he continues

---

6 Mark Twain, "Female Suffrage/The Iniquitous Crusade." St. Louis *Missouri Democrat*, March 15, 1867; Ward, *Works*, 417.

7 As Ward's Betsy Jane threatened to do in "A War Meeting," Ward, *Works*, 251. Louis Budd, *Mark Twain, Social Philosopher* (Bloomington: University of Indiana Press, 1962), 23–24.

8 Mark Twain, "Female Suffrage/Petticoat Government," New York *Sunday Mercury*, April 7, 1867, p. 3.

to make a broad application of the burlesque through the overly rhetorical complaint of Mr. Slawson, of St. Genevieve, that the tirade on fashions was "a matter trivial enough at any time, God knows, but utterly insignificant in presence of so grave a matter as the behests of the Great Pacific Railroad." Add plot continuity and setting to this sort of humor, and the texture of *The Gilded Age* or some portions of *Roughing It* is present in mature form. In *The Gilded Age*, the antirailroad populism was converted into the symbolic encounter between Philip Sterling and Conductor Slum; the rhetoric went to Senator Dilworthy and his cohorts.

The legislative burlesque, which gave Twain scope for ironic exaggerations in diction, was a seductive medium for literary comedians, and Twain was no exception. He already knew that satire could succeed as travesty, as in "The Petrified Man" and the "Bloody Massacre" story, if the travesty did not overwhelm the satire.[9] In "Cannibalism in the Cars," Twain's ability in this area reached its most sophisticated level of expression.

"Cannibalism in the Cars," published in England somewhat later than the other burlesques in this series, is based on an inversion of social and political formality. Here, Twain used political hypocrisy in a more generalized manner than local issues such as Barnum and suffrage allowed. The representatives themselves are the subjects for discussion as various candidates for a cannibal stew. "I liked Harris," or "I have conceived an affection for you. I could like you as well as I liked Harris himself, sir," become dubious compliments.[10] When the narrator of the cannibalism story remarks to his auditor, "This decision created considerable dissatisfaction among the friends of Mr. Ferguson, the defeated candidate," the ironic reversal shows how political terms mask distorted purposes—and also shows how vanity can be contradicted by reality.

9 "Memoranda," *Galaxy*, IX (June, 1870), 858, reprinted in *Contributions to "The Galaxy*," 47.
10 Mark Twain, "Cannibalism in the Cars," reprinted in *Sketches, New and Old*, 339–51. It originally appeared in *Broadway*, November, 1868, a house organ for the publishing firm of Routledge, Twain's British publisher at this time. An analogue for this story, which Artemus Ward created in London in 1866, appears in "Artemus Ward and Mark Twain," by Aaron Watson, *The Savage Club* (London: T. Fisher Unwin, 1907), 120–22, and anticipates the story in many details. Twain reduced the story to a one-line joke in "Riley—Newspaper Correspondent," *Contributions to "The Galaxy*," 90: "had a grand human barbecue in honor of [the cannibal flag], in which it was noticed that the better a man liked a friend the better he enjoyed him."

The sketch is actually more generalized than earlier related pieces through its comic diction. The frame is unobtrusive, and the story begins in a sublime suspense, in which such phrases as "eternal night" and "in the shadow of death" mark the early going. As the parliamentary rhetoric increases, however, the disjunctions between language and events become more grotesque. Even nature is personified, dragging in a sort of antipastoral element: "Nature had been taxed to the limit [by hunger]—she must yield. RICHARD H. GASTON of Minnesota, tall, cadaverous, and pale, rose up.... Only a calm thoughtful seriousness appeared in the eyes that were lately so wild."[11] The formal "yielding" of nature is between high comedy and pun. When the narrator comments, following the nomination of prospective dinners, that "some little caucussing followed," the diction holds the deadpan pose essential to a burlesque of democratic formuli. Human nature is actually at issue, for it is the catastrophic event and the passengers' response which is the action of the story. Cannibalism establishes the importance of the events to the nominees in exaggerated form.

Twain's diction, which seems the source of his humor, is actually subordinated to plot development as Ward's was not. The frame sequence, as with the jumping frog story, has removed the anecdote from the author's own mouth. The "member of Congress" who tells the story deserves a place beside Simon Wheeler, however, for he too is using digression and the deadpan as a means of stating his "experience." Even more significant is Twain's combination of the storyteller with a burlesque based on contemporary American materials; appropriate to the milieu of the literary comedians, the story takes place in a railroad car rather than in the backwoods. Hank Morgan, Huck Finn, and a number of lesser characters grow out of similar combinations. Because the experience is a narrated story, it has only a nominal reality; as fantasy, the social irony of self versus manners underlies the humor. The story is no more a characterization of its teller, really, than is the frog story of Simon Wheeler. Cor-

---

11 Twain uses names of friends Dan Slote and Charles Langdon. Ward's "The Fair Inez" supplies a precedent for this coterie device in using names of his Cleveland friends, and the practice was probably a common one.

porate ethics are at issue just as vanity is at issue in the "Jumping Frog." Many episodes in Twain's longer works depend on this effect; they are applicable as philosophical experience even though the reader knows they are unreal.

Twain is creating literature out of the material of the 1860s in "Cannibalism in the Cars." Egalitarian notions of government offer a comic mode for treating situations, and Twain is able to use such notions outside the Civil War context of Kerr and Nasby. Yet Twain's irony is inescapable. When "on the sixth [ballot], Mr. Harris was elected, all voting for him but himself," the point is again made that no amount of parliamentary rhetoric obscures the practical consideration of an individual's well-being; and so it was when Artemus Ward stepped forward and offered the vicarious sacrifice of his brother-in-law and uncle if need be to win the Civil War. The frame sequence that ends the story allows this "slurred nub" to remain an abstraction, clearly untrue but still horrifying to the auditor in the car. The texture of Twain's fiction, created by his diction and irony—his persona—appears in finished form in this short story. To understand how comparable materials condition a reader's understanding of Twain's viewpoint, it is necessary to examine the open framework for humor which Twain's travel fiction provided, and which became part of his machinery for creating the novel.

THE TRAVEL NARRATIVE

The Innocents Abroad and the material related to it provide particularly clear relationships between literary tradition, Twainian pose, and ethical intention. In these relationships, the extension of the narrative into a rudimentary story foreshadows the novels' picaresque structure, as the material just studied foreshadows their texture. Twain's intention as a writer of literary comedy was set when he undertook the *Quaker City* voyage, and the writer's problem was thus to fit actual experience into a preconceived pose—a thoroughly literary exercise. Allusions to the Ward-Barnum tradition helped establish his viewpoint, and the interplay between the persona and the foreign milieu establish the tension between Old Europe and the new American viewpoint for which the book became famous. The book's events also coalesced around this viewpoint, however, and developed an increasingly serious demonstration of humanitarian qualities.

The book *The Innocents Abroad* was preceded by travel letters that were varied in quality but maintained the flexibility of persona and voice distinguishing his other work. Phoenix had written travel burlesques, as had Ward. Mortimer Thomson, whom Twain corresponded with about the *Quaker City* voyage, had published comic and burlesque travel adventures as early as 1855 in *Doesticks, What He Says*. Twain's own intention is shown most clearly in his letter describing Bierstadt's picture of Yosemite, which was on display in New York when he was there: "It is more the atmosphere of Kingdom-come than of California. As a picture, the work must please, but as a portrait I do not think it will answer. Portraits should be accurate. We do not want feeling and intelligence smuggled into the pictured face of an idiot, and we do not want this glorified atmosphere smuggled into a portrait of the Yosemite where it surely does not belong. I may be wrong, but still I believe that this atmosphere of Mr. Bierstadt's is altogether too gorgeous."[12]

Twain's sense of the Old Masters, as shown in "The Second Advent," applied the same realistic test to sentimentalized religion. Twain's notebooks show this skepticism toward the Holy Land even before he had been there, as Dewey Ganzel has pointed out, and he had already bracketed passages in guidebooks for special treatment. The literary comedian expresses his vision by describing, in Mr. Ganzel's words, "Missouri in Venice, the commonplace surroundings of the exotic, a pattern he was to use again and again in *IA*."[13] The vulgarian's commonplace, almost the viewpoint of the low thief, would control the responses of the American vandal abroad and reveal the psychology of "Mark Twain."

The beginning complaint of Twain's letters is almost an unnecessary vehicle for expressing his American vision through comedy. He

---

12 "Letter 24," *Alta California* (dated New York, June 2, 1867), in Scrapbook Seven, Mark Twain Papers, University of California, Berkeley.

13 John S. Tuckey (ed.), *Mark Twain's Fables of Man* (Berkeley: University of California Press, 1972), 50–68; Dewey Ganzel, *Mark Twain Abroad* (Chicago: University of Chicago Press, 1968), 146, 221.

complained that the travel books had shamefully deceived him, in a passage that was dropped from the Turkish Bath sequence before it went into *The Innocents Abroad*: "What is a Turkish bath in Constantinople to a Russian one in New York? What are the dancing dervishes to the negro minstrels?—and Heaven help us, what is Oriental splendor to the Black Crook?" To flesh out this view with humor, Twain borrowed freely from the tradition of literary comedy. Ward complained that all the jugs in the British Museum were of uncertain age—which did not affect him until he discovered that his chicken at lunch was also "of a uncertain age." Twain captured the same experience in a "Turkish Lunch" (II, 86–87) and expanded upon it with "euchre" terms from the American frontier. "Bishop Southgate's Matinee," in the *Alta* letters, copied Ward's burlesque panorama, which featured a drunken projectionist, from his 1866 tour. Both writers drew comic relationships between religious quackery and the Constitution. P. T. Barnum, earlier, and Twain, later, tested guides for truthfulness in the same way, and both found they lied.[14] Other jokes follow the same tradition.

The circus motif, which Barnum and Ward had developed as an American literary tradition, influences Twain's pose significantly, particularly in the crucial area of religion. In the opening sequence of the book, he masquerades as a minister with claims to the "missionary business" looking for a "show," a sort of Simon Suggs-Artemus Ward compound. Perhaps due to the presence of a Barnum agent on the *Quaker City*, many of Twain's reports reflected the circus. The cathedral at Milan was "bossed" by a "gorgeous old brick" who was mummified and displayed: "It's not part of the regular circus, you know, and so you have to pay extra." Other priests run little sideshows and perform as if they were performing outside a menagerie. Recapturing his Barnum items from St. Louis, Twain said that an Italian dwarf wouldn't stand any "show" in Constantinople: "a beg-

14 Daniel Morley McKeithan (ed.), *Traveling with the Innocents Abroad* (Norman: University of Oklahoma Press, 1958), 132; Ward, *Works*, 444; *Travels with Mr. Brown*, 95–97. Compare Ward, *Works*, 44, on the Shakers, "said world continners to revolve round on her own axletree onct in every 24 hours, subjeck to the Constitution of the United States," with Twain's more refined *addition* to his letter in *The Innocents Abroad*, I, 68–69; "Antiquarians . . . agree that [Hercules] was an enterprizing and energetic man, but decline to believe him a good, bona fide god, because that would be unconstitutional." Barnum, *Life*, 268.

gar has to have exceedingly good points to make a living" there.[15] The diction serves a distinct function in such passages, reflecting the outraged humanity of the narrator. Such brief encounters, exaggerated through ironic diction, also pile up a series of episodes that establish tension between European civilization and the angry, show-conscious traveler. The traveler finally becomes an antagonist, and his travels take on some of the aspects of a plot in which corporate Europe is the enemy.

Twain's treatment of Constantinople offers another point that indicates his method of converting the materials of the comic tradition to fit his own persona. After labeling gilt script inside the dome of St. Sophia "as glaring as a circus bill," he turns his attention from the shoddy atmosphere to the "old-master worshippers from the wilds of New Jersey," combining in a phrase the ideas of art, religion, false reverence, and provincialism. Ward, treating such persons and their entertainers in "The Show Business and Popular Lectures," complained that nine out of ten people "don't have no moore idee of what the lecturer sed than my kangeroo has of the sevunth speer of hevun." Twain complains that his set of traveling American farmers "don't know any more about pictures than a kangaroo does about astronomy."[16] Ward's showman idiom has been altered in tone and generalized to express a yankee cosmopolitanism.

Not only in single lines but also in set pieces and comic vignettes does the tradition contribute to "Twain's" experience. Barnum in Liverpool was assaulted by beggars whom he took for nobility in his innocence; and after him Artemus Ward in London said, "I don't remember a instance since my 'rival in London of my gettin into a cab without a Briton comin and purlitely shuttin the door for me, and then extendin his open hand to'ards me, in the most frenly manner possible. Does he not, by this simple yit tuchin gesture, welcum me to England?" Twain, sharing the American background of Barnum and Ward, shows the same surprise at European beggars, but extends his dramatization in an *Alta* letter: "A crowd of bare-footed

---

15 Ganzel, *Mark Twain Abroad*, 54; McKeithan (ed.), *Traveling with the Innocents Abroad*, 50–51, 115–16.
16 Ward, *Works*, 83; McKeithan (ed.), *Traveling with the Innocents Abroad*, 117.

and ragged and dirty vagabonds, of both sexes, received us on the wharf, and with one hospitable impulse held out their hands. With one grateful impulse we seized the hands and shook them. And then we saw that their hospitality was a vain delusion—they only extended their hands to beg."[17] The earlier travelers had stopped their narrative after showing their own naïveté; Twain continues to define the community—"eminently Portuguese—that is to say, it is slow, poor, shiftless, sleepy and lazy." Continuing, Twain even locates a villain: "The good Catholic Portughee crossed himself and prayed to God to shield him from all blasphemous desire to know more than his father did before him."[18] Burlesque travel narratives take on through such identifications a tension between the narrator —Twain the American—and the milieu—dominated by static religiosity, the corporate church.

Before finishing the discussion of this nascent plot structure in the travel narrative, one or two other crucial borrowings from the tradition need to be developed as sources of the "American" persona, "Mark Twain." In Ward's London letters, the stealing of spoons, as Ward's "Uncle Wilyim" does, burlesques types who try to place themselves in an elevated social context, and newspaper items in Twain's era treat the subject of spoon stealing as comedy rather than with the life-and-death seriousness of *Moll Flanders*. Ward's letters and the Jim Griggins item use the joke as a representation of the venality of the small crook and to indicate his relative harmlessness—a sort of innocence. Twain used the "spoon stealing" joke three times in *The Innocents Abroad*, making it into a *motif* underlying the meeting between the *Quaker City* pilgrims and the Russian Czar. Twain had called into question the good sense and Christian charity of his fellow travelers early (I, 130), and here turns to satire, including through his special flexibility of voice even himself in the group. In the first reference, Twain states that he wants to steal the emperor's coat, claiming, "When I meet a man like that, I want something to remember him by (II, 110)." Then he described the tour by the *Quaker City*

---

17 Barnum, *Life*, 250–51; Ward, *Works*, 437; McKeithan (ed.), *Traveling with the Innocents Abroad*, 4.
18 McKeithan (ed.), *Traveling with the Innocents Abroad*, 16, 17.

party: "We spent half an hour idling through the palace, admiring the cozy apartments and the rich but eminently homelike appointments of the palace, and then the imperial family bade our party a kind good-by, and proceeded to count the spoons" (II, 110). The implication of the passage is that such travelers as the pious voyagers were "low" and vulgar, sharing the traits that Jim Griggins blamed on his lack of education. Twain's borrowing from Ward thus strikes at the essence of the trip, a social pretension by upwardly mobile post–Civil War Americans. And Twain thus develops a theme. Visiting the Russian grand duke, "We bade our distinguished hosts good-by, and they retired happy and contented to their apartments to count *their* spoons" (II, 114). The ship's sailors are even supposed to expand the burlesque of the Russian reception when the third cook—Twain would make it the *third* cook—of the *Quaker City* plays the Czar, damns the formal speech of the visitors and tells his first groom to "proceed to count the portable articles of value belonging to the premises" (II, 121). There is little likelihood that such events occurred as narrated, particularly since there is a literary tradition behind Twain's line. The "low" characterization is no longer attached to a low figure—it has become almost philosophical in its ironic implications about social vanity, and Twain thus reasserts the values of the American comedians even while traveling in a cosmopolitan guise and speaking in a normal colloquial voice.

A second borrowing from Artemus Ward is equally illuminating. Artemus Ward's "Is he dead?" joke shows a British landlord's skepticism about spiritualism in "The Green Lion and Oliver Cromwell." The landlord didn't want to speak to the spirit of the historical figure, he only wanted the spiritualist's room rent. This sort of aggressive practicality, intolerant of historical humbug, is the fund upon which Twain was drawing when in *The Innocents Abroad* he shows his "boys" confronting the guides with the same question. As the guides make a sideshow out of Columbus and an Egyptian mummy, Twain's characters play credulous naifs: "Christopher Columbo—pleasant name—is—is he dead?" (I, 305). The one-line joke is elaborated into a scene and into a motif, as with the spoon-stealing joke. It appears twice in the last chapter of Book I and again in the opening chapter of Book II (I, 305, 307; II, 5). The transference of the joke from the municipal palace of Genoa (and before that from Ward's London surroundings) through the Vatican Museum at Rome and finally to the catacombs under the Capuchin Convent gradually extends Twain's irony about historical showmanship into the area of European Catholicism. The elaboration of the joke is more sophisticated than Ward's digressions, and the turning of the joke from European fraud to the church's view of man is appropriate to Twain's moral and humanitarian concerns in his fiction. Rather than signifying merely a verbal relation cloaking disparate and antagonistic intentions, as Bernard DeVoto has written, such open borrowings of jokes like the "Is he dead?" formula reflect the unity of viewpoint underlying the various American humorists generally.[19] Twain's elaboration and expansion of such jokes in language and format is his development of the tradition into a vision beyond the level of contemporary newspaper humor.

Finally, Twain's social reflections and religious commentary are pulled together in the Holy Land in burlesque scenes such as the Tomb of Adam sequence and in genteel statements such as those on

---

19 DeVoto, *Mark Twain's America*, 220–21. More recently, Edwin H. Cady, *The Light of Common Day* (Bloomington: Indiana University Press, 1971), 80, has said that this "seems to me one of the classic instances of American humor, especially as it peaks in Chapter XXVII of *The Innocents Abroad*." Twain later took this same "Is he dead?" formula one step further in fabricating a story to define his attitude toward John Altgeld, who was running for the Illinois governorship on the platform that he would enforce all the laws of the state fully. Twain pretended that his anecdote was an actual experience from a circus in Little Rock, Arkansas, which was displaying an Egyptian Mummy:

As the guide was giving (his talk) to the party of ten-cents-apiece customers, pointing out the various features of interest, a solemn-looking fellow, Bert Wheeler, interrupted him.

"Is this man dead?" he asked.

"Oh, yes, of course. He—"

"How did he die?" persisted Bert.

"Don't know," returned the attendant. "He—"

"Ever been an inquest held over him in this county?" broke in Bert.

"No, you see, he's been dead for a long time," said the attendant. "Maybe four thousand years. So you see—"

"Makes no difference," snapped Bert. "I'm the coroner of this county, and if you haven't already a certificate on this man's death, he's got to have an inquest. That's the law. Boys, bring the deceased along. The laws of this county must be upheld." Opie Read, *Mark Twain and I* (Chicago: Reilley & Lee, 1940), 119. This story was presented as a "real" experience, even though the "Is he dead?" element identifies it as an extension of the traditional skepticism of the literary naif. So completely does Twain come to believe in the literary expression that it finally becomes a new anecdote from the "old" Southwest to express his political views. One must not underestimate the value of this insight into Twain's use of local and vernacular-seeming materials.

Godfrey of Bouillon. The rhetorical highpoint, however, comes during the race into the Holy Land before the Sabbath. Twain's outrage at this point proves the value of his flexible voice, for his statement is intended to be taken seriously and is not burdened with a comic pose or inflection. He had made sarcastic comments about the Plymouth Collection of Hymns dominating ship life and remarked that Balaam's ass was "The patron saint of all pilgrims like us" (II, 173). He is beyond this sarcasm and outside of his fictional character in attacking formulaic Christianity as he saw its immediate consequences in the Holy Land:

> They *must* press on [the "pilgrims" trying to reach a holy point before Sunday]. Men might die, horses might die, but they must enter upon holy soil next week, with no sabbath-breaking stain upon them. Thus they were willing to commit a sin against the spirit of religious law, in order that they might preserve the letter of it. It was not worth while to tell them "the letter kills." I am talking now about personal friends; men whom I like; men who are good citizens; who are honorable, upright, conscientious: but whose idea of the Savior's religion seems to me distorted. (II, 172)

Josh Billings had commented in *His Sayings* in 1865 that "Heathen are alwus kind tew hosses, it iz only among Christian people, that a hoss hez tew trot 3 mile heats, in a hot da, for $2500 kounterfit munny," and other analogues to the attitude, notably in Dickens' *Hard Times*, predated Twain.[20] Yet so directly is the ethical position stated that problems of pose and persona become largely irrelevant. Twain has shifted from the literary comedian to the "real" (equally literary, of course) persona without apology and caused the hidden plot-action to appear in a single episode. His flexibility of voice allows for the expression of his own ethical background, fixed in his

---

20 Cited in Jesse Bier, *The Rise and Fall of American Humor* (New York: Holt, Rinehart, and Winston, 1968), 84. Sleery, the showman in Dickens' novel on factory life in England, expresses his humanity in his treatment of horses, so this idea can be seen as a cosmopolitan metaphor rather than a strictly western American one. Sleery delivers the following speech while offering to apprentice the orphaned Sissy Jupe, thus providing her with a permanent home and security: "But what I thay, Thquire, ith, that good tempered or bad tempered, I never did a horthe a injury yet, no more than thwearing at him went, and that I don't expect I thall begin otherwithe at my time of life, with a rider. I never wath much of a Cackler, Thquire, and I have thed my thay." Charles Dickens, *Hard Times* (New York: Holt, Rinehart and Winston, 1963), 35. To find an analogue for Twain's statement in a "vulgar" character such as Sleery reinforces the difference between "genteel" religion and the blunter humanism of the Twain persona as expressed in *The Innocents Abroad*.

childhood and in the West as well as inherited from the comic tradition of egalitarianism. Burlesque donkey-riding sequences in Fayal at the opening of the book come to have a foreshadowing thematic relationship to the rest of the travels, and the ethics which underlie the narrator's viewpoint—the viewpoint which rejects corrupt corporations and governmental bodies in the novels, and dissents from a host of social and religious vanities—protest the treatment of animals in a brief moment in the travel narrative.

There are a number of comparisons between the works of Artemus Ward and Mark Twain, but the most significant comparisons are those that show Twain's growth as an independent process. He was developing a sustained vision of society and an ethical stance out of the materials and techniques available in American literary comedy. Twain's innocent faces a more sophisticated environment than Ward's showman, and Twain's techniques are more mature and more flexible. His experiments with burlesque dramatization, as in "Barnum's First Speech in Congress," show him developing fictional characterizations to express the broad social and aesthetic criticism that distinguishes the literary comedians from the Yankee correspondents, and Twain from the literary comedians in turn. The continuing presence of Ward's humor in Twain's mind through the writing of *The Innocents Abroad* is an indication of how much the tradition offered Twain in the expression of his own ethics. As he developed into a writer of books, he began to sustain and elaborate these themes from the comic tradition in his own way, deepening the form of the cosmopolitan travel burlesque as we have seen. He became capable of expressing a variety of sentiments in a variety of comic and serious modes. His writings of the 1860s are thus clearly the products of the school of literary comedy in America and just as clearly foreshadow the voice of the novelist.

SEVEN

Humor and Social Criticism
The Gilded Age and *The Prince and the Pauper*

TWAIN'S EXPERIMENTS in form in the 1860s reveal him combining the techniques and themes of the literary comedians with the extended framework of the travel narrative. His early novels show him attempting to use the same combination for the purpose of sustained fiction. Because his narrators are not located at the center of the dramatic action, however, the early novels were only partly successful. Nevertheless, Twain's use of literary comedy in the novelistic setting made his works unique examples of the American democratic consciousness expressed by the comedians. *The Gilded Age* fails to unite its humorous points into a coherent structure, something Twain had already achieved through the flexible persona of *The Innocents Abroad*, but it still provides fascinating individual types in Colonel Sellers and Senator Dilworthy and a remarkable burlesque milieu of post–Civil War corruption. Twain subdued his humor in favor of nostalgic storytelling in *Tom Sawyer*, but in *The Prince and the Pauper* he came substantially closer to blending the voice of the American literary comedian with the techniques of the novelist in his narrative style and through the viewpoint of the hero, Miles Hendon.

The Gilded Age begins with local color sequences from the Mississippi River, moves to Washington, D.C., to follow the doings of the United States Congress in regard to the Sellers and Hawkins family hopes, and digresses to Philadelphia to follow the lives of a family of

Quakers named Bolton. Philip Sterling, joined with the Bolton fortunes, is a lackluster model for a young hero; Colonel Sellers is a burlesque of the vulgar officeseeker of Lincoln's era matured into a nascent corporate developer; Senator Dilworthy, an opportunistic and corrupt Washington politician, is an almost melodramatic villain. The story ends with the death of Laura Hawkins, who has been the protégé of Sellers and Dilworthy, with Congress in turmoil, and with the discovery of a coal mine in Pennsylvania that will rescue Sterling and the Boltons from destitution. Altogether, the book is a panorama, as it was intended to be, rather than a contained narrative.[1]

The Gilded Age describes a series of milieus and one or two central characters that inhabit them. The milieus—Obedstown as a symbol of backwoods America and Washington as a symbol of corporate political corruption—are as important to the plot of the story as are individual actions by the characters. Appropriately, considering Twain's history as a travel writer, Gladys Bellamy finds the backwoods at the root of all the life of the novel, including Washington itself.[2] Actually, the protective local coloration of the small-town early in the book disguises the centrality of Washington as a target of Twain's burlesque. Colonel Sellers comes to personify the connection of the two milieus, and central incidents reinforce the linking. The book's publisher, Elisha Bliss, concentrated almost solely on the localist portions of the book in advertisements—Obedstown, the steamboat race, and Col. Sellers' turnip dinner—completely ignoring Washington and the portions of the book by Twain's coauthor, Charles Dudley Warner.[3]

Twain managed the localist setting to include a variety of comic

---

1 In part this may be due to the problem of joint authorship, as some contomporary reviewers suggested. The passages cited here are usually from the chapters that Twain claimed, as amended by Ernest E. Leisy, "Mark Twain's Part in *The Gilded Age*," *American Literature*, VIII (January, 1937), 445-47. Leisy feels that when there was a chance to expose abuse or to enliven dialogue it was generally taken up by Twain. The Ward joke at the end of Chapter 26 on "owing two millions" bridges the respective chapters by Twain and Warner and could be from either author. All references to *The Gilded Age*, I and II, are to the Harper & Brothers 1917 text, "Author's National Edition," Vols. X and XI.

2 Gladys C. Bellamy, *Mark Twain as a Literary Artist* (Norman: University of Oklahoma Press, 1950), 292-93.

3 Hamlin Hill, *Mark Twain and Elisha Bliss* (Columbia: University of Missouri Press, 1964), 83-84.

and sentimental motifs. Early in the story, the readers are shown the fire-belching Mississippi steamboat and the children and darkies who are frightened by it. Untroublingly conventional in its condescending treatment of childlife, the sequence was easily transformed into verse by Sidney Lanier for a *Lippincott's* issue in 1875.[4] Obedstown, with its loafers and dogfights, resembles other villages in Twain's novels. Some elements, however, reflect the literary comedian's observations in *Roughing It*, such as the descriptions of stagecoaches racing in and out of town for effect and then jogging the rest of the route. Ironic revelations of local attitudes are more intrusive than in *Tom Sawyer* later but not fully developed. Hawkins and Sellers family women in particular are noted for their self-effacing love of their irresponsible husbands.

Washington, D.C., is an expansion of the localist experience through burlesque, with corrupt elements added. Laura's involvement with Washington lobbying, and with the symbolic southerner, Colonel Selby, destroys her in the end. The setting itself reflects the literary comedians' antagonism toward social and political corruption. Lincoln is "petrified by a young lady artist" for ten thousand dollars. The Washington monument is a "memorial chimney" with cow sheds lending a pastoral air to its base (I,236–37). Molasses-candy Parthenons dot the landscape, along with lunatic asylums. The president lives in a "white barn." Washington, in other words, is a gigantic Hawkeye gone to political seed; although according to one buried disclaimer, "To a large portion of the people who frequent Washington, or dwell there, the ultra fashion, the shoddy, the jobbery are as utterly distasteful as they would be in a refined New England city" (II, 61). Reviewers were attracted by the crudeness of characters and the portrayal of the American experience, however, and the picture of Washington certainly corresponds to the burlesque of social parvenus such as Oliver Higgins, who "had always been regarded as the

---

4 Representative reviews are Howells' "The Play from *The Gilded Age*," reprinted in William Dean Howells, *My Mark Twain* (Baton Rouge: Louisiana State University Press, 1967 [1910]), 97–100, and the review in *Appleton's Journal*, XII (October 3, 1874), 446. Reviews of the book appear in *Appleton's Journal*, XII (January 10, 1874), 59; *The Athenaeum*, No. 2411 (January 10, 1874), 53; *Galaxy*, XVII (March, 1874), 428; *Old and New*, IX (March, 1874), 386–88; *Saturday Review*, XXXVII (Feburary 14, 1874), 223–24; and *Graphic*, IX (February 28, 1874), 199.

most elegant gentleman in his Territory, and it was conceded by all that no man thereabouts was anywhere near his equal in the telling of an obscene story, except the venerable white-haired governor himself" (II, 22).[5] When the voters discover the thievery of Patrick O'Riley and Boss Weed they elect them to "their proper theater of action, the New York legislature" (II, 25) and then on to Congress.

Washington family life mirrors its political corruption. Laura is described as leading a life of intrigue, and much of the book's drama springs from this source, but her social experience is developed through literary comedy. In their undemocratic orbit, important families trouble themselves little about the "other orders of nobility" (II, 28–29). Mrs. Fulke-Fulkerson views Cape May with the attitude of this gilded minority: "Nobody goes *there*, Miss Hawkins—at least, only persons of no position in society. And the President" (II, 14). Corry O'Lanus had described an Irish milliner as naming herself Mme. D'Oshaughnessé; Twain pointedly refers to "The Hon. Patrique Oreillé . . . a wealthy Frenchman from Cork" (II, 17). As Washington Hawkins' fortunes rise in relation to Laura's manipulation of this elite, he is looked on "as if he were one of those foreign barbers who flit over here now and then with a self-conferred title of nobility and marry some rich fool's absurd daughter" (II, 34).

Twain and Warner meant such humor to be identified with popular opinion and the traditional American literary comedy that was the mode in which they wrote. After spending three chapters describing the economic situation in Philadelphia and Washington and its negative effects on promising young people like Philip Sterling and Ruth Bolton, they conclude their description with a borrowed anecdote: "Beautiful credit! The foundation of modern society. Who shall say that this is not the golden age of mutual trust, of unlimited reliance upon human promises? That is a peculiar condition of society which enables a whole nation to instantly recognize point and meaning in the familiar newspaper anecdote, which puts into the mouth of a distinguished speculator in lands and mines this

---

[5] *Athenaeum*, No. 2411 (January 10, 1874), 53, *Graphic*, IX (February 28, 1874), 199, and *International Review*, I (January, 1874), 386–88, all commented on these characteristics as dominating the uncoordinated plot.

remark: "'I wasn't worth a cent two years ago, and now I owe two millions of dollars'" (I, 263). Even into the 1890s, Enoch Knight relished this joke from an Artemus Ward lecture, although Ward gave the figure of only two hundred thousand dollars instead of two million and made the speculator undistinguished—not part of the ruling clique.[6] In *The Gilded Age* the reader is expected to know that the subjects under discussion have been commented upon before—the only alteration is to identify the swindler more completely with the upper levels of society. This is a plot-making theme as well, for Philip and Harry Brierly follow this course, as does Sellers. Such an obvious borrowing, however, makes the reader more conscious of the work as a contrived experience, ordered by the philosophy of the humorist.

Sellers is one of the focal points of the gilded age experience. He is always the hawker, even of such places as Corruptionville: "And patriotic?—why, they named it after Congress itself" (I, 270). Sellers is an albatross to the poor Hawkins family, particularly to Washington, whom he involves in a variety of frauds; they admit, "Nobody can help liking the creature, he means so well—but I do dread to come across him again" (I, 12). Even his own family is victimized as he heats his house with a candle inside the stove door, which gives the appearance of fire but no heat (I, 72–73). Sellers shares some of the characteristics of the literary comedian's persona, but he does not possess the comedian's pragmatic and egalitarian stance. Unlike the old showman, Jim Griggins, or the innocent Twain, Sellers himself seldom suffers when others do, yet he is too naïve to be a Sut Lovingood either.

Sellers as a dramatic figure tends to combine the small town with the milieu of Washington. Although he is a showman, unlike Ward he lacks a "moral show." Consequently he ends up as a sort of appendage to Dilworthy as a corrupt power, as when Dilworthy speaks in Hawkeye and Sellers is master of ceremonies: "He escorted the band from the city hotel to Gen. Boswell's; he marshaled the procession of Masons, of Odd Fellows, and of Firemen, the Good Templars,

---

6 Knight, "The Real Artemus Ward," 58. The joke also appears in Ward, *Works*, 394, in the original program for his Mormons lecture.

the Sons of Temperance, the Cadets of Temperance, the Daughters of Rebecca, the Sunday-school children, and citizens generally, which followed the Senator to the court-house; he bustled about the room long after every one else was seated, and loudly cried 'Order!' in the dead silence which preceded the introduction of the Senator by Gen. Boswell. The occasion was one to call out his finest powers of personal appearance, and one he long dwelt on with pleasure" (I, 200–201). The third-person narrative lacks the viewpoint of the Ward figure but allows for a narrative development. Sellers is more peripheral than Ward would have been, and the rest of the chapter is given to Dilworthy's hypocritical speech.

Despite the above problem, Sellers was hypnotic for critics of the book, and their fascination was due to his irrepressible expansionism. His ethics are a reversal—as in the Nasby letters—of those held by the literary comedians as a school. Much as Ward had described his conversation with Lincoln, Sellers talked to Grant, but aligned himself with a corporate crassness which is even tainted by association with the Confederacy: "We played for a big thing, and lost it, and I don't whine, for one. I go for putting the old flag on all the vacant lots. I said to the President, says I, 'Grant, why don't you take Santo Domingo, annex the whole thing, and settle the bill afterwards.' That's my way. I'd take the job to manage Congress. The South would come into it. You've got to conciliate the South, consolidate the two debts" (II, 79–80). Howells analyzed this antidemocratic character in reviewing the play from *The Gilded Age*: "Some extremely good suggestions give the ease and composure with which these Missourian ex-slave-holders adapt themselves to the splendors of Washington: once the first people in their own neighborhood, they are of the first people anywhere, and in arriving at luxury they have merely come into their own."[7] Sellers thus has a somewhat different role from the central figure in literary comedy, who is usually an outsider sharing the biases of the popular audience from the lower and middle classes. His proposition comes out of the Southwest of Baldwin's Ovid Bolus and is fused to the manner of the literary co-

---

7 Howells, "The Play from *The Gilded Age*," 100.

medians Ward and Nasby: Sellers is indeed a new figure in American literature.

Sellers' confrontation of the jury in Laura's trial for the murder of Colonel Selby, at the end of the book, is his climactic moment as a burlesque figure. At this point, he draws together the strands of the novel in a grotesque bonanza of set speeches, suspense, and caricature. Two previous episodes citing juries—the steamboat explosion jury and the juries owned by the railroads—establish the motif of corrupted judicial processes. After the final jury sequence, Twain and Warner even intrude themselves into the plot to burlesque their own portrayal of the verdict, indicating how intellectual the humor actually is in the book. When Sellers himself addresses the jury, a string of burlesque conclusions in proof of Laura's insanity is offered; she is said to seek a lame man resembling her father (who has never been seen or identified). Colonel Sellers is the digressive comic lecturer par excellence, although his motives are to free Laura unjustly. His last full statement to the jury, that he believes Laura's father to be alive because he has never heard of his death (II, 251), is a borrowing of Mark Twain's joke from Adam's tomb in *The Innocents Abroad*. The fool narrator is thus fused with the corruption of the gilded age at the height of the novel's melodrama; burlesque comedy feeds into the themes of the novel.

Senator Dilworthy is the most corrupt figure in the novel, far more so than the feckless Sellers. Dilworthy has to be discredited to some extent at the end of the novel, but the authors take care to show that he is brazen and unabashed to the end of his stay in Congress. Generally, in other words, his sleazy motto stands: "I never push a private interest if it is not justified and ennobled by some larger public good" (II, 40). The placing of the self first in this speech follows the pattern developed in "Barnum's First Speech in Congress." Dilworthy, however, manifests the terminology of the Sunday School rather than the "show." He remains ostentatiously pious, his diction emphasizing his hypocrisy rather than his materialism. He does not see himself with any redeeming innocence. In response to Harry Brierly's remark that thieves might have been around the house, since none of the Congress was detained by night sessions—a remark reminiscent of Ward's wishing to own a house as nice as some western bankers would break into—Senator Dilworthy uncomprehendingly admonishes him that he does not like to hear newspaper slang (II, 67).

Unlike Ward the showman, who undercuts his own venality by cacography and anticlimax, there are few overt indications in Dilworthy's speech of an alternative ethic, except in the exaggeration of the rhetoric itself. Consequently, Twain develops dramatic incidents and interchanges that elaborate motifs of the novel, something impossible in the newspaper letter format used by Ward. One of the most noticeable themes is the suggestion that the corrupt are firmly in power and the skeptical represent a handful of powerless outsiders, as in the following response to one of Dilworthy's particularly pious paragraphs:

"Fellow citizens: it gives me great pleasure to thus meet and mingle with you, to lay aside for a moment the heavy duties of an official and burdensome station, and confer in familiar converse with my friends in your great State. The good opinion of my fellow citizens of all sections is the sweetest solace in all my anxieties. I look forward with longing to the time when I can lay aside the cares of office—" ["Dam sight," shouted a tipsy fellow near the door. Cries of "Put him out."] (I, 201)

In Ward pieces, the showman is beaten up; in this case the drunken skeptic is ejected. Corruption holds power; innocent venality of the vulgar type finds no place. The speech is linked to government through a reference to the *Congressional Globe*, assuring the reader that it is a manifestation of the corporate government. The episode also foreshadows the attempt to put Dilworthy out of the Senate for bribing "Mr. Noble," an attempt which ends in the trial of Noble. After this speech, Dilworthy delivers a Sunday School address which is similarly successful. Traces of skepticism in the audience are described as changing into plans to run for the Senate (II, 216–21), showing the common man to be corrupted like the senator.

Sellers and Dilworthy are comic creations whose corrupt viewpoints dominate the novel but do not really focus it. In Ward's letters, either the showman stated his ethical viewpoint or else he revealed his own naïveté. Authorial narrative compensates for much of the loss, but the various subplots do move away from the two figures. Sentimental matters such as the fortunes of the Bolton family were Warner's responsibility, but Laura was Twain's, and her objectivity, as when she labels Washington lobbying a "weary, sordid, heartless game" (II, 58), separates the reader's sympathy for her from the comic matter that characterizes her work with congressmen. J. W. DeForest, with somewhat less discontinuity, managed similar material in "An Inspired Lobbyist" (1872) and *Honest John Vane* (1875) by putting the corrupt figure at the center of the action and limiting the story to legislative events. Consequently, the plot did not escape. DeForest, however, lacked the color, scope, and sentimentalism of Twain and Warner in *The Gilded Age* and failed to achieve their popularity.

One or two highpoints in the novel's action deserve special comment, Philip Sterling's confrontation with Conductor Slum and Laura's trial—both climaxes in their respective volumes. In Philip's episode, the railroad as a corporate symbol is brought into the plot. Twain injected the story into Warner's portion of the novel as an isolated episode; in later novels such atrocity stories are more firmly connected to the main plot. Ward had joked, "I have allers sustained a good moral character. I was never a railroad director in my life," and Jim Griggins, the thief, had wished that he had something to do with state governments or banks or railroads.[8] Twain expands on the theme dramatically—much more dramatically here than with the rude clerks sketched in "Traveling with a Reformer."[9] Melodramatically, Twain shows a lady almost killed by the callous orders of the mean-spirited Conductor Slum. Saving the life of the lady, heroically, Philip upbraids Slum and finally hits him in anger, for which he is thrown off the train by Slum and two brakemen; other passengers remain ineffectually indignant at Philip's predicament.

As a result of the encounter with the conductor, the railroads, newspapers, and court system are seen as interlocked. When the Hooverville *Patriot and Clarion* covers the story the next day, the details are reversed. Philip is supposed to have been beaten and is caricatured

---

8 Ward, *Works*, 254 and 150, respectively.
9 Reprinted in *Literary Essays*, Vol. XXII, "Author's National Edition," 78–99.

as "a young sprig, from the East"—like the "man of Bostin' dressin'" in Artemus Ward's story; Slum is described by the newspaper as "gentlemanly and efficient." Meanwhile, Twain depicts Philip walking out of the swamp where he had landed, wondering "if the company would permit him to walk over their track if they should know he hadn't a ticket" (I, 288–89). Meeting a kindly justice of the peace, Philip retells his story and is advised, "Suin's no use. The railroad company owns all these people along here, and the judges on the bench, too" (I, 290–91). But the episode is not thoroughly disconnected from major motifs. It is very much like the melodramatic steamboat disaster of Laura's appearance, where Twain had balanced a dying engineer's curse on the foolhardy captain against the "inevitable American verdict" of the jury for the steamboat company, that there was "NOBODY TO BLAME" (I, 38). Carelessly caused human suffering and corporate irresponsibility are intertwined and restated through these episodes, and humorous clichés are transformed into fictional experience holding the novel's main themes. As Twain particularizes the violence, he adds a dimension of reality to the comic action of the comedians, which is *not* to say that his plotting more closely corresponds to literary "realism."

Laura's trial for murdering her false lover, Colonel Selby, provides a climax for the whole novel, conjoined as it is with the defeat of the Knobs Industrial College bill on which so much time and corrupt practice have been spent. It is a summary of main themes. Colonel Sellers emerges at the trial as an orator in caricature. The jury shows little more than low animal cunning. Ward had his boots repaired by a penitentiary graduate and felt uncomfortable, but Twain's juries were earlier said to have "three graduates from Sing Sing" (II, 19). At the trial this strand of the novel is fleshed out by a jury that boasts a saloon-keeper, a "showy genteel" contractor, and assorted other misfits. Consistent with Congress' venality, Judge O'Shaunnessy sits in a courthouse which he helped build, a spittoon beside his feet that cost the city a thousand dollars (II, 226). Laura's lawyer, whose Irish brogue is almost unnoticeable, brings the jury back to the original steamboat disaster and then looses Sellers on them. Finally, Laura is acquitted and taken away to a lunatic asylum

—"But this is history and not fiction," the authors intervene. She is rescued and put on the lecture platform, a place about which Twain was always ambivalent; humiliated by a small but disorderly audience, she dies of heart failure, closing the action.

The Gilded Age is finally a congeries of literary comedy, local color, sentimental plotting, and overt burlesque. Sellers is an amalgam of Southwestern "Flush Times" and the platform comedian, but the political and social ethics of the comedians are retained in the narrative voice of the novel. Consequently, the milieu is more characteristic of the book's philosophy than is any single character. In turn, this allows the plot to wander, much as a travel narrative might. Yet, when highpoints occur, as they do around Philip and Laura, those climaxes gather together a range of themes and motifs and condense the ideals of the authors into comic moments. Humor is used to foreshadow plot developments, and convincing scenes are created in burlesque and caricature. This achievement is not to be undervalued, for it proves that literary comedy could be fused with the novel, and it provided the comic author with encouragement to use his own comic voice to create fiction, rather than attempting to achieve "realism" by suppressing his comic persona. Twain's later novels continue this experiment, an experiment at which he alone of the literary comedians succeeded.

II

The Adventures of Tom Sawyer bears traces of *The Gilded Age* and casts further light on it. Humorous material is much more completely subordinated to the boy's novel themes of the small town. The author is "aware" of the future gilded age, chronologically, and foreshadows it without directly pointing to its coming. Thus, *Tom Sawyer* maintains a different mood, considerably more in the vein of local color, from that of *The Gilded Age* but is not wholly unrelated to it.

As Walter Blair has noted, burlesques of children's novels were written by Max Adeler, T. B. Aldrich, M. Quad, and the Danbury News Man in the 1870s, and their approach seems to have been fairly popular. Shillaber's Mrs. Partington with her troublesome boy Ike had been well known since the 1850s and was particularly influential on the early descriptions of Aunt Polly in relation to Tom. The structure of the novel emphasizes "real" boy traits, however, so the literary tradition must be carefully blended with local setting; burlesque is deemphasized.[10] The story is sustained as a narrative stressing alterations of character—the sense of milieu which dominates *The Gilded Age* is now subdued background color. Contemporary reviewers, such as the London *Athenaeum*, are in agreement with Professor Blair's findings. *Tom Sawyer* is seen as "an attempt in a new direction. It is consecutive, and much longer than the former books, and it is not put forward as a mere collection of 'screamers.'"[11] Scattered literary humor, however, still finds its place in the work.

Tom is brought up, as was Harry Brierly, to be a "heedless lad" like the rest of his generation of boys (146).[12] Coinciding with *The Gilded Age*, where young men are supposed to be taught to expect easy money by their environment, Tom comes into a large fortune through adventure rather than labor, and is admired by the town. These correspondences are not accidental but rather seem to foreshadow the failures of the coming era; the older era has the seeds of the 1870s within it. The Knobs Industrial College is a swindle disguised as aid for the Negro freedman; in almost unnoticeable foreshadowing, verbal irony appears in Twain's description of Tom washing dirt off of his face, becoming "a man and a brother, without distinction of color" (32). Contemporary readers would have recognized this allusion to one of the most widespread of the English antislavery mottoes of the 1830s, dating at least to 1791 in American experience. No corruption is implied, but irony is present. Twain's use of the phrase is verbal merely, indifferent to the ethics involved. Such low-keyed humor creates the pre–Civil War, pre–Gilded Age milieu underneath the run of boyhood adventures with cats and schoolmasters and playmates who white-wash fences. Tom's early likeness to Ike Partington in the episode with the cat and the pain killer (108–109) fixes him clearly in the small-town milieu of the 1850s, with its

---

10 Walter Blair, "The Structure of *Tom Sawyer*," *Modern Philology*, XXXVII (August, 1939), 75–88.
11 *Athenaeum*, No. 2539 (June 24, 1876), 851.
12 *Adventures of Tom Sawyer* (New York: Harper & Brothers, 1917), "Author's National Edition," Vol. XII. All references are to this edition.

boyhood pranks and irresponsibility. Yet Tom is otherwise described as representative of his age, particularly in his desire to show off (38). His attitude toward church, for example, mirrors the mild hypocrisy with which the rest of the townspeople tolerate the dullness of the experience, and they prove to be as grateful as he is for any distraction (47–49). In fact, every person involved in the Sunday School is involved also in "showing off," the small-town vanity which portends the grotesque social climbers of the 1870s. The teachers, the girls and boys, the superintendent, and even the great man—the country judge—"was 'showing off,' too" (38). In scriptural memorization Twain even turns to the reader: "How many of my readers would have the industry and application to memorize two thousand verses, even for a Doré Bible?" (34), to establish *their* relationship to this world. Tom's notoriety comes in fact through a flashy swindle: the 1850s boy is father to the 1870s man after all. Perhaps Twain's comedy might be taken as more pointed in this novel than it is usually given credit for being.

Tom Sawyer also provides an opportunity to assess how influential the flexible narrative voice of "Mark Twain" is in making his works unique. Even with the local color scenes, Twain's exaggerated diction builds narrative themes through contemporary analogy, as with the Doré reference. Twain's description of the reading of pastoral notices in church can be compared with an identical description in Max Adeler's *Captain Bluitt* (1901). Adeler writes in a relatively noncomic voice: "The preacher, Reverend Dr. Frobisher, began by giving out notices. Drury did not heed them. He simply thought the proceeding tiresome and concluded from the sound of the doctor's voice that he must be a dull preacher, although he was a man of fine appearance."[13] Twain's description is distinctively social and historical in comparison with Adeler, crammed with his characteristic attitudes and dictional implications: "After the hymn had been sung, the Rev. Dr. Sprague turned himself into a bulletin-board, and read off "notices" of meetings and societies and things till it seemed that the list would stretch out to the crack of doom—a queer custom

---

13 Charles Heber Clark [Max Adeler], *Captain Bluitt* (Philadelphia: Henry T. Coates, 1901), 4.

which is still kept up in America, even in cities, away here in this age of abundant newspapers. Often, the less there is to justify a traditional custom, the harder it is to get rid of it" (45). Even while the book treats "local color," a sense of the urban milieu is implanted in the reader's mind. The Twain persona is apparent in the colloquial "till" and "crack of doom," as well as in the turn of phrase applied to Mr. Sprague. Intensified and magnified, such passages would have made *Tom Sawyer* more like *The Gilded Age*.

Tom Sawyer draws in a contemporary milieu through Twain's voice, but it is otherwise a smoothly consistent production. It might be inferred in comparison that *The Gilded Age* is an exaggerated social caricature due to the conscious intrusion of Twain's style into the narrative. Moreover, the fragmentation of that book, although undoubtedly due in part to its joint authorship, may also have been due to the author's intention to mirror in style the chaotic world created by their caricatures. Laura and Clay Hawkins are given origins in the same local experience as Tom Sawyer, but they emerge into the modern industrial world as understood by the literary comedians and must make their adjustments to it. The perception of change first seen in Mrs. Partington and Frank Forrester must be carried out in their plot experience whereas Tom remains fixed in a past time that holds the future subordinated in an artfully manipulated tone. Had Twain wished to make the later book more fully reflect the world of the 1870s, he might easily have done so through his usual comic devices, as he proved with the "medieval" *Prince and the Pauper* a few years later.

III

In *The Prince and the Pauper*, literary comedy is brought substantially closer to creating a complete novelistic medium. Egalitarian ethics are developed through Twain's combination of "gilded" government and violent rabble against a representative common man. This is obviously a very specialized, perhaps even reversed, egalitarianism, but it is in keeping with Mark Twain's own bias toward professionals who make their way in the world through apprenticeship and virtuous hard work. Scene and characterization echo the American experience in form and individual passages. Charlotte Yonge's *The Prince and the Page* may have provided direct motivation, but the prince-pauper theme had been developed by the comedians as well, particularly in Artemus Ward's interview with the Prince of Wales. The deadpan irony of the platform humorist, and even some Southwestern anecdotes, infused the "medieval" experience with democratic naïveté. Law and law officers and the institutional church, in the person of a mad "Archangel," are melodramatic villains. Consequently, Twain is close to individualizing antidemocratic institutions as antagonists to his heroes—the point at which his literary comedy truly becomes sustained fiction.

Twain's conception of the community of London Bridge offers the most flagrant example of his transformation of feudal England into the Baldinsville or Dawson's Landing of the nineteenth century. American small-town values, provincial and materialistic, dominate, and even the Western tall-tale finds a place:

> The Bridge was a sort of town to itself; it had its inn, its beerhouses, its bakeries, its haberdasheries, its food markets, its manufacturing industries, and even its church.... It was a narrow town.... Its population was but a village population, and everybody in it knew all his fellow-townsmen intimately, and had known their fathers and mothers before them—and all their little family affairs into the bargain. It had its aristocracy, of course—its fine old families of butchers, and bakers, and what not, who had occupied the same old premises for five or six hundred years, and knew the great history of the Bridge from beginning to end, and all its strange legends; and who always talk[ed] bridgy talk, and thought bridgy thoughts, and lied in a long, level, direct, substantial bridgy way. It was just the sort of population to be narrow and ignorant and self-conceited (77).[14]

To speak of fourteenth-century burghers as having an "aristocracy" is to apply to them a nineteenth-century metaphor meaning "socially influential people," and Twain applies the term to Washington society in *The Gilded Age* in that sense. Similarly, it was her unknown parentage and family affairs which spoiled Laura's life in the

---

14 *The Prince and the Pauper* (New York: Harper & Brothers, 1917), "Author's National Edition," Vol. XV. All references are to this edition.

small town of Hawkeye, *circa* 1870, and those elements are stressed here, as Twain draws a portrait understandable to his own readers in his own colloquial language. The whole scene is typical of the "irreverence" of the literary comedians which allows the portrait to become a comic American scene—Flush Times on the London Bridge.

As might be expected in a work of literary comedy, the bridge also has political-social significance which welds it to Twain's plot. Immediately following the identification of the bridge with an American village scene, an overly coy narrative voice points up the meaning of the locale in respect to persons: "In the times of which we are writing, the Bridge furnished 'object lessons' in English history, for its children—namely, the livid and decaying heads of renowned men impaled upon iron spikes atop of its gateways. But we digress (78)." The final three words, of course, are ironic emphasis; the central motif of the novel is the cruelty of the established government and the kindness of outside individuals. Various incidents reproduce this theme. The specific connection between the localized bridge and its historical meaning will be brought back to introduce the climactic action of the novel: a severed head falls and hits Hendon's arm, causing him to return to this theme in his musing: "So evanescent and unstable are men's works in the world!—the late good king is but three weeks dead and three days in his grave, and already the adornments which he took such pains to select from prominent people for his noble bridge are falling (232)." The traveler-naif thus brings the perceptions of the literary comedian back into the novel. In fact, it is actually the omniscient narrator making these observations, having coopted Hendon's persona. Twain is closer than ever to the mode of Huck Finn.

Contemporary critics, with good reason, were quick to see the essential Americanness of Twain's writing. Joe Goodman, who supported Twain's development as a literary comedian in Virginia City, wrote to Twain protesting his departure in writing a historical English novel, but his concern was wasted.[15] Astute critics quickly iden-

---

15 As recorded in Kenneth Andrew's study of the background of the novel in *Nook Farm: Mark Twain's Hartford Circle* (Cambridge: Harvard University Press, 1950), 192.

tified the tendency of the plot to move toward the "extravaganza" of Twain's other works:

> We can imagine a lover of the old Mark, the Western humorist (as distinguished from the new Mark, the romancer), hailing with uproarious delight his familiar friend in the two passages we are about to quote.... Speaking of the perils of the office of royal taster, the author observes: "Why they did not use a dog or a plumber seems strange; but all the ways of royalty are strange." Again in the description of the people who lived upon London Bridge, we recognize the old familiar manner: "They always talked bridgy talk."[16]

The plumber suggests the American milieu through anachronism. Such lapses of tone in the omniscient author's voice are Twain's control of the novel, as in the remark that the "First Groom of the Chamber, was there, to do goodness knows what" (45). Similarly, speeches and characterizations are Americanized: the pauper Tom Canty, learning to be prince, gets over "snags and sandbars" (39) just like a cub pilot on the Mississippi; his father shouts in fury over the real prince who seems to be performing a mad act, "let the show go on" (59) like a circus ringmaster; and, on two occasions, the soldier Miles Hendon strikes for "the capital" (23, 231) like any other favor-seeking veteran of the Grand Army of the Republic.

Twain's plot depends on such contemporary elements, and even related items from the Southwest, to generate a democratic atmosphere against which he can raise an aristocratic world in opposition. Southwestern episodes like the boy-bull-bees wedding scene from Sut Lovingood might be rejected—at least until *Joan of Arc* called them forth[17]—but others were not. Southwestern folktales come into play when Tom Canty drinks sop from the fingerbowl, and the scene expresses the naïveté of the common man of England just as it did for his backwoods American counterpart. A social milieu is created which is a modified burlesque. In opposition to the common man there exists a medieval counterpart to the gilded age: a frowning, colossal stone gate, guarded by stone lions, "with its gilded

---

16 *"The Prince and the Pauper," Critic*, I (December, 1881), 368.
17 Albert E. Stone, *The Innocent Eye: Childhood in Mark Twain's Imagination* (New Haven: Yale University Press, 1961), 96–97.

bars," separating the countryfolk and townspeople from royalty. "At each side of the gilded gate stood a living statue, that is to say, an erect and stately and motionless man-at-arms, clad from head to heel in shining steel armor. . . . Splendid carriages, with splendid people in them and splendid servants outside, were arriving" (11). Such imagery should carry the point to the reader, at least subconsciously. In case it does not, the meeting of the prince and the pauper through the universal understanding of boyhood is a bridging of economic and social class: "The soldiers presented arms . . . as the little Prince of Poverty passed in, in his fluttering rags to join hands with the Prince of Limitless Plenty" (12). The stage is thus set for an examination of humanity in relation to economic status, the chief concern of postindustrial America.

There are two chief villains in *The Prince and the Pauper*—the state through its laws, and the church—but neither are as completely dramatized as they were to be in *A Connecticut Yankee*. Nevertheless, the high points in the novel's melodrama come in relation to such things as the burning of suspected witches or widows who have committed minor thefts. Twain's most striking and most simplistic statement on the state occurs in Yokel's speech at the thieves' revel. At several points in the narrative, as in the chapter "In Prison" (219–24), commoners are given opportunities to express themselves on the injustices of the law and abuses of feudal power, power which equates with corporate power and civil power in *The Gilded Age*. The scope of the novel now allows a change from the irony of the comic letter to the direct statement of grievance. Thus, Yokel, an outcast in the rogues' band, delivers a speech on English law which brings the position of Jim Griggins, Ward's "low thief," into the main arena of the drama:

I am Yokel, once a farmer and prosperous, with loving wife and kids—now am I somewhat different in estate and calling; and the wife and kids are gone; mayhap they are in heaven, maybe in—maybe in the other place—but the kindly God be thanked, they bide no more in *England*! My good old blameless mother strove to earn bread by nursing the sick; one of these died, the doctors knew not how, so my mother was burned for a witch, whilst my babes looked on and wailed. English law!—up, all, with your cups!—now all together and with a cheer!—drink to the merciful English law that delivered *her* from the English hell! Thank you, mates, one and all. I begged, from house to house—I and the wife—bearing with us the hungry kids—but it was a crime to be hungry in England—so they stripped us and lashed us through three towns. Drink ye all again to the merciful English law!—for its lash drank deep of my Mary's blood and its blessed deliverance came quick. She lies there, in the potter's field, safe from all harms. And the kids—well, whilst the law lashed me from town to town, they starved. Drink lads—only a drop—a drop to the poor kids, that never did any creature harm. I begged again—begged for a crust, and got the stocks and lost an ear—see, here bides the stump; I begged again, and here is the stump of the other to keep me minded of it. And still I begged again, and was sold for a slave—here on my cheek under this stain, if I washed it off, ye might see the red S the branding iron left there! A SLAVE! Do ye understand that word! An English SLAVE!—that is he that stands before ye. I have run from my master, and when I am found—the heavy curse of heaven fall on the law of the land that hath commanded it!—I shall hang! (140-41)

This poor beggar's speech, which so fully indicts inhumanity in law, converts the comic stance of the comedians into a medodramatic vignette—one of the most powerful in the novel. Barnum's burlesque speech has been transformed into a deadly serious dramatic moment. And the speech is immediately affirmed in the plot as the Prince, emerging from the shadows to declare an end to the laws that have victimized Yokel, distinguishes the individual ruler from the governmental mechanism. Nor does Twain leave Yokel's speech in isolation, for Yokel, like Hendon, elsewhere appears in the nick of time to save the prince from disfigurement by the wicked thief Hugo. Yokel's humanitarian action thus validates his stand as an outraged individual against the law. Ruffler, the leader of the band of thieves, gives a sort of moral summary when the Prince responds angrily to taunts after his own sympathetic declaration for Yokel: "*Be* king, if it please thy mad humor, but be not harmful in it" (142).

As government and law are indicted by the vulgar criminal, the church—religious authority—is also called into question through a burlesque episode. The prince meets a mad hermit in an unabashedly melodramatic encounter and is rescued by the chance passing of Miles Hendon. Unlike the prince's other misadventures, when he announces himself to be the king, he finds himself accepted with enthusiasm. The hermit sees him as a king who has cast worldly wealth away and come to mortify the flesh; the madman then reveals to the king his "secret" in a whisper, topping the king's self-identification: "I am an archangel!" (167). As the religious fanatic traps, ties up, and prepares to murder the prince, his musings, reiterated over and over as a litany, take the form of a comic device, the ironic anticlimax: "Yes, I am an archangel; *a mere archangel!*—I that might have been pope!" (168). Twain converts the comic line into a characterization of the church's preference for worldly power. Vanity, power, and religiosity—Twain's major themes—are dramatized by his joke.

Three figures—all of whom adopt the role of innocent travelers—are central to the action of the novel, the pauper, the prince, and the soldier, Miles Hendon. Tom Canty, elevated from rags to riches, takes the role of the vandal, not in Europe and the Holy Land this time but in gilded halls of royal pomp. He expresses the vandal's perspective on independence from the attention of courtiers, "I marvel they do not require to breathe for me also!" (41), and the vandal's mystification with etiquette, "I crave your indulgence; my nose itcheth cruelly. What is the custom and usage in this emergence?" (46), and the southwesterner's practicality, as noted in the fingerbowl incident, "Nay, it likes me not, my lord; it hath a pretty flavor, but it wanteth strength" (47). Characterization is achieved by a string of one-line jokes, and the tension between simplicity and social grandeur is hinted.

As the plot develops, Tom Canty's naïveté is expressed in more significant set pieces that imply the basic difference in attitude between the pompous rich and the practical commoner. When Tom learns that the dead king's funeral is some time off, he replies, " 'Tis a strange folly. Will he keep?" (102). Twain clarifies the social irony involved by referring to the rapid burial of residents in Offal Court. Shortly afterwards, Tom, upon being instructed about the royal budget, gives a response which reflects a middle-class ethos, not a peasant point of view: " 'Tis meet and necessary that we take a smaller house and set the servants at large. . . . I remember me of a small house that standeth over against the fish-market, by Billingsgate—" (103). Of course it is not sufficient that he merely deliver the line; it is characteristically exaggerated by including the fish market, as a truly vulgar counterpoise to the royal situation. The humor of the naif is again used to contrast values. Pomp, power, and debt as corporate tools of power are foreign to the naif as an individual. The most immediate expression of this juxtaposition comes early, when the usurper wonders about his own status: "Might they not hang him at once, and inquire into his case afterward?" (25). Modern existential man has the same concern.

Tom's early anxiety about life and death and government establishes the motif which most of his episodes in the plot center upon. The naif's ethics are such that he spares lives rather than destroys them—an affirmative stance. The Duke of Norfolk is an early beneficiary, and old Andrew recalls the event later in his praise of the usurper to Miles and the prince: "He began humanely, with saving the old Duke of Norfolk's life, and now he is bent on destroying the cruelest of the laws that harry and oppress the people" (218). In Chapter XV, "Tom as King," the youth finds, true to Artemus Ward's spirit towards a dukedom, that being king "hath its compensations" (114). He rescues one old man from boiling in oil, for he had seen him risk his life to save a drowning boy, and frees a woman from the charge of witchcraft because it seems unbusinesslike that she could sell herself to the devil but not to an Englishman—why waste privileges on the devil? Thus the naïve humorist becomes the active humanist. His ultimate guilt at this life-change, when he denies his mother with the melodramatic declaration, "I do not know you, woman!" in the closing pages of the book, reassures the reader that such power for good is not cheaply bought in human terms.

The real prince provides answers to two problems about monarchy and aristocracy which interested the democratic Ward in the 1860s. The Prince of Wales confided to Ward that he wished to travel through Canada unknown and be treated like other boys. Tom Canty correspondingly wishes he were in the fields and "free" air (103–104). For Prince Edward, the reality is somewhat harsher, thereby allowing an answer to the second question. Ward's statement was on the prince Napoleon, whom he wanted to see "becaws I'm anxious to know how he stands as a man ... onless he is *good* he'll come down with a crash." The prince, dressed in Tom's rags out of a playful but sympathetic interest, is hurled among the mob, where he quickly distinguishes himself and is, in the course of events, singled out by Miles Hendon for his "gallant" courage. Falling in with the robber band, soon after, Prince Edward hears Yokel's story and comes forth to abolish the laws which caused it; for this mad statement, he is described as a "manikin" and derided by the thieves (141). Nevertheless, he is going to school to suffering. He soon requites himself and wins the title King of the Game-Cocks for defeating Hugo's "'prentice work" with the quarter-staff (180). Immersed in the reality of kitchen work in a farmer's cottage, he learns the truth about "showy menial heroisms that would read picturesquely" and is tempted to resign that sort of duty (162). It is "In Prison," Chapter XXVII, that the king's humanity is most fully touched by the stories, and later by the tortured deaths, of his cellmates. He declares: "The world is made wrong, kings should go to school to their own laws at times, and so learn mercy" (224). So it is that when a "great dignitary, some gilded vassal" makes argument against leniency, the tested democratic king turns compassionate eyes on him, acknowledging that "I and my people know, but not thou" (274). The throne is democratized through the king's travels, just as the vandal was elevated through travel, and just as the traveling showman Ward would have predicted.

Miles Hendon's role in the novel is the most significant; for though not the central character in the plot, his role looks forward to Huck Finn and Hank Morgan in later novels. Indeed, as I noted earlier, Hendon and the omniscient narrator are almost the same voice; it is but a small step from their shared point of view to the invention of a first-person narrator. Hendon himself is distinguished by the manners of the complete literary comedian. He views himself in deadpan, as when stuck with a needle: "It matters little . . . yet 'tis not a convenience, neither" (93). What Phoenix and Harte called "scrambled sesquipedalianism" is ready in his mouth to save the prince a whipping: "In the law this crime is called *Non compos mentis lex talionis sic transit gloria mundi*" (194–95). Led to what he thinks is his hanging, he muses with a detachment similar to that of Artemus

Ward in Dixie: "An I were not traveling to death and judgment, and so must needs economize in sin, I would throttle this knave for his mock courtesy" (266). Such detachment gives Twain's humor a philosophical impact beyond its force as fiction, for as fiction merely—without humor—it borders on the maudlin and sentimental.

Hendon also expresses the major positive themes of the book. It is he who portrays the manliness which the comedians' philosophy saw as crucial. Years at war "might make a soldier and a man of me" through long probation (86). He adopts the prince because he recognizes his soldierlike bravery. Hendon reveals his own ultimate pragmatism, when, granted any boon he wishes, he merely asks the prince for the right to sit in his presence: " 'Twas a brave thought, and hath wrought a mighty deliverance; my legs are grievously wearied" (90). As time passes, Hendon participates in various adventures and is raised by the little king to knighthood and earldom. He reflects not upon the form but on the meaning of the whole process: "An this go on, I shall presently be hung like a very Maypole with fantastic gauds and make-believe honors. But I shall value them, all valueless as they are, for the love that doth bestow them. Better these poor mock dignities of mine, that come unasked from a clean hand and a right spirit, than real ones bought by servility from grudging and interested power" (229). If the king's standing as a man is verified by his clean, *i.e.* powerless hand and right spirit, Hendon's idealism is illustrated by his attitude toward power. Edward, too, has made a recognition: "Kings cannot ennoble thee, thou good, great soul, for One who is higher than kings hath done that for thee; but a king can confirm thy nobility to men" (228). Such recognitions, perhaps permissible in a novel addressed to the "young people of all ages," nonetheless reflect sentimental and genteel idealism stripped of the transforming power of humor. Such is the basis, however, of the ethics of the 1850s and 1860s out of which this literature sprang.

One last theme deserves mention, although it has little place in the discussion of literary comedy—the dream identity theme. Twain had used spiritual telegraph to obtain Barnum's speech and others in the 1860s, but *The Prince and the Pauper* is somewhat deeper. The prince is taken to be mad in his reversed role, and is labeled "Foo-foo the First, king of the Mooncalves" (143). Hendon doubts him throughout and sees himself as "become a knight of the Kingdom of Dreams and Shadows!" (90). Twain heavily emphasizes the irony of this situation as Hendon himself is denied *his* identity by Hugh and Edith, in Chapter XXV. The king affirms his belief in Hendon and queries, "Dost thou doubt *me*?" (203) in a parry which makes Hendon the more naïve-seeming of the two. Dragged into the reality of the full-panoplied court, Hendon is shocked, "Lo, the lord of the Kingdom of Dreams and Shadows on his throne.... But these are *real*—verily these are *real*—surely it is not a dream" (267). The poignance of this reversed reality is clearer when one compares it to Hank Morgan's predicament, or to Mark Twain's deepening concern with the whole problem of reality and dream in the gloomy later fiction. The mooncalf confusion is a surface of thin ice over a void, and the only test applicable is the pragmatism of a "mannerless clown"; Hendon plants his chair on the floor and sits down on it (268).

The Prince and the Pauper is a full fusion of literary comedy with the novel form. The modes of comedy are employed to build plot and theme. Characters lacking humor themselves, such as Yokel, correspond to the comic devices that Twain had practiced in previous newspaper writings. Major figures embody the innocence and the pragmatic humanism of the comedians to the fullest, and their standing as men is justified in the action. Humor takes its place as an expression of social ethics, sustained in fiction of significance. The masterworks that followed raise this expression to vision.

EIGHT

Adventures of Huckleberry Finn
The Literary Comedian Within the Novel

HENRY NASH SMITH has suggested that, at least in the beginning of the period in which Twain wrote *Huckleberry Finn*, Twain's conception of his writing was "even more ambiguous than it had been eight years earlier when he began composing *The Innocents Abroad*."[1] Even though he was still thought of as a disciple of Artemus Ward, he now could "hold his own" with the genteel audience of the *Atlantic Monthly*. Twain's treatment of the river in *Huckleberry Finn* is not unlike his attitude toward it in "Old Times on the Mississippi," which he had published in the *Atlantic*; and his treatment of Jim's humanity, like the pathos of "A True Story" (also published there and praised to Howells by John W. DeForest for its realism), is an indication of the human sympathies that could be taken more seriously as local color than as literary comedy.

The main theme of the book revolves around freedom of belief and action.[2] Social mores and the rascals who profit by them and suffer from them provide the main components of this theme. The evils of corporate authority are subsumed in characterization and in the description of milieu. In Huck, a sympathetic stance derived from the professional showman or newspaper reporter establishes Twain's

---

[1] Smith, *Mark Twain, Development of a Writer*, 92.
[2] John C. Gerber, "Mark Twain," *American Literary Scholarship, 1967*, ed. James Woodress (Durham: Duke University Press, 1969), 69, sums all of the themes up: "freedom, slavery, religion, money, illusion, the family, superstition, loneliness, death and moral growth."

positive moral beliefs. The book combines literary comedy and realism and local color fiction. The ambiguity sensed by Professor Smith may partly account for this mixture, but it is also a natural culmination of Twain's development.

Adventures of Huckleberry Finn represents the point at which Twain most completely merged the practices of the literary comedians with the possibilities of the tradition of the novel as a genre stressing observed scene and continuing action. While literary comedy as such can be seen as little more than a collection of devices, the persistent humanism of the comedians lies behind the novelistic action of *Huckleberry Finn*. Huck holds, "intuitively" and passively, all of their antagonism toward fixed social institutions. Huck himself is characterized through the same devices that Ward and Twain employed to establish naïveté in their traveling showman and traveling reporter personas in the 1860s. Social caricature also appears, although more muted than in *The Gilded Age*, and is balanced against the raft and the natural aspects of the river.[3] Fabricating these traditional materials in the dryly ironic humor of Huck's narrative prose, Mark Twain even risked the burlesque ending of the novel, which has caused distress to many "serious" readers.

Huck is an offspring not only of the literary comedians generally but of Twain's own personal background. Huck's idiom is thus flavored with a cosmopolitan experience. Cold meat is described as no better than "a hunk of old cold cannibal in the morning" (319),[4] a metaphor consistent with the Sandwich Island travel reporter's interests and "Cannibalism in the Cars" but not necessarily with a backwoods Mississippi River boy. Similarly, Twain's piloting background is reflected in the paragraph describing Jim's prison bed in which Tom Sawyer's spiders and snakes "took turn about," "come on watch," "was on deck," and "crossed over" (368-69). Even as it

---

[3] Although I will not extensively treat here the problem of Huck's valuation of the natural, the centrality of this matter is evident in the essays in Barry A. Marks (ed.), *Mark Twain's Huckleberry Finn* (Boston: D. C. Heath, 1959). For a full debate on the nature of this novel, which raises most of the pertinent problems of its construction and meaning, the reader is referred to this anthology of criticism.

[4] All footnotes are to Volume XIII of the "Author's National Edition" (New York: Harper & Brothers, 1912).

echoes the serious themes of personal relations and the river journey, Mark Twain's imagination infuses Huck's somber reflections with comic analogies.

There is, for example, a faint hint of Ward's formulations in "Show Business and Popular Lectures," which had earlier influenced Twain in the *Alta* letters. When Huck describes the Duke and Dauphin's attempts to succeed in various kinds of shows, Ward's reference to his kangaroo and the general public shows up as part of a series of humorous reversals:

> First they done a lecture on temperance; but they didn't make enough for both of them to get drunk on. Then in another village they started a dancing-school; but they didn't know no more how to dance than a kangaroo does; so the first prance they made the general public jumped in and pranced them out of town. Another time they tried a go at yellocution; but they didn't yellocute long till the audience got up and give them a solid good cussing, and made them skip out. (290)

The language here is fairly convincing due to its restraint, a point that has been applied to Huck's diction generally.[5] Taken out of context, however, it is clearly a literary fabrication. The weak dialect joke "yellocute" is forced by its appearance twice in five words. Huck is more of a deadpan literary humorist than is apparent in the more finely wrought passages of nature description elsewhere in the text.

Many of the word changes in the manuscript and proof of *Huckleberry Finn* which Bernard DeVoto describes as "softenings" of Twain's writing are actually conversions of flatly realistic words into the sort of humorous description seen in the yellocution passage. Such substitutions as *various* for *rancid* smells and "Tighter . . . mellow . . . mellower" for "drunk . . . drunk . . . drunk" in treating Pap Finn may be more accurately described as the employment of ironic euphemism rather than evasions of realism. If this is the case, it may help to explain Huck's apparent maturity and objectivity. Henry Nash Smith has suggested that Twain's satiric method requires that Huck Finn be his mask rather than a fully developed character.[6] Al-

---

5 Bridgman, *Colloquial Style*, 87, 115–16.
6 DeVoto, *Mark Twain at Work* (Cambridge, Houghton Mifflin Sentry Edition, 1957), 82–84; Smith, *Mark Twain, Development of a Writer*, 118.

though the ironic force that Twain develops by means of this strategy may inhibit Huck's "moral development," it nonetheless establishes the flexibility of voice that Ward, the vulgar showman, lacked and is thus crucial to the development of Huck's *skeptical maturity*. Had Twain attempted sterner realism, Huck would have lost his personal voice and become only another false-sounding authority. Huck's humor, even when it is forced in diction, frees him.

There is further evidence that Huck's dialect masks the social vision of Twain, the literary comedian, in countrified metaphors. The psychology of the traveling American abroad, and particularly his skepticism, was the central point of development that distinguishes Twain's writing in *The Innocents Abroad*. The attitude toward churches which appeared there in showman's speech appears in *Huck Finn* as well, but in backwoods vernacular: "So I slid out and slipped off up the road, and there warn't anybody at the church, except maybe a hog or two, for there warn't any lock on the door, and hogs likes a puncheon floor in summer-time because it's cool. If you notice, most folks don't go to church only when they've got to; but a hog is different" (153). Huck caricatures Protestant "manners." Apparently only a passing observation, the observation expands the viewpoint toward religion of *Tom Sawyer*. The joke is not only characteristic of Huck's personality—the narrative persona—it also contributes to the central motif of the novel, the struggle between the two providences. One side is static, doctrinaire, and institutional, like "most folks" filling social requirements; the other side is individualized and grossly human, or animal, but wholly sincere; it is the American vandal fableized into a pig. So Huck's offhand manner characterizes his mind, offers a comic viewpoint toward society, and plays on a major motif of the novel. This is the most striking aspect of Twain's development of literary comedy into the novel form.[7]

Huck's persona can be seen in terms of other conventions of the platform humorist as well. Take, for example, Huck's memorable

---

[7] The Huck Finn-Mark Twain persona may be even closer than this indicates. Huck comments that he didn't believe the saying that bees wouldn't sting an idiot because he had tried it and they wouldn't sting him (63). Twain borrowed this from Huck in his own *Autobiography* (141), saying, "The proverb says that Providence protects children and idiots. This is really true. I know it because I have tested it," essentially the same joke.

"No'm. Killed a nigger" (306–307) following a query whether anyone was hurt and preceding a long burlesque digression by Aunt Sally. Although the language is freely Huck's, the attitude is not. Huck says the *words*, but the comic irony of the scene enables the humorist's audience to exempt Huck from responsibility for the attitudes. Or take Huck's tale of Hank Bunker. It is profoundly related to the story of William Wheeler (in *Roughing It*) who was woven into fourteen yards of carpet and buried straight up at full length (in the climax of "The Story of the Old Ram"): "Old Hank Bunker done it once, and bragged about it; and in less than two years he got drunk and fell off of the shot-tower, and spread himself out so that he was just a kind of layer, as you may say; and they slid him edgeways between two barn doors for a coffin, and buried him so, so they say, but I didn't see it. Pap told me" (74). Effortlessly blended into Huck's comments on omens of bad luck, this anecdote disappears in the run of his talk. Such stories, however, help to establish his naïve objectivity as the narrator of the novel, just as they help the innocent-seeming tenderfoot establish his pose as Mark Twain in *Roughing It*.[8] Huck's disclaimer of certain knowledge about the incident employs the joke to build the plot of the novel. Huck's relationship to Pap as a moral instructor is burlesqued. At the same time, Huck's statement that he "didn't see it" reconfirms his truthfulness and his emphatic preference for immediate experience. Twain successfully subordinates the humor to Huck's psychology on one hand and to plot development on the other.

Huck's pretense to naïveté is based on the voice created by such

---

[8] Mark Twain's lecture from *Roughing It*, in 1871–1872, reconstructed by Fred Lorch in *The Trouble Begins at Eight* (Ames: Iowa State University Press, 1968), 311, shows an equally striking point in Twain's description of camping and boating on Lake Tahoe:

We used to foot it out there, taking along provisions and blankets—camp out on the lake shore two or three weeks at a time; not another human being within miles of us. We used to loaf along in the boat, smoke and read, sometimes play seven-up to strengthen the mind. It's a sinful game but it's mighty nice. We'd just let the boat drift and drift wherever it wanted to. I can stand a deal of such hardship and suffering when I'm healthy. And the water was so wonderfully clear. Where it was 80 feet deep the pebbles on the bottom were just as distinct.

It would appear from this passage that Huck's idyllic raft experience has its roots in the western experience of Twain when he used the lake as an escape from the booming atmosphere of the silver rush—an experience polished ten years later by his platform presentation. Huck even uses the phrase "If they could stand it I could" (104), while rowing his boat in search of the drowned robbers on the *Walter Scott*.

passages. Subjected to his conflicting apprenticeships under Widow Douglas and Pap on good breeding, Huck resolves the conflict by formulating a pragmatic ethic. When Pap and the Widow are in conflict on "borrowing," for instance, Huck and Jim create a third ethic which makes of the raft a microcosmic world more self-contained in regard to universal needs than Ward the showman achieved with his profit-seeking, consciously patriotic show. Through this means Huck escapes the limits which "vulgarity" would seem to place on him. His ethics, in the plot, reflect the potential inherent in the flexible persona, reinforced by his Twainian diction. As Edgar Branch notes, Miss Watson, Pap, the Duke and the Dauphin, and other believers in social respectability all live by a rigid code.[9] When these codes conflict the result is intellectual humor, and it serves to create Huck Finn as the actor who wishes to swap books and morals for picks to dig Jim out of prison with.

Other elements in *Huckleberry Finn* are also traceable to the tradition of literary comedy. Jim's description of Solomon's harem as a boarding house containing rackety times in the nursery and wives who make noise like a boiler factory (107–108) is the same sort of juxtaposition of historical statement and "realistic" localized viewpoint that Twain had experimented with in "Another Bloody Massacre" and a number of pieces on San Francisco in the early 1860s. It resembles Twain's treatment of Brigham Young in *Roughing It*, which resembled, in turn, Ward's and Max Adeler's treatment of the Mormons. Jim and Huck's discussions on Solomon and the French language and on Jim's "stock investment" in a cow are close in format to the minstrel humor of M. Quad in books like *Brother Gardner's Lime Kiln Club* (1883) as well as to the earlier minstrel show tradition. Among the characterizations, Aunt Polly has been compared to B. P. Shillaber's Mrs. Partington, whose picture is even used

---

9 One of the passages in Huck's consideration of Pap's ethics reverses the terms of goodness in Mrs. Partington's experience with the stolen turkey: "Pap always said, take a chicken when you get a chance, because if you don't want him yourself you can easy find somebody that does, and a good deed ain't never forgot. I never see Pap when he didn't want the chicken himself, but that is what he used to say, anyway" (91). Mrs. Partington's creator was trying to show her emerging into the urban situation. Huck is breaking out of the same situation and developing an antisocial ethic akin to the antisocial ethic of the reporter who would rather break the Sabbath than kill his horse. Branch, *Literary Apprenticeship of Mark Twain*, 204.

to represent her in one instance, and the southwestern grotesques in "Simon Suggs Attends a Camp-Meeting" seem to have been taken into Chapter XX of *Huckleberry Finn* as part of the Dauphin's experience.¹⁰

Many of the elements in Huck's speech are verbal humor drawn from comic literalism. He describes Mrs. Loftus' relations as being better off than "they used to was" (78). His description of the unshakable Duke and Dauphin at the Wilks's is in the diction of the old showman: "I reckoned they'd turn pale. But no, nary a pale did *they* turn" (271). The Duke's advertisement of the Royal Nonesuch over the rubric "Ladies and Children Not Admitted," though frequently taken as particularly American in its cynical attitude toward the flatheads of Arkansas, has a literary analogue in the introduction to *Father Tom and The Pope* (New York, 1868): "At last one afternoon, after the battle of the day was over, Gregg raised his mighty arm high in the air, and said 'that on the next day, the secrets of the confessional would be the subject of the discourse,' and warned the ladies, 'that no modest woman would appear, or could appear, while he revealed the secrets of that powerful instrument of the Romish Church.' The consequence may be imagined. he Hall was packed to overflowing by the gentler sex" (10).

Twain can thus be seen as transforming already extant humorous conceptions into his depiction of rural Arkansas, for the purpose of the novel. The Mississippi River culture that Twain appears to describe so accurately and realistically has within it literary elements that owe a great deal to the traditional craft of the humorist and through which the mixed skepticism and humanism of the literary comedian pervades the tone of the supposedly regional elements. Pascal Covici has noted that Huck's needle-threading experience, when he learns to thread "the way a woman most always does," is exactly the reverse of the manner described as a woman's way in

---

10 Robert Rowlette, "Mark Ward on Artemus Twain: Twain's Literary Debt to Ward," *American Literary Realism, 1870–1910*, VI (Winter, 1973), 13–26, outlines a number of these parallels. Blair, *Native American Humor*, 151–52. Lynn, *Mark Twain and Southwestern Humor*, 80–82, analyzes this transference and its possible implications for the "honest" cynic who dupes the religious enthusiasts.

The Prince and the Pauper.[11] The point is that Twain wishes for the appearance of realism but is not interested in the actual mechanics of the problem. He is concerned with establishing a believable social framework in which to work out his hero's ethics.

Episodes throughout the novel identify it as a work of literary comedy and thus carry their own irony within the nominally realistic experience. Pap's "Call this a govment!" speech reflects this irony. As an isolated episode it could be inserted anywhere in the story. Presented early in the novel, it accompanies Miss Watson's grim description of hell, foreclosing both church and state to the innocent who only wishes for immediate comfort and kindness. The comic statement is transformed into thematic material by its effect on Huck —since Pap, like Miss Watson, is seeking to exploit Huck for his own egotistical satisfaction. The bitterness of the speech is a considerable deepening of Neal's and Ward's portrayals, as in Peter Brush and Jim Griggins, for dramatic purposes. Huck becomes a positive alternative to this exploitation by preferring Tom Sawyer or freeing niggers, and his responses become the underpinnings of the social theme of the novel.

The ethics of the literary comedian provide Huck's perspective. Much of the business early in the novel is intended to establish this perspective. If Ward had declined to worry about the murders of long-dead kings, Huck "don't take no stock in dead people" (2).[12] The ferryboat full of townspeople hunting Huck's "carcass" do, however, and almost create the corpse which they value so highly. Huck's characteristic interest in the concrete and pragmatic is more fully established through this ironic episode. Since the interplay between Huck and Tom Sawyer in the concluding fifth of the novel is based on Huck's pragmatism versus Tom's fantasy world such episodes significantly foreshadow the outcome of the novel.

---

11 Pascal Covici, Jr., *Mark Twain's Humor* (Dallas: Southern Methodist University Press, 1962), 62.

12 The Artemus Ward analogue to this statement appears in the London letters when Ward comments on the Tower of London in roughly the same way that Huck comments on "Moses and the Bulrushers": "The early managers of this institootion were a bad lot, and their crimes were trooly orful; but I can't sob for those who died four or five hundred years ago. If they was my own relations I couldn't. It's absurd to shed sobs over things which occurd during the rain of Henry the Three." (Ward, *Works*, 433)

Lionel Trilling has commented on Huck's quick sympathy for humanity as opposed to the respectable Christianity and morality of his society. Twain integrates this opposition into Huck's episodic river journey, yet each of these episodes contain traditional humorous elements. The Pap and Miss Watson scenes, the Boggs-Sherburn episode, the *Walter Scott* incident, the Grangerford-Shepherdson feud, and the Duke and Dauphin's invasion of the raft all provide dramatic action into which the ethical presuppositions of literary comedy blend naturally. Because Twain retains Huck's flexibility he is able to blend ethical and natural reality without making Huck completely incongruous, as Leo Marx has demonstrated.[13] The raft, in conjunction with Huck's persona, provides the medium through which he can become a traveling observer like the reporter of *The Innocents Abroad* and *Roughing It*, and, like them, he has ironic comments to make about religion and history in the course of his movements. Ward's "moral show" lacked the flexibility that Huck achieves in his description of natural settings and town experiences. Huck's world is actually an extremely sophisticated one, and it is perhaps for this reason that many readers are uncomfortable when the Duke and the Dauphin vulgarize it and Tom Sawyer degrades it to childish game playing.

Huck's speeches are the high points of the novel, particularly his definition of two providences, his recognition of the beauty and mystery of a starry night, his statement of the raft ethic, and his decision to go to hell. Each carries the stamp of the ironic literalism which literary comedy applied to social institutions. Huck can recognize the vulgar level of experience by observation even when he himself has just narrated a dramatic or sublime experience, as when he observes on the river, "No; spirits wouldn't say, 'Dern the dern fog,'" (165) or reports the Dauphin's remarks, "I've done considerable in the doctoring way in my time. Layin' on o' hands is my best holt—for cancer and paralysis, and sich things" (169). In lengthier speeches, the irony of *The Gilded Age* appears in dramatic sequences which

---

13 Lionel Trilling, "The Greatness of *Huckleberry Finn*," in Marks (ed.), *Mark Twain's Huckleberry Finn*, 46–49. Leo Marx, "The Pilot and the Passenger: Landscape Conventions and the Style of *Huckleberry Finn*," *American Literature*, XXVIII (May, 1956), 129–46.

Huck hears, overhears, or observes. Aboard the *Walter Scott*, Huck listens to a violent argument: "Hear him beg! and yet if we hadn't got the best of him and tied him, he'd a killed us both. And what for? Jist for noth'n. Jist because we stood on our *rights*—that's what for" (95). And "I'm unfavorable to killin' a man as long as you can git aroun' it; it ain't good sense, it ain't good morals. Ain't I right" (97).

When Huck has to state his ethical position, however, he almost never uses such terms as appear in these passages; his own dialect is a careful mixture of dialect and common words that do not suggest the ironic problems inherent in his recorded observations, as when he explains his position to Mary Jane Wilks:

"Well," I says, "it's a rough gang, them two frauds, and I'm fixed so I got to travel with them a while longer. Whether I want to or not—I druther not tell you why; and if you was to blow on them this town would get me out of their claws, and I'd be all right; but there'd be another person that you don't know about who'd be in big trouble. Well, we got to save *him*, hain't we? Of course. Well, then, we won't blow on them." (261)

Even here, where Huck is evading the mention of Jim, his speech is clear and the dialect is muted, a *them* for a *those*, *claws* for the *clutches* of melodrama, *blow* for *tell*, and little else. Dramatization replaces—personalizes—moral abstractions. It appears that literary comedy is used to characterize the negative aspects of Huck's milieu and to illustrate the objectivity of his persona. It may be for this purpose that one of Huck's most literary-seeming non sequiturs —"it belonged to one of his ancestors with a long wooden handle" (356)—appears in the area of the novel where Huck has become subordinate to Tom's search for "glory." The more positive elements of his philosophy, which provide the tension of the novel, are couched in relatively normal colloquial English. Humor is integral in Huck's world, and certainly with certain aspects of Huck himself; Huck is also the deadpan humorist with many of the features of Twain and Ward, the professional comedians, which such a role implies. The travels on the raft provide the medium in which the professional humorist then becomes the chief actor. Hank Morgan shows the same trait even more obviously than does Huck.

The Duke and the Dauphin serve a vital function in the novel through their successful invasion of the raft, which has constituted a community in many ways less viable than Hank Morgan's industrial utopia will prove to be in Arthurian England. In their royal claims, the two tramps are examples of the vulgar pretension that appeared in the willingness of Artemus Ward to become a duke if the opportunity was offered, an attitude copied by Col. Sellers in *The American Claimant*. Huck, a good deal less naïve than the townspeople in the next few places visited by the tramps, readily sees them for what they are:

"It ain't my fault I warn't born a duke, it ain't your fault you warn't born a king—so what's the use to worry? make the best o' things the way you find 'em, says I—that's my motto. This ain't no bad thing that we've struck here —plenty grub and an easy life—come, give us your hand, duke, and le's all be friends."
The duke done it, and Jim and me was pretty glad to see it. It took away all the uncomfortableness and we felt mighty good over it, because it would a been a miserable business to have any unfriendliness on the raft; for what you want, above all things, on a raft, is for everybody to be satisfied, and feel right and kind toward the others.
It didn't take me long to make up my mind that these liars warn't no kings nor dukes at all, but just low-down humbugs and frauds. But I never said nothing, never let on; kept it to myself, it's the best way; then you don't have no quarrels, and don't get into no trouble. If they wanted us to call them kings and dukes, I hadn't no objections, 'long as it would keep peace in the family; and it warn't no use to tell Jim, so I didn't tell him. (173–74)

The above passage gives evidence of the two most important themes of the novel, one used by Twain to complete the development of the raft experience in the last fifth of the book in the context of Tom's burlesque activities, the other the social theme that dominates all of Twain's novels. Huck's acquiescence is the central feature of the moment, and Tom Sawyer will take advantage of it later.[14] The practices of the Duke and the Dauphin as humbugs are part of the inescapable political impositions of life. Antagonism toward such self-assured pretentiousness underlies Twain's conception of the Holy

---

14 It is possible to guess that Huck's use of "family" reflects Twain's ironic treatment of Barnum's "Happy Family," since the cases parallel each other, but the likeness is too tenuous to merit extended consideration.

Land, of the Samson story, and of every locale that he treats in humorous form. Their actions are consistent with the pattern of royalty developed in Barnum's attitudes and Ward's burlesque letters and thus are drawn directly from the view of royalty established by the egalitarian literary comedians. Huck's recognition of the need for "peace in the family" is a positive element in this experience, however, and generates a tension between his desire and those around him. This is the basis for the plot of the novel—the desire to free Jim and recognize him as an equal human being. Although the point hardly needs to be stated again, the transformation of literary comedy into the novelist's vision occurs in this tension, a tension which Orpheus C. Kerr, Max Adeler, and the other comedians who attempted the novel form were never able to create. The position that Huck takes will, in fact, be restated twice by the end of the novel, once in terms of Jim (in the speech to Mary Jane Wilks already discussed) and once by Jim in burlesque terms (in describing his prison bed after the intrusion of Tom Sawyer's snakes and spiders).

Twain's theory relating to society and government finally causes him to abandon even so impermanent a structure as the raft. In *A Connecticut Yankee*, his hero described the governing structure as springing from the seizure of power by the gilded minority, the nobles and the church. Similar theories are broached in *The American Claimant* and *The Prince and the Pauper*. *The Gilded Age* suggests corresponding corruption in a democracy. The raft, apparently like any other social form, is susceptible to this usurpation by false nobility. The whole duke and dauphin sequence is a translation of literary humor into fictional narrative. Huck calls the King "your majesty" throughout, and the foreshadowing lesson which he had given Jim on the nature of kings and nobles reinforces Twain's meaning where such material in Ward's letters served only the purpose of the individual letter. The return of the Duke and Dauphin to the raft, after the Wilks episode, is marked by the climactic lightning effects that echo the first destruction of the raft by a steamboat, and here again the end of the raft world is imminent. Like the facts relating to the missing Wilks brothers, or as with democratic rhetoric, the raft has proved capable of misuse and can no longer serve the good and freeing purposes of Jim's escape. Twain's theme as it appears in the burlesque Duke and Dauphin represents a refinement of the royalty themes posed by Ward in the 1860s. Twain surpasses Ward in the development of short items and comic phrases through which Ward initially stated his viewpoint into plot material carrying on his main themes. Thus, Twain freely develops the two mountebanks into backwoods scoundrels, well adapted to prey upon the towns whose ethic they share and understand, while maintaining between them and Huck a burlesque of the monarchial organization. With the addition of natural elements, a further physical dimension is added that is a positive alternative to social corruption.

In the last portion of *Huckleberry Finn*, Tom Sawyer reemerges as the leader of the gang composed of himself, Huck, and Jim. Twain returns to the burlesque form in this portion of the book in order to restate as humor the serious themes that have emerged in the course of the novel. From the first, Tom has been associated with the element of literary burlesque in the novel. As early as the second and third chapters, Tom shows so complete a dependence on the "pirate" books and "robber" books as to create difficulties between himself and the more pragmatic Huck. It was at this point that Huck, having already repudiated Miss Watson's Bible stories, remarked sarcastically of Tom's stories about Arabs and elephants that they "had all the marks of a Sunday-school" .(20). (The equation of Sunday-school with Tom's play-acting, part of Twain's rejection of formal Christianity in *Huckleberry Finn*, must have been an offensive element to his contemporaries.) In the final section of the novel, Tom is still identified with the prescriptive morality of St. Petersburg when he reasserts the earlier definition of Huck's "borrowing" as nothing but a soft name for stealing (91 and 335). Tom's insistence on developing difficulties and solutions for freeing Jim "the *right* way" according to books puts him, and Huck and Jim as well, at the center of an extended literary burlesque.

In a sense, Twain's extensive writing of political and literary burlesques in the late 1860s makes the final turn in the development of the novel understandable. As with Ward, Twain not only did not segregate the burlesque from social criticism, but he could freely write his own literary persona into a burlesque sequence and expect it to be believable in the literary sense. *A Connecticut Yankee* is just such a convincing literary burlesque carrying a serious social message. In the last fifth of *Huckleberry Finn*, Huck's realistic attitude remains in effect, and even at the height of the comedy it is Huck who recognizes the danger and says to himself that "we'd overdone this thing" (376). Consequently it should not be too surprising to find in a comic sequence dealing with the prison-cabin full of insects and snakes the serious reechoing of the raft ethic of toleration expounded by Huck, here stated in response to Tom's advice on the soothing of prison pets:

"You want to set on your bed nights before you go to sleep, and early in the mornings, and play your jews-harp; play 'The Last Link is Broken'—that's the thing that'll scoop a rat quicker'n anything else; and when you've played about two minutes you'll see all the rats, and the snakes, and spiders, and things begin to feel worried about you, and come. And they'll just fairly swarm over you, and have a noble good time."
"Yes, *dey* will, I reck'n, Mars Tom, but what kine er time is *Jim* havin'? Blest if I kin see de pint. But I'll do it ef I got to. I reck'n I better keep de animals satisfied, en not have no trouble in de house." (364)

At this point, the literary comedy of *Huckleberry Finn* and the thematic intention of the novelist are run together. The experience of Huck's journey becomes Jim's refuge in the midst of the literary burlesque reimposed by Tom's dominance. River terminology also appears in Huck's speech at this time, reinforcing the reader's recollections of the raft experience. The subjection of Huck and Jim to Tom is a parallel to the capture of the raft by the Duke and Dauphin. Neither persons nor societies nor vehicles of flight are immune to domination by false imposers of power, regulations, royal privileges, or false literary ideas—only the ethics of the individual remain untouched. This final point is the source of the power, as well as the poignance, inherent in Huck's final determination to renew his flight from "sivilization" as an individual. The appearance of the burlesque at the end of the novel is appropriate to this meaning.

The chorus of rustics who attempt to appraise the romantic paraphernalia involved in Jim's escape serve as a reminder that Twain's theme is not the apotheosis of the vernacular figure as such. Brother

Marples is simply a caricature of the cruel loafers around Bricksville. Aunt Sally's susceptibility to talk of spirits proves her to be less shrewd than was Huck on the foggy Mississippi. As in Artemus Ward's letters, the use of the vulgar dialogue and caricatures of figures in the novel serves to emphasize the comedy of stereotyped thought; it implies to the reader that there is a value that is being missed, that of the honest individual with plain and direct vision and action. It may be that this section is close to the superior viewpoint of the southwestern humorists, but S. J. Liljegren's study of Twain's antiromantic burlesque newspaper writings of the 1860s indicates that Twain could use burlesques as a serious form of dissent —as it is used in the last portion of the novel.[15]

The last fifth of *Adventures of Huckleberry Finn* will remain a problem for critics of the work, but it is worth noting that the concluding portion of the book is understandable in terms of the practice of literary comedy as we have discussed it. In criticizing society, literary comedy from the 1840s and 1850s through the 1890s makes little or no distinction between orthodox literary forms and burlesque, parody, and exaggeration. It is for this reason, in fact, that many items in the *Carpet-Bag* of B. P. Shillaber's day could be made to bear directly on Twain's humor—even more than the central themes isolated earlier. Huck can distinguish between certain experiences which are burlesque and those which are rational, however, and he thus comments on Tom's "intellectural" fun that it was "one of the most jackass ideas I ever struck" (344–45). This is unusually strong language for a novel of the 1880s, and it should caution critics about the degree of sensitivity Twain had in developing his main character as an antagonist toward formalized conventions. If anything, the employment of a dramatic character like Huck has freed Twain to express feelings more openly than he might in the omniscient "Mark Twain" persona. The book's final line, "Yours truly, Huck Finn" compared to the widely known "Yours trooly, A. Ward," seems almost a challenge to relate the novel to the attitudes found in the tradition.

The strength of the positive themes in Huck Finn is due in large

---

15 S. J. Liljegren, *The Revolt Against Romanticism in American Literature as Evidenced in the Works of S. L. Clemens* (New York: Haskell House, 1970 [1945]).

part to the successful characterization of Huck. Huck's attention centers on revelations of human quality. Part of his difficulties spring from his overreadiness to credit people, like a true naif. He rescues the Duke and Dauphin without question when they beg to have their lives saved—"said they hadn't been doing nothing, and was being chased for it" (167). He continues to credit Pap long after the reader has seen through Huck's account of the "call this a govment" speech that Pap is interested in property and rights and ownership, not egalitarian democracy or demonstrated qualities such as those held by the Negro professor. Huck thinks about men, as when he tries even to rescue the thieves on the *Walter Scott*, in terms of himself: "Now was the first time that I begun to worry about the men.... There ain't no telling but I might come to be a murderer myself yet and then how would I like it?" (100). Huck's self-effacing humanism, which recurs later in his option for Jim, is an elevation of the Twain of the spoon-stealing jokes; intensified and made conversational, this figure's vision is at the center of the fictional plot, and the working out of this vision against social dogma provides the major plot tension.

Huck also espouses his own unique philosophy. Persistently, he stands for humanity and nature over social experience. He admires the stars and the beauty of the river; he gourmandizes on Jim's home cooking; he enjoys Tom's imagination, and he enters into ready sympathy with a vast number of diverse types. Most of all, of course, he establishes an affirmative ethic in his love of freedom from smothery convention to enjoy the natural life on the raft, and the raft consequently becomes the book's chief symbol. He is also intensely human and personal as a character. Tom Sawyer and Miss Watson both leave Huck feeling lonely, and Pap abandons him in an isolated cabin only to return drunk to try to murder him. Huck and Jim together recognize a sort of loneliness in nature, as demonstrated in the stars that get "spoiled" and "hove out of the nest." Jim and Huck's friendship, however, is the counterstatement for the two of them as social rejects. Huck sympathizes with Jim's love for his family and recalls at crucial points Jim's favors and services to him as friend, standing watch, caring, but most of all uniting with Huck in human terms, "talking and singing and laughing." It is on this basis that Huck makes his choice to forget about right and wrong and do "whichever come handiest at the time" (128), a remarkably antisocial statement which makes sense in the context under discussion but otherwise requires deeper ethical inspection than it is usually accorded.

The climax of the novel comes in Chapter XXXI when Huck makes his final decision in favor of Jim. The final decision to go to hell is the high point in the development of Huck's affirmative position against society. In this instance, Sunday school, prayer, and "sin" are the representatives of corporate belief. Alternatively, Huck visualizes Jim "before me all the time," standing watch, expressing joy at Huck's return, "and how good he alway was" (296)—Jim's standing as a man. And he remembers Jim's statement to him that Huck is his best and only friend. Thus Huck comes to a choice "forever, betwixt two things": man and social obligation, seen by Huck as the choice between heaven and hell. Opting for hell, he decides further to steal Jim out of slavery, and go the "whole hog." The major success of the novel here is to translate the social concerns of the comedians and their sense of being outside corporate government into the broader metaphor of freedom and slavery and the question of the cruelty of human beings toward each other. Twain used the slavery theme extensively in three novels, not just in Huck's Southwest but also in medieval Britain, twice, to maintain this same dramatic tension. No other comedian caught up this theme with Twain's intensity, even when they wrote of foreign places and times or dropped back into an American historical setting; it is Twain's unique vision.

Finally, it is Huck's relationship to Jim as a man—Jim's standing as a man and a brother beyond social and color caste—which determines Huck's standing as a man. Huck makes his decision for human relationships against what Twain has depicted, episode by episode, as overwhelming social and religious authority. Nature and personal freedom on the raft have coalesced into an alternative world. Twain's development of this phenomenon has leaned heavily on borrowings from the tradition. Huck's persona is an elaboration and expansion of Twain's own. His deadpan accounts carry the ethics and attitudes of the literary comedians into the novel, and even into areas of the novel that appear most realistic and regionalistic. Nor is it easy to be satisfied with critics who dismiss the end of the book, for it carries out major themes and undercuts some localist aspects of Huck, as a type, which might otherwise dominate him. Huck is not the hero because he is an unspoiled local; he is altogether spoiled by society, as a character. He becomes unspoiled through his positive human situation, which he both participates in and observes objectively, like the travel narrators of literary comedy who are his ancestors. It is for these reasons that Huck is a figure of major significance and a new voice in American fiction.

NINE

A Connecticut Yankee:
A Culmination of American Literary Comedy

TWAIN'S MOST COMPLETE translation of social commentary into literary burlesque is *A Connecticut Yankee*, and every level of the novel holds contemporary elements from the American 1890s in juxtaposition with the plot material derived from King Arthur's medieval round table. Huck Finn is Twain's most successful blending of the themes and techniques of literary comedy with a visionary hero, but Hank Morgan, the Connecticut Yankee, is the most didactic representation of Twain's social philosophy in humor, and he is also the most active and economically powerful of all Twain's heroes. The *failure* of all of the strands of political argument, economic reasoning, professional ethics, comic humanism, and literary burlesque to contribute to a plot victory—a success for the Yankee against the forces of feudalism—is more than a mere necessity of historical verisimilitude. The Yankee's destruction and the destruction of his modern democratic civilization are an admission of futility that Huck Finn had been able to duck by heading out for the territories. Too much of Twain's own thinking and experience as a literary comedian is tied up in the novel for his readers to lightly dismiss the work's implications.

Twain first used the term *Connecticut Yankee* in referring to the shrewdness of Heber C. Kimball, in *Roughing It* (I, 96), with the intention of relating Kimball's managerial abilities, as seen in the Mormon utopia, to his Yankee geographic background. P. T. Barnum was another Connecticut Yankee very much in Twain's consciousness in the 1880s who also manifested such traits. In developing his fictional Connecticut Yankee, Twain drew extensively on the fund of diction established through Barnum and Ward's burlesque of the Barnum figure. Around this central showman, Twain developed his elaborate burlesque of an England that is defined through American comic conceptions (causing it to be offensive in the extreme to English critics). The more elaborate showmanship of Hank Morgan and the more extensive burlesque episodes of *A Connecticut Yankee*, however, do not necessarily indicate that Twain was more successful in combining humor and the novel form than he appears to have been in *Huckleberry Finn*.

The Yankee is a Connecticut mechanic who is crowbarred back to the sixth century during a fight and encounters, and almost masters, Arthurian England. The reader is introduced to the narrator through a frame sequence. The plot is thus the equivalent of a diary filtered through two narrators. The Yankee's purpose, when he locates himself in Arthurian England—a madhouse and circus combined, in his view—is to establish a nineteenth-century industrial nation-state, displacing the two backward forces of the church and nobility. Twain's themes are thus similar to those of *The Innocents Abroad*, *The Prince and the Pauper*, and *Huckleberry Finn*, and even his imagery cleaves to the diction and metaphor of those works. Hank Morgan, the Yankee, represents the traveling Mark Twain persona in feudal England. He goes through a series of adventures, including travel vignettes during a journey as a slave, a meeting with Morgan le Fay and her dungeons, a visit to the Valley of Holiness where he studies the church in burlesque and defeats Merlin, and similar adventures. He also attempts to build "men" with a man factory—recapturing the major theme of American literary comedy, and he finally applies that same yardstick to King Arthur. Industrial growth, however, has been identified by the comedians as altering such humane values in favor of nonindividualized machinery, and the same proves true here, as Hank's own civilization is destructive and is finally destroyed. The Yankee achieves a partial victory in asserting democratic values, but the plot expresses inescapable contradictions, and Twain's concern with the lost soul of the individual is somewhat more obvious in this later book than it was in *Huckleberry Finn*. Still, the Yankee is a significant achievement as a comic narrator.

The Yankee's interest in various aspects of business, particularly the commercial side, seems as much or more in keeping with the Yankee type created through the figures of Sam Slick, P. T. Barnum, and others, as with the background of Hank Morgan the arms-factory mechanic, described in the opening of *A Connecticut Yankee*. W. T. Stead, the English progressive, noted this relationship as a main point in Twain's attack on the semifeudal paraphernalia which Henry George and Edward Bellemy had already undermined in the popular conception: "There is something infinitely significant in the very form of his satire. If there is nothing sacred to the sapper, neither can there be anything sacred to the descendent of the [man] of the *Mayflower*, who has all the fervour of Mr. Zeal-for-the-Lord-Busy and the confident, complacent assurance of Sam Slick, who dismissed unceremoniously the authority of Plato or Aristotle with the observation that we need not heed what they said since there were no railways in their times."[1] The correspondence between Hank Morgan and Sam Slick noticed here extends to their overall attitude toward business as well; the Yankee also shows aspects of Barnum, Ward, and Twain himself, which seem to be consciously intended.

Hamlin Hill has identified one of the links between Hank Morgan and P. T. Barnum in the opening sequence of the novel. The Yankee mistakes Camelot for Bridgeport—a reasonable mistake for a Connecticut man to make only when Barnum's oriental mansion, *Iranistan*, overlooking that Connecticut city, is taken into account.[2] As Professor Hill suggests, other parallels may be discovered between Hank Morgan and Barnum. On the business side of Hank's personality is an aggressive interest in business opportunities and advertis-

---

[1] W. T. Stead, "Mark Twain's New Book," *Review of Reviews*, I (February, 1890), 144.
[2] Hamlin Hill, "Barnum, Bridgeport, and *The Connecticut Yankee*," *American Quarterly*, XVI (Winter, 1964), 615-16. Laurens D. Mason, "Real People in Mark Twain's Stories," *Overland Monthly*, LXXXIX (January, 1931), 12-13, 27, has also noted that when Twain wrote about the Yankee he was "thoroughly familiar" with Barnum's autobiography, and the Yankee has a strong element of Barnum in him.

ing. One of his early perceptions about Arthurian England is a burlesque businessman's opinion: "Look at the opportunities here for a man of knowledge, brains, pluck, and enterprise to sail in and grow up with the country" (60).[3] Another instance appears in the eclipse that saves the Yankee's life; it is not only a great triumph, but, as Morgan comments, "in a business way it would be the making of me" (43). These are very much like the sentiments of Barnum as he describes his greatest triumphs in *The Life of P. T. Barnum, Written by Himself*, the exploitations of Tom Thumb and Jenny Lind; and Twain's hero holds the same mood in his manuscript treating his own adventures and successes. Barnum's penchant for blatant advertising is reflected in the Yankee's attitude toward his restoration of the fountain in the Valley of Holiness: "You can't throw too much style into a miracle. It costs trouble, and work, and sometimes money; but it pays in the end" (213). The showmanship of the Yankee seems here, as elsewhere, to be an inheritance from Barnum rather than anything inherent in his own presumed background or with the covert industrializing of England.

Hank Morgan's showmanship appears in his language even in diction, indicating further his debt to the tradition. He complains that one of his horses belongs in a circus (119). He compares himself to an elephant in a menagerie and calls the hermits in the Valley of Holiness "a most strange menagerie" (204); he also wonders, reflecting Twain's burlesque of Bishop Southgate's Matinée for the *Alta California* in the 1860s, whether there is a matinée for the hermits (202), thereby reducing them to the level of one of Barnum's exhibits. The examination of a military cadet is introduced by the Yankee's ironic comment, "and the circus began" (239). The phrases characterize the Yankee's attitude toward his surroundings—Arthurian Britain is a circus show or a humbug. As in *Huckleberry Finn*, humor is directed toward those things that are objectionable hypocrisies, most particularly the Valley of Holiness. The Yankee's irreverence comes out of his recognition of the showmanship and commercial-

---

[3] Citations are from Volume XVI of the "Author's National Edition" (New York: Harper & Brothers, 1917).

ism bound up in the medieval world in the same ways it was bound up in Washington, D.C., or Hannibal—that is, largely, in the terms of the later nineteenth-century culture.

The Valley of Holiness shows a compound of such elements at work. In the plot it gives the Yankee an opportunity to show that his technology is superior to the church and Merlin, as well as to a random mountebank or two. It directly follows scenes of whippings that indict the cruel people who make pilgrimages. When the well of holy water is discovered to be dry, the Yankee comments "How odd to find that even this industry has its financial panics, and at times its assignats and greenbacks languish to zero, and everything comes to a standstill" (185). This description of a financial crisis would make sense to American readers; at the same time it places the church in a critical light as a commercial enterprise. St. Simon Stylites, who had been burlesqued in similar terms in the *Knickerbocker* in 1854, becomes the Yankee's enterprise when his "pedal movement" is employed to manufacture shirts, "patronized by the nobility" (206).[4] Burlesque, diction, and theme are united in the interplay of these elements to show that the Yankee is a more aggressive exploiter of the already corrupted experience than are its own proprietors. He

---

4 The American analogue for Twain's treatment of Saint Simon features the same attitudes which Morgan expresses. It is "Saint Simon Stylites and the Flea," by J. H. A. Bone, *Knickerbocker Magazine*, XLIII (March, 1854), 243–44, including these verses:

    Saint Simon knelt on his pillar of stone,
      Where, let the weather be fair or foul,
    Bishop butler declares that, for several years,
      The Saint had perched like a holy owl.
    On the top of his pillar, (just three feet wide,)
      The Saint had perched, (unless the fibs are told,)
    Till his joints were rusty, and his brain was musty,
      And his nostrils were stuffed with a terrible cold.
    . . . .
    Though his knees were sore, and his legs were cramped,
      The Saint still knelt with his arms in the air;
    Oft his body twitching, for his back was itching,
      And he durst not scratch it while saying his prayer:
    . . . .
    'Paters' and 'aves,' how fast they flew!
      Ne'er had he prayed with such speed before;
    His 'Credo' he told while the sweat-drops rolled—
      He was bitten so bad that he almost swore!

The Saint's dirtiness is also stressed. The poem describes the attack of Satan in the form of a flea on Saint Simon, who frantically speeds the prayers and catches the flea in fingers moistened with spit that has become holy water.

encourages bathing and pities slaves with almost equal enthusiasm. His own idealistic sentiments are identifiably separate from his English peers, and he is distinguished even from other potential business proprietors like Bors de Ganis, who purchases Saint Simon just before the business collapses.

The Yankee's business diction, as casual in tone as Twain's own in conversation, is the most important aspect of the transference of diction between nineteenth-century America and medieval Britain, for it is this conjunction that subjects both American business and the sublimity of the past to ironic incongruity. As early as 1886 Twain had been experimenting in platform readings with business slang, apparently using Launcelot, and the juxtaposition is reported to have been striking at that time.[5] Most noticeable in the novel is the term *man factory*, closely related to the plot of the book and used several times. There is also a "teacher factory" (77) and Sunday schools and grade schools are in "full blast" (77) like an industrial furnace helping to create a new industrial age. Hank becomes the "proprietor" (116) of some knights (whom he calls "cowboys") like an American storekeeper; appropriately one knight is in "the gentleman's furnishing line" (190). Sandy's "mill" shuts down for repairs when she is asked about her age (166). There is also talk of trade unions to Dowley the artisan (332) among other arguments on economics that are "pile-driver" arguments (324). Most obvious are the running references to Merlin's "stock" (59, 396, *et passim*), which culminate in the establishment of a stock exchange with bulling and bearing of stocks (403). Baseball, with one team named the "Bessemers" (405–406), is connected to Merlin's "innings" (57). Such diction should not be undervalued, for it is directly connected to the humanistic professionalism derived from Twain's own background; the Yankee is an aggressive organizer-investor, not unlike Twain considered himself. Determined to start a newspaper, one of the preconditions for a free nation, Hank seeks an apprenticed "local" reporter to train

---

[5] "Twain's Yankee Knight," Keokuk (Iowa) *Weekly Gate City*, November 25, 1886, in Scrapbook Twenty, pp. 62–63, in Mark Twain Papers, Berkeley, contains a review of Twain's platform reading to a West Point audience in which Twain used boss-contract diction in Launcelot's speech as well as describing a hero named "Smith," and this same reading also used the anecdote about hearing a joke for the thousandth time and disliking it.

into the business, as Twain had been trained (70–71). Later in the plot Hank even plans to reform the gilded nobility when, after Arthur, "nobility (is) abolished, every member of it bound out to some useful trade, universal suffrage instituted, and the whole government placed in the hands of the men and women of the nation there to remain" (302). Such diction may indicate that Twain still believes in the nexus of the 1850 and 1860 comedians, even though the coming of the railroads and kindred corporations has established an industrial milieu in which his plot must be worked out.

The world of *A Connecticut Yankee* is a welter of elements that burlesque each other in cross-cultural terms in the Yankee's breezy commercialism. Many comic items, however, also establish his high ethical standards. Pascal Covici suggests that Hank's poker talk is one of the elements which guarantees his Americanism as he roams the streets of England, but as the foregoing indicates, his Americanism appears in all of his plans.[6] The industrial, mercantile, and sports diction in Hank's dialect add support to this philosophical stance. They complement the themes of the book without validating vulgarity any more than Huck's speech validates the yokels who collect at the Phelps farm. When the slang of the Yankees was emphasized in the stage play, Twain even complained that the actor had captured only "one side of the Yankee's character—his rude animal side, the good heart & the high intent are left out of him; he is a mere boisterous clown, & oozes slang from every pore."[7] Such a comment indicates Twain's awareness of the burlesque effect of Hank's language and his discomfort when the burlesque tone was exaggerated without some compensating ideal statement. As he had learned with his newspaper hoaxes, satire and caricature could exist side by side if one did not overwhelm the other.

Although much of the Yankee's diction is based on his attitude toward England, other aspects of the Yankee's language reflect Twain's own idiom as it developed through his background on the Mississippi. Hank Morgan talks about the "starboard side" of his horse, for

---

6 Covici, *Mark Twain's Humor*, 27, 39.
7 *Love Letters of Mark Twain*, 257–58.

example (176). He refers to himself as having to "be on deck and attending to business" (232). His destruction of knights in armor is stated in a metaphor that suggests the Mississippi River experience openly: "Yes, it was a neat thing, very neat and pretty to see. It resembled a steamboat explosion on the Mississippi; and during the next fifteen minutes we stood under a steady drizzle of microscopic fragments of knights and hardware and horseflesh" (272-73). Twain's intention in this passage may be to reemphasize the fact that his story deals with the opinions of a contemporary man of the age of steamboats in nineteenth-century America. As a means of emphasizing this, Twain draws on his own experience and makes the Yankee approximate his own persona.

Elsewhere the Yankee breaks into nautical language to present a fashion burlesque which sounds quite foreign to his normal dialect: "As it extended, I brought out a line of goods suitable for kings, and a nobby thing for duchesses and that sort, with ruffles down the forehatch and the running-gear clewed up with a featherstitch to leeward and then hauled aft with a back-stay and triced up with a half-turn in the standing rigging forward of the weather-gaskets. Yes, it was a daisy" (206). The last sentence holds the only idiom recognizable as Hank Morgan's; all the rest—the scrambling of terms, the use of nautical dialect, and the burlesque of fashionable dress—are from Twain's literary comedy of the 1860s. The irreverent burlesques of the Civil War era are repeated as part of a Yankee mechanic's treatment of royalty in feudal England. The original attitude of the comic writer is a means of characterizing the writer's hero, and the literary comedian's desire to satirize and burlesque, stated explicitly by Twain as early as the "Preface" to *The Gilded Age*, becomes one of the sources of tension between the hero of *A Connecticut Yankee* and the social and moral environment in which he finds himself. The fashion burlesque is only one indication of this tension; it is also evident in the chapters dealing with another anachronism from Twain's early writing—the Arkansas newspaper, published by the irrepressible scoffer, Clarence. Twain identifies Hank's experience with his own, an identification that points toward the final assimilation of comic irony into the omniscient authorial voice in *Pudd'nhead Wilson*—and the submergence of its comedy in the increasingly obvious pessimism of Twain's plots.

Other sequences in *A Connecticut Yankee* suggest how much Twain was relying on his own background as a humorist in the formation of the Yankee's character. Artemus Ward, and others, described Horace Greeley's wild stagecoach ride with Hank Monk on Greeley's much publicized overland journey to California in the late 1850s; and Twain himself mentioned this story in his newspaper writing[8] and retold it in *Roughing It* (I, 136–43). In November of 1866, Twain experimented with the story of Greeley's ride by retelling a dull version of it over and over until it became funny by repetition, on one occasion repeating it five times before bringing the house down.[9] Hank Morgan repeats Twain's experience when he tells an unnamed story to monks in the Valley of Holiness:

> At last I ventured a story myself; and vast was the success of it. Not right off, of course, for the native of those islands does not, as a rule, dissolve upon the early applications of a humorous thing; but the fifth time I told it, they began to crack in places; the eighth time I told it, they began to crumble; at the twelfth repetition they fell apart in chunks; and at the fifteenth they disintegrated, and I got a broom and swept them up. This language is figurative. Those islanders—well, they are slow pay at first, in the matter of return for your investment of effort, but in the end they make the pay of all other nations poor and small by contrast. (198)

The anecdote serves to suggest the slowness and dullness of the English while showing the final strength of their responses in some situations—and this point is reiterated in the Yankee's education of King Arthur in the matter of human slavery. This anecdote thus serves multiple functions. First, it establishes a character for the Yankee, as a patient deadpan platform lecturer, seeking a satisfying response from his audience—based on Twain's early efforts as a platform humorist. Second, it shows the English as responsive to hu-

---

8 *Mark Twain of the Enterprise*, 99.
9 Fatout, *Mark Twain on the Lecture Circuit*, 56. As with Yankee business diction in Launcelot's speech, Twain had this story on his mind in the middle 1880s. Notes for a book on lecturing in Notebook Nineteen, Mark Twain Papers, p. 24, for May 28, 1885, indicate plans for a chapter on English and American lecture audiences.

morous repetition, which in Twain's experience connects them with Americans, though the relation is not overtly stated. Third, it foreshadows the Yankee's drawn-out education of the king, one of the most important positive statements of Twain's humanism in the book. The story might also be taken as an excuse for the redundancy of some of his burlesques of commercialism and knighthood.

Twain intended that the Yankee be connected with the tradition of the literary comedians, even if only to emphasize how far beyond that school he had gone in his own works. The social criticism of the literary comedians provides some precedent for Twain's burlesques of and attacks on certain classes of society. The lineage of one joke that the Yankee tells, even while he complains about it, is explicitly traced through Artemus Ward:

If by malice of fate he knew the one particular anecdote which I had heard oftenest and most hated and most loathed all my life, he had at least spared it me. It was one which I had heard attributed to every humorous person who had ever stood on American soil, from Columbus down to Artemus Ward. It was about a humorous lecturer who flooded an ignorant audience with the killingest jokes for an hour and never got a laugh; and then when he was leaving, some gray simpletons wrung him gratefully by the hand and said it had been the funniest thing they had ever heard, and "it was all they could do to keep from laughin' right out in meetin'." (73)

This piece is inserted into the narrative to explain why the Yankee likes Sir Dinadan, the dull humorist of the Arthurian court. Its function, however, is to maintain the atmosphere of literary comedy in the novel while simultaneously seeming to deny it. Morgan's relationship to this same story is fully established later in the novel, when Sir Dinadan produces the first volume of jokes in Arthur's realm and Morgan comments, "If he had left out that old rancid one about the lecturer I wouldn't have said anything; but I couldn't stand that one. I suppressed the book and hanged the author" (398), just as the tenderfoot Mark Twain had scalped a sarcastic Indian for a humorous remark in *Roughing It* (I, 123).

The Yankee's maturation beyond 1860s literary humor seems intended as a universal touchstone. Twain uses his own experience of thirty years of writing to indicate the nineteenth-century Yankee's superiority over his medieval counterparts. The lineage of the joke itself is traceable—Paul Fatout has pointed out how Twain's "A Wicked Fraud," an analogue of this story published in 1868, was probably based on Artemus Ward's "How the Napoleon of Sellers was Sold," in which the quiet audience is represented by a deaf and dumb man.[10] The maturation of the joke in Twain's experience being a product of twenty years, he has the Yankee expect that the maturation of English society will be similarly measurable. When Sir Dinadan does not show this development and refinement of taste, he becomes of the same class as the slave drivers and the corporate feudal and religious entities; consequently, the Yankee destroys him without compunction, whereas toward other individuals, such as King Arthur, he can be as flexible in his attitudes as Ward was toward Prince Albert Edward. Elsewhere, growth beyond overt literary comedy also indicates ability to develop. The Yankee's view of Arkansas journalism, in the chapter titled "The First Newspaper," suggests that he has undergone a "considerable change." His maturing attitude towards flippant backwoods American journalism corresponds to his growth beyond the literary jokes of the 1860s. The two aspects of Twain's literary background, his apprenticeship and his early career as a humorist, thus seem to function correspondingly in his treatment of the Yankee's intellectual position as a traveler in feudal English society.

There are, in fact, so many elements reflecting Twain's literary background that there seems to have been a concerted effort on his part to introduce and apply them. The monks in the Valley of Holiness who tell questionable stories (198) reecho the description of the governor in *The Gilded Age*. The Yankee's digression on art and the old masters, in which he comments that angels are as fond of being included in pictures as are members of a local fire company (199), echoes both *The Innocents Abroad* and *A Tramp Abroad*. The title of "Boss," which is given by the nation rather than the king and to which he is "Elected by the nation" (67), is like the title of "Admiral" in *Roughing It* (II, 165), which was the "voluntary offering of a whole

---

10 Fatout, *Mark Twain on the Lecture Circuit*, 109.

nation," direct from the people, without red tape, to an old salt. In constructing a platform for the show in the Valley of Holiness, Hank, playing the showman, says, "My idea was, doors open at ten-thirty, performance to begin at eleven-twenty-five sharp. I wished I could charge admission, but of course that wouldn't answer" (213). Last, and most subtle, is the replay of Twain's "Golden Arm" story, which he describes in "How to Tell a Story"; it is reenacted by Clarence in describing the substitution of cats for kings—so convincingly that Hank is shocked when Clarence comes out with a hideous series of yowls to describe the results (401).

Such willful intrusions into the Yankee's persona by Twain's own persona as a literary comedian serve a purpose. They alter the "realism" of the novel, giving the narrator some distance from it. His attitude is so independent, like Miles Hendon's in some cases, that he appears free from real consequences. The plot becomes a philosophical representation of the literary comedian's viewpoints, ensured by his persistent pose. Confirming evidence of this point is the Yankee's tendency to become a travel reporter where a more compact plot might have been developed had he stayed in one place. His travels, however, give him the same opportunity for humorous social commentary, exaggeration, and burlesque as do the travels of the Twain reporter. Henry Nash Smith has complained that the identification of the author and narrator destroys the fictional integrity of the novel,[11] yet it is just as possible to maintain that this was Twain's intention. By refusing to confine Hank to consistency of character, Mark Twain freed his point of view to entertain a wide spectrum of social and intellectual issues. Such breadth and freedom enable Mark Twain to suspend belief as well as disbelief in a confined "fiction." Thus, when Clarence numbers Hank's dead friends at the end of the novel, Hank resorts to thoughts of baseball teams (415–16) to escape the full fictional imprisonment of the moment. This escape is similarly necessary when the Yankee describes a number of atrocities during his travels.

The format of a modern viewpoint applied to medieval concep-

---

11 Smith, *Mark Twain: Development of a Writer*, 144.

tions of chivalry and human responsibility, directly allied to literary comedy as it is, may underlie the nature of the Yankee's humor. Twain had tentatively broached the idea in "The 'Tournament' in A.D. 1870" in the *Galaxy* years before.[12] At the time, Twain had commented sarcastically on the intrusion of romance among the rolling mills and factories of the North, noting the absurdity of sentimentalizing such chivalry as was possessed by a half-savage people. He suggested that the next event be a wholesale burning and butchering of Jewish women and children. This sarcastic rejection defines the Yankee's philosophy. His mood and diction were foreshadowed as well in B. P. Shillaber's "Modern Chivalry":

> Then knightly heads did all the needed thinking;
> The people in benightedness were hid:
> Fighting and robbing, sleeping, eating, drinking,
> Comprised the active business that they did.[13]

Since Shillaber's book of verse was published in 1874, it is apparent that a critical conception of chivalry in relation to modern times was current early in that decade. Another of the literary comedians, Max Adeler, wrote an extended treatment of an American scientific man in medieval settings, "The Fortunate Island," which appeared in 1881.[14] Technology is intruded into the chivalric world in essentially the same terms as Twain employed, although with somewhat less harshness. Thus, although George W. Cable may have started Twain's thinking about a book of this nature by his interest in Malory in 1884, a number of analogues already existed. The sources indicate the viability of the modern-medieval juxtaposition at the same time that they indicate the need for an individualistic treatment of the subject—and this also may account for Twain's intrusion into the Hank Morgan persona.

Hank persistently introduces contemporary reference points into his medieval experience, requiring his reader to generalize episodes

12 *Contributions to "The Galaxy,"* 59–60.
13 Shillaber, *Lines in Pleasant Places*, 61.
14 See Edward F. Foster's excellent, brief study of these correspondences in "*A Connecticut Yankee* Anticipated: Max Adeler's *Fortunate Island*," *Ball State University Forum*, IX (1968), 73–76.

of the novel into social principles: "It reminded me of a time thirteen centuries away, when the 'poor whites' of our South who were always despised and frequently insulted by the slave-lords around them, and who owed their base condition simply to the presence of slavery in their midst, were yet pusillanimously ready to side with the slave-lords" (298). Similarly, after recording an incident when a priest took a pig for tithes, leaving its owner's family to starve, the Yankee commented: "How curious. The same thing had happened in the Wales of my day, under this same old Established Church." With these remarks, deeper and more directly stated complaints about the organization of society appear in the mouth of Twain's character. The social criticism moves beyond the area of comedy. Twain's feelings about the church are further developed through burlesque in the treatment of religion in the Valley of Holiness.

William Dean Howells recognized *A Connecticut Yankee* as a novel about contemporary America allowing Twain further scope than had *The Prince and the Pauper* and *Huckleberry Finn* for an "object-lesson in democracy." Part of the interaction between present and past is an outcome of the characterization of Hank Morgan, which has already been discussed. But the interaction of past and present is also a product of Morgan's sarcastic jokes, which, like those of Ward the old showman, appear in combination with open diatribes against inhuman social practices. Howells pointed out this pattern in *A Connecticut Yankee* and went on to point out, in his review, the similar overall patterns of the book: "The elastic scheme of the romance allows it to play freely back and forward between the sixth century and the nineteenth century; and often while it is working the reader up to a blasting contempt of monarchy and aristocracy in King Arthur's time, the dates are magically shifted under him, and he is confronted with exactly the same principles in Queen Victoria's time."[15]

Twain's lighter humor, as it applies to this elastic scheme noticed by Howells, corresponds to his statements of social doctrine. Twain went so far as to claim that he was "only after the *life* of that day . . .

15 Howells, *My Mark Twain*, 124-28, reprinted from *Harper's Magazine* (1890).

to try to get into it; to see how it feels and seems," and went on to say that he would be sorry if he lost the pathos of the round table's destruction.[16] Twain's belief that he was localizing medieval experience makes sense only if this anachronistic insertion of American experience is allowed to be a description of the comedian's sense of universal "human natur'." The feel of life was to be achieved by translating the experience, as in *The Innocents Abroad*, into the language and thought patterns of the skeptical American traveler (Hank's persona appears obviously in his realist complaint on art—Raphael puts three men in a canoe that wouldn't hold a dog without upsetting, in the "Miraculous Drought of Fishes" [52]). Elsewhere the psychology of the Yankee in England is translated through the consciously American experiences of Twain, the platform humorist and newspaperman. The humorist is to create realism by asserting the likeness of various ages, and the materials of the literary comedians are taken as universals.

Parallel passages in Twain's own speeches indicate how closely the Yankee's feelings about the feudal order, reflecting Sam Slick's skepticism, are actually literary transcriptions of Twain's own sentiments and diction. In 1886 Twain delivered a paper titled "The New Dynasty" on the subject of the rising labor unions. In that paper he stated the basic ideas that underlie the Yankee's opposition to medieval institutions of church and state. Commenting generally, he suggested that "power when lodged in the hands of men, means oppression—*insures* oppression." Although stimulus for Twain's speech was the appearance of a labor leader before a committee of the United States Senate, he went on to attack "gilded idlers" by using feudal terms: "Who are the oppressors? The few: the king, the capitalist, and the handful of other overseers and superintendents. Who are the oppressed? The many: the nations of the earth; the valuable personages; the workers; they that MAKE the bread that the soft-handed and the idle eat."[17] Essentially the same social structure, and even the same terms, occur in the Yankee's diatribe on Arthurian

---

16 Mark Twain to Mrs. Fairbanks, ed. Wecter, 257–58, letter dated November 16, 1886.
17 Mark Twain, "The New Dynasty," reprinted in Paul J. Carter, Jr., "Mark Twain and the American Labor Movement," *New England Quarterly*, XXX (September, 1957), 582–88.

England. Although the idea of "non-resistance under oppression" is reserved for the teachings of the Church, the concept of aristocratic "gilded idlers" versus the nation of workers is plainly stressed:

> Seven-tenths of the free population of the country were of just their class and degree: small "independent" farmers, artisans, etc.; which is to say, they were the nation, the actual Nation; they were about all of it that was useful, or worth saving, or really respectworthy, and to subtract them would have been to subtract the Nation and leave behind some dregs, some refuse, in the shape of a king, nobility and gentry, idle, unproductive, acquainted mainly with the arts of wasting and destroying, and of no sort of use or value in any rationally constructed world. And yet, by ingenious contrivance, this gilded minority, instead of being in the tail of the procession where it belonged, was marching head up and banners flying, at the other end of it; had elected itself to be the Nation, and these innumerable clams had permitted it so long that they had come at last to accept it as a truth; and not only that, but to believe it right and as it should be. (102–103)

The Yankee is here translating the burlesque comedy of the story into openly stated political principles. Recognizable are the images and even word choices of *The Prince and the Pauper*, centralized in the narrator's vision. The Yankee had earlier elaborated a "new country's" need for a patent office, school system, and a newspaper. Thus the Yankee speaks for Twain's own beliefs about free press, inventiveness, and other frontier virtues of the American system.

Episodes in the novel dramatize the political and social principles. Plot is advanced and themes are built, for example, through Hank Morgan's visit to Morgan le Fay's castle. In this episode the themes of social order are applied, through humor, to the social experience of the individual. Morgan le Fay is a grotesque whose dungeons contain "assets" from the previous royal firms. As Hank frees these human assets, he discovers each story and offers it as a vignette to show the enmity between power and human dignity. He takes into his own experience the social viewpoint of a Yokel or a Jim Griggins. One particular incident stands out as a blending of the subtlest elements of American humor. One of the freed prisoners had said that if you were to strip a "nation" naked, you couldn't tell a king from a quack doctor, or a duke from a hotel clerk (157). He is sent to Hank's man factory as Hank proceeds to a second prisoner, whose story was given a foreshadowing political overtone by the first: "But for me, he never would have got out. Morgan le Fay hated him with her whole heart, and she never would have softened toward him. And yet his crime was committed more in thoughtlessness than depravity. He had said she had red hair. Well, she had; but that was no way to speak of it. When red-headed people are above a certain social grade their hair is auburn" (159). All the comedians' themes are involved —the sense of corporate social power, the operation of vanity, the passivity of the egalitarian innocent, and the pragmatism of the deadpan reporter. Charles Dudley Warner had made jokes about the social standing of redheads in *Backlog Studies*, fifteen years earlier, but without Mark Twain's multiplicity of dimensions.[18] The joke is almost in the tone of Potiphar in the 1850s, in fact, and it consequently takes on added irony from Twain's exaggerated diction, which uses words like "crime" and "depravity" to describe the act. Social caricature and the speaker's diction blend into the development of motifs of social oppression. One might see the humanist, libertarian attitudes of the 1850s being redrawn to suit the conditions of the modern age, all in a *joke*. Thus we see the novelist Twain adapting into fiction the deadpan monologue of the comedian.

Similarly impressive is Twain's use of other sequences that are very much like atrocity stories employed for purposes of wartime propaganda. One of the most notable of these melodramatic vignettes appears when Hank and Arthur witness the whipping of a young mother in a chain of slaves. She seems "but a girl," to the two men who watch as her child is seized from her. Yet, she is thrown to the ground and whipped without mercy until her back is flayed. Other travelers comment on the expertise of the whipper; another slave who turns his face away, her husband, is whipped for his "humanity"; they are soon sold away from each other. The late passage on horses in *The Innocents Abroad* is reechoed in Hank's remark on the attitude of the observers, "These pilgrims were kindhearted people,

---

18 Charles Dudley Warner, *Backlog Studies* (Boston: James R. Osgood, 1873), 257, burlesques Emerson in having the red-haired son of an Emir, ashamed of his red hair, counseled to behave so that all fathers would wish their sons to have red hair.

and they would not have allowed that man to treat a horse like that" (189). Elsewhere, young girls are hung for petty thefts (358–62) while their babies cry for them, and worse cruelties are described in the dungeons of Morgan le Fay. It is bizarre to consider such episodes as literary comedy, but they provide evidence of the same sort of social experience that Ward describes in his letters; and they are based on the same intention—to provide an emotional context for the egalitarian humorist to assert his positive ethic. Moreover, they are in the same format—vignetted observations comparable to Yokel's compacted indictment in *The Prince and the Pauper*.

The broadest statement of this egalitarianism appears when the Yankee and King Arthur are sold as slaves, late in the novel, and the Yankee's penchant for business terminology leads into a distinction between a man and his aristocratic position. His speech is reminiscent of Ward's treatment of Prince Albert Edward and Prince Napoleon. The Yankee had earlier referred to his knights as "assets" (116), called Morgan le Fay's prisoners "assets inherited, along with the throne, from the former firm" (160), and complained, when he himself was sold into slavery, that the sellers were trying to "force a sale on a dull market" (352). Out of this last statement, however, comes the Yankee's comment on himself and King Arthur that "there is nothing diviner about a king than there is about a tramp, after all" (352). Like the egalitarian old showman Ward, the Yankee places primary value in the individual. If Ward had inquired how Louis Napoleon "stands as a man,"[19] the Yankee observes of Arthur: "A king is a mere artificiality, and so a king's feelings, like the impulses of an automatic doll, are mere artificialities; but as a man, he is a reality, and his feelings, as a man, are real, not phantoms" (353). This distinction is typical of the stance of the literary comedians, and it expresses their essential optimism about man, once he is distinguished from the political and social corporations that so frequently own the lesser members of society. The business ethics burlesqued by the Yankee thus hold one key to the workings of the novel as literary

[19] Ward, *Works*, 131.

comedy, for out of the Yankee's sarcastic reduction of Arthur and his minister to the business commodities of the feudal world comes the affirmative statement about humanity.

The conflict between the humanity of the individual and the corruption of power, so central to the plot, is dramatized in terms of the comic humanist in dissent from institutions. After defining the manly individual power of Arthur and himself, Hank contends that the institutional church was "stronger than the both of us put together" (62). The tension is thus established for the final struggle of the novel, which comes after Arthur is dead and the church and the nobility are combined against Morgan and his boys. Dan Beard's illustrations for the original edition of the novel make the point of this arrangement clear—the opposition of financial and social interests against the downtrodden was the main theme of the novel. The Yankee reports that a man's feelings are real when he and Arthur are sold as slaves, but it is only after seeing the king refuse to relinquish his "style" under a slavemaster's whip that he declares, "The fact is, the king was a good deal more than a king, he was a man, you can't knock it out of him" (355). Hank's acknowledgment that the king was sublimely great in the smallpox hut (284), one of the book's most melodramatic scenes, foreshadows this moment and establishes the basis for the polarity between individual and corporation.

The tension of the novel is inherent in the contrasting portraits of Hank Morgan, King Arthur, and Morgan le Fay. King Arthur, like the royal figures of the 1860s, must justify his humanity, which he does in the smallpox hut most completely. The plot of the novel is elaborated around such human justification as the Yankee's advocacy of democratic civilization. There are other influential sources to be discovered for the elaboration of plot in the novel—Howard Baetzhold has discussed the most important British sources, particularly Carlyle and Dickens, in his recent study of Twain's relationship with England.[20] All these materials, direct sources and indicators of a traditional mode of thinking, were combined in the essentially digressive pattern of the platform humorist, along with yet other jokes

---

20 Howard G. Baetzhold, *Mark Twain and John Bull: The British Connection* (Bloomington: Indiana University Press, 1970), 102–61.

of Twain's own contriving.[21] Literary comedy, however, has come to serve a different function in *A Connecticut Yankee* than it had earlier. It had, for Twain, burlesqued an opposing cultural standard or embodied humanistic skepticism in a seemingly naïve framework. The naïve persona was retained along with some of its most characteristic comic representations. In *A Connecticut Yankee*, however, the naïveté is largely gone from the comic devices. Where Hendon's feeling that he was an earl in the Kingdom of Dreams was modified in the plot to the more material reward of public status as a return for his humanity and loyalty, Hank Morgan is described as increasingly involved in a dream experience in which the humor of his viewpoint is much more frequently balanced by stark portraits of human viciousness. Ultimately, the Yankee's specific programs for creating counterinstitutions bring about the greatest and most murderous effect in the plot. Figures of solitary dissent, reminiscent of Ward's Jim Griggins, are scattered through the novel, submerged in the "innumerable clams" of Britain. The showman himself, the Yankee, is the most subversive figure. He takes over the viewpoint of the outsider and adds to it his political and industrial power. Huck Finn acted with more individuality in his concentration on Jim; Hank, bound to his complex organization, has to destroy it to free himself. Where Civil War literary comedians used humor to attack the corruption in institutional ideals, Mark Twain uses it to confront the results of the urban-industrial social problems in a historical format. The failure of the Yankee in the plot, despite Twain's freedom in personalizing him with his own ethics and diction, and with the Barnumesque powers of the industrial magician, may indicate Twain's feeling that such social problems were no longer susceptible to the humanist remedies implicit in literary comedy.

Howells recognized even in minor scenes the Yankee's demands for a sort of patriotic justice, his complaint "that the laws are still

21 When the Yankee talks about "a man who had two thumbs on each hand and a wart on the inside of his upper lip, and died in the hope of a glorious resurrection" (305), he is not only expressing himself in the non sequitur of the fool comedian as Ward had done in his speeches, but is also borrowing from *Adventures of Huckleberry Finn*: "Yes, it was mortification that was it. He turned blue all over, and died in the hope of a glorious resurrection" (307). The persistence with which Twain maintains literary formulations is again in evidence in this case of burlesque religiosity.

made for the few against the many and that the preservation of things, not men, is still the ideal of legislation."[22] In fact, Twain shares with Browne the willingness to make his persona speak as humanist, even when the character's own entrepreneurial bent seems at variance with this stance. In *A Connecticut Yankee*, Twain's strength as a novelist may lie in his readiness to adopt the self-contradictions some critics have discovered in Artemus Ward and develop them into a full-scale amalgam of comedy, burlesque, social criticism, and personal diatribe—not only realizing some of the qualities implicit in the Ward persona but adding to them broader and more insistent social demands and the deeper sense of a social alternative, the special product of Twain's background. Literary comedy has come much farther here than might be indicated in the original notebook entry describing the difficulties of a suit of armor that had no pockets for a handerchief.[23]

Arthurian England is combined with nineteenth-century America in ways that cannot be thought of in "realistic" terms. Events translate the egalitarianism of the literary comedians into dramatic action through burlesque, caricature, or melodrama. Morgan le Fay and Hank Morgan, sharing part of their names, uncomfortably share an allegiance to absolute power, one democratic and one feudal; the reckless destruction of lives as mere housekeeping foreshadows Hank's last chilling effects. In fact, his cleaning of her dungeons is a dubious victory, as Pudd'nhead Wilson's victory will later prove to be. The convictions of the humorist-humanist are subservient to the complexities of the historical power of church and state.

The Yankee himself is a curious subordinate to his own ethics. The frame describes him as modest and simple and his behavior toward his wife Sandy is Victorian in the extreme. His love for "Hello Central" is also particularized as a feeling. This seems a strange figure for a *picaro*, which the Yankee is in many respects, and it is all the more poignant when he reenters the darkened castles of England toward the end of the action, and later in his still dark exile and death

22 Howells, *My Mark Twain*, 125.
23 This entry is reprinted in Hamlin Hill's useful Introduction to the Chandler Publishing Company's facsimile edition (San Francisco, 1963), ix–x. The episode was included in the book in the Yankee's journey (93–101).

in the modern world from which he had come. Ultimately, he represents a conflict between the beliefs of the antislavery comedians and the emerging world of the later nineteenth century, an existential problem still present in American self-awareness.

The localism of the literary comedians, although retained in Hank's mind in realistic references throughout—many of which, such as the comparison of a knight in armor to a sunstruck man being carried into a drugstore (91), have not even found a place in the discussion here—gives way to a pessimistic universalism early in the novel, foreshadowing his doom. In referring to the tedious, ostentatious, and unprofitable development of the human race, terms that themselves restate the main themes, the Yankee makes his baffled plea: "All that I think about in this plodding sad pilgrimage, this pathetic drift between eternities, is to look out humbly and live a pure and high and blameless life, and save that one microscopic atom in me that is truly *me*: the rest may land in Sheol and welcome for all I care" (150). The Yankee appears, as pilgrim, to be less well anchored than Huck Finn, who at least had specific moral choices to make. Finally the novel demonstrates the consequences of Hank's problem. The naif abandons much of his naïveté in this pessimistic philosophy, and this loss signals the end-point of Twain's expression of his humanism through humor, with the exception of the sarcasm of *Pudd'nhead Wilson* and the poorly integrated burlesques of *An American Claimant*. Twain's Yankee is his last representation of a figure approximating his own persona and holding, even as he abandons them, the traditional values of the comic figure developed through the traditional mode.

TEN

The American Claimant
and *Pudd'nhead Wilson*

THE INCOMPLETELY synthesized materials of *The American Claimant* and the pessimistic main character and plot outcome of *Pudd'nhead Wilson* indicate the disintegration of the potential for literary comedy in the construction of Twain's novels. In both novels the central figure is less successful in presenting ethical stances through humor than were Twain's major heroes. Although Twain's philosophy intrudes in many areas, it is seldom advanced into a sustained voice for his characters. This would seem to be why the elements of the literary comedians' viewpoint are present but do not achieve the sort of commentary that would typify the tradition as Twain had previously depended on it. The basic conception of *The American Claimant* was borrowed directly from literary comedy, but this fact did not make a coherent book, and he was not successful in combining his growing skepticism about democracy with his humor, which is ultimately pessimistic about the perfectability of the human condition. Pudd'nhead Wilson's stance is largely at variance with Hank Morgan's determination to make Arthur better as a man through insights into the meaning of slavery. The optimism of the naif underlies the comedy of earlier works; later, Twain's scorn for venality and inhumanity seems to persist without the supporting affirmation which literary comedy had provided. Both the flexibility and the positive humanism of earlier narrator-heroes are lost. Where *A Connecticut Yankee* was existential, these two later novels are a series of elements that are philosophically pertinent to Twain's major themes but dramatically unprepossessing.

I

THE AMERICAN CLAIMANT

The American Claimant, like *The Prince and the Pauper*, is based on traveling characters who exchange economic and social experiences. In the later book, however, once the exchange is made the characters become geographically immobile in the boardinghouse and neighborhood milieu of Washington, D.C. Pudd'nhead Wilson is similarly located in Dawson's Landing, and in the case of Mulberry Sellers, Howard Tracy, and Wilson there are comparable losses of freedom. The format in which social vignettes and cultural burlesques could be intruded is lost, and there is little room for the appearance of figures such as Yokel to establish in melodramatic terms the consequences of the presumably humorous narrative. Colonel Sellers is an overt copy of the Ward showman with the addition of some of Twain's ideas; and his location in Washington helps to place him with the literary comedians of the Civil War era, who also focused on that city. Although literary comedy does not contribute as much to the novel as it might, many of the jokes developed in the novel still represent the comedians' underlying interests. Unfortunately, the milieu of the 1890s is not clearly described through this humor, and the complicated plot adds little in this respect.

The young Viscount Berkeley, taking the American name of Howard Tracy, rejects his English earldom in favor of the experience of egalitarian democracy in an American boardinghouse. Eventually, he finds this experience to be full of commonplace hardships and vulgar melodramas which are more pretentious than are the ways of the aristocracy. The juxtaposition, however, provides a framework for a number of episodes and set speeches elaborating on the nature of democracy and monarchy. Colonel Sellers, a burlesque opportunist carrying on a variety of humbugs, seeks to acquire the earldom of Rossmore, which Tracy has abandoned. Sellers also, following his bent as shown in *The Gilded Age*, toys with schemes for reforming the world in ways profitable to himself. In this framework,

Sellers as politician-inventor has license to contrive his own burlesque fantasies—thus doubly removing the comedy from contemporary experience and making it identifiably different from Finley Peter Dunne's newspaper columns or even the interminable *Samantha at Saratoga* series by Marietta Holley, which took a vernacular-speaking farm woman to the centennials and expositions of the 1890s and made socially oriented comments about them. Twain's plot is finally resolved when Tracy decides to retain his earldom and marry Sellers' daughter, Sally, a resolution that is only partly satisfactory.

Colonel Sellers is even more the central figure of *The American Claimant* than he had been in *The Gilded Age*. Twain and Howells, working together in 1883, had developed much of the story as a farce for the stage, featuring Sellers in a role that potential producers felt bordered on the lunatic.[1] Traces of this character remain in a burlesque materialization scheme and elsewhere. Preeminently, however, Sellers is an old showman of the Ward variety, as the London *Spectator* recognized fully in its review of the novel: "He is not an absolute extravagance; he is a caricature indeed, but then a caricature is nothing without it suggests a truth. This is what the Colonel does; we see in him something of the qualities which make 'spread-eagleism' in politics and in private life create a curious combination of boundless self-belief and conscious imposture."[2] Artemus Ward in London provided essentially the same figure in 1867. His own dramatized function is that of political and social commentator, whatever his claimed role as showman or lobbyist might indicate. Furthermore, in the context of Howellsian realism, or even the realism of *Huckleberry Finn* and *A Connecticut Yankee*, the Sellers figure might be labeled irresponsible in providing his own support—one means by which other Twain heroes are frequently related to the world around them. Sellers thus criticizes the absolutism of Russia, but his own counterproposal is a burlesque scheme for spiritual materialization that *he* will totally dominate. Earlier heroes caricatured their milieu; Sellers burlesques himself.

---

[1] Clyde L. Grimm recounts the history of the play in *"The American Claimant*: Reclamation of a Farce," *American Quarterly*, XIX (Spring, 1967), 86–103.

[2] "The American Claimant," *Spectator*, LXIX supplement (November 19, 1892), 714.

Sellers has frequently been described as culturally split. In part he is no better as a potential advocate of democracy than is the young English earl, and he expresses himself cynically about the workings of the federal government, which men attend solely because they "want" something (14).[3] Nevertheless, as Warner Berthoff has noted, one of Sellers' speeches echoes the terms of the letter which Twain had written in 1889 to extol American progress on the occasion of Whitman's birthday.[4] The duplicity of Twain's views is evidenced by the subject that Sellers chooses as distinguishing his civilization —sewer gas, for which he sees tremendous potential in the service of mankind. When Hank Morgan was given a Twain speech, it became his viewpoint. In Sellers there appears to be an ambivalence indicated by the conversion of the original expression into a total absurdity.

Clyde Grimm has defended the novel as a reclaimed farce which converts humor into meaningful satire by infusing Twain's political beliefs into the plot of the work. Grimm sees Howard Tracy's experiences as exposing a discriminatory system in democratic experience. Sally Sellers' choice of Tracy as a lover is the alternate expression of preference based on individual worth and moral distinction rather than appearance and social standing. In the original farce, Sellers' claim to a title was a sham. In the novel, however, it is justified, and the colonel consequently appears more honest and objective than in the original. Professor Berthoff, although agreeing that meaningful themes are developed as Tracy discovers the instinctive servility of the American masses and their conformism, complains that "the chance for a satire on the illusion of democratic freedom is wasted as the narrative bogs down in elaborate corpse-and-ashes jokes and in a long farce sequence about materializing dead spirits, which no actor or manager who read the original play could persuade Twain to give up."[5] In part, these sequences are elaborations of literary comedy ideas that link irony and political implication,

---

3 All page references to *The American Claimant* are to Volume XXI, "Author's National Edition" (New York: Harper & Brothers, 1899).
4 Warner Berthoff, *The Ferment of Realism/American Literature, 1884–1919* (New York: Free Press, 1965), 70.
5 *Ibid.*, 69.

and it is probably for this reason that Twain introduced them into this context, but they actually detract more than they add to meaningful plot development.

The ashes joke to which Berthoff refers is related to material derived historically from the Ward persona, and thus gives evidence of Twain's reliance on the tradition for the purposes of developing the themes of the novel. Sellers visits the site of a hotel fire in which the young earl apparently perished. Believing that the earl *could* have died in any of three separate places, he carries home three baskets of ashes to memorialize his kinsman. Although the sequence burlesques sentimental posturing, it adds nothing to the sense of the Washington milieu, as comparable comedy did in *The Gilded Age*. A train of jokes is initiated, however, that relates the novel to a long-standing metaphor for fraud and unsatisfactory politics. Sellers, on learning of the presumed death of his kinsman, emotes like Ward, "It's true—too true" (59), even while deciding to make it false by materializing the dead spirit. Later, when Tracy is presumed to be a materialized cowboy, Washington Hawkins, Sellers' follower, comments on him as if he were part of Ward's show rather than Sally's lover: "You couldn't expect a person would fall in love with a wax-work. And this one doesn't even amount to that" (203). This terminology is not only applied to Tracy by Hawkins. Even earlier, when Tracy is in his boardinghouse, the American mechanics label his noble father, whom they believe to be fictitious, a "wax-figger" (115, 136). Thus the general tone of Ward the hawker is employed in connection with Tracy, supplying a metaphor for fraud in the vulgarized society, but the only complication is the delay of the love affair of Sally and Howard, a trivial outcome.

The materialization theme and the context supplied by the Ward showman is extended and elaborated by the major episodes of the novel, in keeping with the "wax-figger" metaphor noted above. Twain openly translated one of Ward's most characteristic political jokes into a burlesque episode. Howard Tracy is presumed to be a materialization because Colonel Sellers has devised an extravagant scheme based on this concept. Artemus Ward, in writing about the congressional elections in "Things in New York," claimed to have voted for the dead Henry Clay because "inasmuch as we don't seem to have a live statesman in our National Congress, let us by all means have a first-class corpse."[6] Similarly, Sellers originates a plot to revitalize corpses and materialize spirits to staff Congress and local police forces (28–29). When Hawkins asks, "But will dead policemen answer?" Sellers responds, "Haven't they—up to this time?" Yet Sellers' joke lacks a contemporary social context; instead it is just an expansion of Ward's comment on the Civil War era. "I will dig up the trained statesmen of all ages and all climes, and furnish this country with a Congress that knows enough to come in out of the rain—a thing that's never happened yet since the Declaration of Independence, and never will happen till these practically dead people are replaced with the genuine article." The combination of self-belief and imposture noted by the *Spectator* reviewer in the American character may lie in such jokes with their democratic preoccupation about elective government. Thus they provide democratic motifs—even though their relation to the rest of the novel is tenuous: they do not figure directly in establishing a contemporary milieu in which the young nobleman's actions might take place. The Knobs Industrial Bill in *The Gilded Age*, as a motif, figures much more successfully as a Sellers project than does the later borrowing form Ward.

The central problems of *The American Claimant* are the pursuit of a noble title and Howard Tracy's attempt to justify himself as an individual in a democratic society without aristocratic privilege. Sellers poses his side of the problem in burlesque, as when he explains himself as "being a democrat by birth and preference, and an aristocrat by inheritance and relish" (167). As an alternative to this burlesque stance, Tracy reasons on the problem of aristocracy with a logic reflecting Hank Morgan's thinking about the "innumerable

---

6 Ward, *Works*, 258. Ward, in his turn, may have borrowed the idea for his Henry Clay joke from Phoenix, who told a similar story naming John C. Calhoun:

> This gentleman (a candidate for the Senate), however, in the elucidation of his political principles, declared that he "went in altogether for John C. Calhoun, and nothing shorter." Now I'm no politician, and have no wish to engage in a controversy on the subject; but, God forgive me if I am in error, I thought Calhoun had been dead for some months. Well, I suppose some one is elected by this time, and the waves of political excitement have become calm, but Benecia was a stormy place during the election, I assure you.

John Phoenix [George H. Derby], *Phoenixiana: or, Sketches and Burlesques* (New York: D. Appleton, 1873 [1855]), 87.

clams" who do not rise from their beds to change Arthurian England: "I think I realize that caste does not exist and cannot exist except by common consent of the masses outside of its limits. I thought caste created itself and perpetuated itself; but it seems quite true that it only creates itself, and is perpetuated by the people whom it despises, and who can dissolve it at any time by assuming its mere sign-names themselves" (93). Tracy's ideas not only reflect the Yankee's doctrines; they also reflect Artemus Ward's remarks on Canada when he said, "I wouldn't mind comin over here to live in the capacity of a Duke, provided a vacancy occurs, and provided further, I could be allowed for a few star-spangled banners, a eagle, a boon of liberty, etc."[7] Ward's program would vulgarize the idea of aristocracy. The similarity of Ward's suggestion to Tracy's and Sellers' more abstract statements of the same principle is an indication of how readily Twain expanded upon the theme of democratic pretensions mixed with aristocratic snobbery. And this element of the book *is* sustained in the plot.

As the novel continues, Ward's frequently expressed admission of his own "human nater" in his letters appears in the mouth of Twain's boardinghouse cynic Barrow as an explanation of the normal desire of every man to undertake the wages of what Ward called "the lord bisniss."[8] The passage that follows shows how Twain has transformed Ward's brief joke into the problem of a novel, even making room for Twain's own jokes within the discussion:

"What is it you object to in Tompkin's speech, Barrow?"
"Oh, the leaving out of the factor of human nature; requiring another man to do what you wouldn't do yourself."
"Do you mean—"
"Why, here's what I mean; it's very simple. Tompkins is a blacksmith; has a family; works for wages; and hard, too—fooling around won't furnish the bread. Suppose it should turn out that by the death of somebody in England he is suddenly an earl—income, half a million dollars a year. What would he do?

. . . .

"Fool or *no* fool, he would grab it. Anybody would. Anybody that's alive.

7 Ward, *Works*, 263–64.
8 *Ibid.*, 261.

And I've seen dead people that would get up and go for it. I would myself."
   This was balm, this was healing, this was rest and peace and comfort.
   "But I thought you were opposed to nobilities?"
   "Transmissable ones, yes. But that's nothing. I'm opposed to millionaires, but it would be dangerous to offer me the position."
   "You'd take it?"
   "I would leave the funeral of my dearest enemy to go and assume its burdens and responsibilities." (127)

Twain's funeral jokes establish Barrow's honesty by making him seem a naïve character. Like the Ward and Twain personae, he shows a simple whimsicality that is almost foolishness, and which differentiates him from the churlish egocentrism of many of the boardinghouse people encountered by Tracy. For part of this effect in Barrow, Twain relies on one of his own tenderfoot jokes from *Roughing It*; his desire to attend the funeral of the man who sold him a genuine Mexican plug (*Roughing It*, I, 171) is recognizable in Barrow's conversation. When Barrow says that even a dead man would "get up and go" for an earldom, his comments not only restate the revitalization motif from the Sellers plot but also prepare for the following anticlimax, which suggests that Barrow is like the corpse. The same technique appears as part of Huck Finn's speech. Thus, although Sellers makes statements that echo some of Twain's statements, it is Barrow who inherits his manner. The comic resources that established the psychology of Hank Morgan and Huck Finn as central in their novels are split in this latter work. The sense of a single perception is absent, and with its loss may go some of the force that Twain achieved by employing a first-person narrator like his own persona for the heroes of his novels.

Other comic effects support the main theme of the novel but cannot offset the dispersion of the comic viewpoint into Sellers' extravagant plans and Barrow's irony. Grimm has commented that the combination of an English lord and a western outlaw, as happens in Sellers' and Hawkins' conceptions of Howard Tracy as One-armed Pete, works much the same social juxtaposition suggested in *A Connecticut Yankee*. In one work knights are savages, in the other earls are outlaws. The boardinghouse milieu is also pervaded by parallel suggestions about the mind of the common workman. Just as the nobility in corrupt feudal Europe had their portraits painted, so democratic man pursues aristocracy by having his portrait painted with the symbols of his trade.[9] Nevertheless, this last, seemingly disparate, element allows Tracy to confirm his own identity by painting in the items: "there was something about work—even such grotesque and humble work as this—which most pleasantly satisfied a something in his nature which had never been satisfied before, and also gave him a strange new dignity in his own private view of himself" (153–54).

Tracy's search for himself is central to the contrived romance of the subplot. The romance between Sally Sellers and the young earl borders on the "slop, silly slop" burlesqued by Howells. Sally is an independent girl by temperament, but her only dramatic action occurs in relation to Howard. She does get an opportunity to validate his own search, however, when Howard makes his declaration for equality in place of the privileges and unfair advantages of nobility. Once again, the statement of admiration recalls the concept of a "man": "An earl's son do that! Why, he were a man! A man to love! —oh, more, a man to worship!" (223). Ridiculously, Sally is privately outspoken about her love for Howard because he is weak, not because she believes his pretensions. For the most part, she resists his claims and weeps.

The plot and subplot of the novel come together through the multiple realization of humanity. The English aristocrat and the American pretender are brought together by the romance and like each other due to their oppositeness. The lovers are united, as permitted by the English earl's estimate of Sally's worth—and apparent skepticism about the worth of his own son. Finally, Sellers himself validates the uniting in sentimental love through his last letter. Disappearing even further than Hank Morgan it seems, Sellers leaves to create sunspots on the sun, and this heroic insanity will be his way of throwing a kiss across the universe (249). Thus, the plot problems are resolved, traditional comic issues are stated, and the demands of sentimental readers are met. Yet, in terms of any visionary state-

---

9 Grimm, "*The American Claimant*: Reclamation of a Farce," 99–100.

ment, little of moment occurs. Tracy is cowlike and Sellers lunatic to the end, and the English earl retains his fatherly presence as a mildly persuasive antidemocrat.

Ultimately, the plot is only half sentimental romance and half burlesque Colonel Sellers. In fact, Sally's choice of Howard is undemocratic and demonstrates that the aristocracy really is superior to the commonality. Tracy's growth toward the vulgar wisdom of the boardinghouse is intended to democratize him, bringing him into conformity with the special urban folk wisdom of the comedians, but this remains only partly satisfying. At the very least, the novel proves that joint authorship was not the source of plot weakness in *The Gilded Age*. Rather, the growth of romance fits awkwardly with the experience of the low thief of the Jim Griggins, Huck Finn type. The strongest point in Twain's novels is not their plotting but rather their psychological unity—their representation of a philosophic viewpoint. The greatest loss in this novel is that continuity. The flexibility of narrative voice has not infused the plot structure as in Twain's more successful works.

II
PUDD'NHEAD WILSON

Pudd'nhead Wilson shows traces of literary comedy and these traces continue to influence Twain's presentation of society and of his main characters. The increasing sarcasm of his expression, however, makes the overall work somewhat different from the other novels. In part, this is due to the isolation of the main figure, David Wilson, from the narrator's voice and frequently from the chief events in the plot. The comic preface, as used in *The Gilded Age, Huckleberry Finn,* and *The American Claimant*, indicates the comic intent of the novel, thus freeing Twain at once from the formal restraints of literary realism. As with *A Connecticut Yankee*, an obvious joke at the opening of the book, the "shoot my half" story, reinforces the appearance of comedy while suggesting a Barnumized world through its origin. Ironic diction, however, is restricted to a few pointed occasions, and the social milieu is outlined briefly rather than caricatured. Wilson shows some of Twain's experience, appropriate to the pose of literary comedian as novelist that Twain takes in the preface, but he has a more overtly pessimistic social vision than the voice in the preface.

Henry Nash Smith has pointed out how Pudd'nhead Wilson reasserts a grim social reality while Roxy represents a vernacular figure who wishes to hide the truth, thus dividing the traits united in such a figure as Hank Morgan. In fact, much of the direct involvement of the naif in the social caricature that characterizes Twain in *The Innocents Abroad*, or Huck, Miles Hendon, and Hank Morgan is lacking in *Pudd'nhead Wilson*. Smith rightly finds the social consciousness of the novel grim rather than comic. There is little room left for the idealism of Twain's earlier novels, for even though the novel is cast in the form of local-color fiction, Wilson's inability to free himself from circumstances places the novel close to the determinism of the naturalists. The assertive freedom of literary comedy, indicated by the tone of the preface, does not appear in the hero, although it influences portraits of characters such as Roxy. The exchanged children, Tom Driscoll and Chambers, share Wilson's powerlessness, although his is of action and theirs is of psychology. Wilson is necessarily a major component in the reality of the town, but is only its direct antagonist in the opening and closing sequences of the novel, and in the final court scene he really takes on the function of entertaining it. Twain's irony infuses the novel, but no clear polarity is established between the naïve idealism of the hero and the social corruption he observes, the chief polarity in other novels. With Wilson "merely a lever," to move the plot, there is less chance in the novel to relate humor to an optimistic conclusion of the plot.[10]

David Wilson, on arriving at Dawson's Landing, undergoes an experience that identifies his character at the same time that it stamps him with the nickname "Pudd'nhead." Hearing a dog barking, Wilson comments that if he owned half the dog he would kill his half. Local characters, taking Wilson's joke as an actual proposal, then gave him his new name, which followed him for twenty years (5–7).[11] P. T. Barnum tells a story in his *Life* which closely parallels this one,

---

10 Smith, *Mark Twain: The Development of a Writer*, 181–82, cites Twain's remark on Wilson from a letter in 1894 treating a critic's praise of the character.

11 Page references to *Pudd'nhead Wilson* are to Volume XIV, "Author's National Edition" (New York: Harper & Brothers, 1899).

describing how the showman Hack Bailey was being cheated of the proceeds for exhibiting an elephant in which he owned a half interest. Receiving no satisfaction from his partner, Bailey went to the elephant's barn with a rifle and announced, "You have refused to buy or sell—now you may do what you please with your half of that elephant, but I am fully determined to *shoot my half!*"[12] Barnum relished the success of Bailey's threat, and Pudd'nhead Wilson, as he came to be known, must have misjudged the ability of his audience to appreciate a *Yankee* story in the Sam Slick tradition. Nevertheless, Wilson is marked as a broadly knowledgeable man with some understanding and appreciation of the showman mentality; this creates a subtle bond between him and the Capello twins, who gained their knowledge of humanity, in part, while being exhibited in a traveling museum for two years (45). The half-dog joke also establishes a repeated motif, for Tom calls himself a dog (79) when he learns that he is in reality a slave rather than the master; Roxy later says she would not sell a dog down the river (151); Tom is described as a dog (161); and Twain finally refers to childless couples adopting dogs in a metaphor explaining the Driscolls' acceptance of Tom (165). In the original conception of the novel, as well, the town was supposed to love everything divided by halves, further expanding the irony of the joke.[13] In this context the joke conveys the misery implicit in disregarding the real, living object, a theme which Kenneth Lynn has noted in Jim's attack on Solomon in *Huckleberry Finn*.[14]

Hank Morgan's Bridgeport-Camelot mistake was integral to his own mentality. From Hank's original misconception Twain developed the ensuing intrusion of the nineteenth century into Arthurian England. David Wilson's joke is, on the other hand, a mechanism that separates him from Dawson's Landing in the 1850s. Southern

---

12 [Barnum], *Life*, 114–15. Another variant of the joke appears in "Yankee Humor," *Quarterly Review*, CXXII (January and April, 1867), 221, in which a minister asks blessings on "his half" of a negro slave. Wilson's joke is closer to Barnum's, however. Kenneth Lynn, in *Mark Twain and Southwestern Humor*, 262, indicates that Perry Miller has also found the joke in Porter's *Spirit of the Times*, from which it was copied into the *Knickerbocker Magazine*.

13 The holograph of "Those Extraordinary Twins" in the Berg Collection, New York Public Library, makes this clear on page 3, although the "shoot my half" story does not appear until pages 118–24 at the end of the manuscript. Twain's description of the Dawson's Landing Fire Company retains this motif in the novel.

14 Lynn, *Mark Twain and Southwestern Humor*, 264.

critics have disputed Twain's application of the joke in this fashion since locals should have liked it. The possible Yankee identification of the story, however, makes Twain's application of the story to disrupt Wilson's relations with the townspeople understandable. Unfortunately, the joke separates Wilson from the action and thus plays a part in disrupting the normal travel pattern that distinguishes Twain's first-person narratives.[15]

David Wilson himself is somewhat ambiguous as a humorous figure. In his notebook in 1879 Twain had commented that speech in the third person was detestable and Josh Billings', or Robert Burdette's, or the Danbury News Man's remarks could not be imagined except in the first person.[16] Even Colonel Sellers, in *The American Claimant*, has a considerable voice in elaborating his own burlesque conceptions. Wilson, however, is not dominant in the plot and is generally a serious speaker in his interchanges with other characters. "Pudd'nhead Wilson's Calendar," a series of mottoes at the head of each chapter, is Wilson's comic contribution in his own voice. The calendar was singled out by reviewers as one of the funniest parts of the book.[17] Presumably, mottoes are directly related to the text by the Capello twins' flattering request for the manuscript of Wilson's calendar (83). Specific mottoes reflect the post–Civil War literary comedians and serve the function, as does Twain's humor elsewhere, of making the novel carry overtones that are contemporaneous with the experience of Twain's readers. For example, one motto describes Fijians as using plumbers rather than turkeys on Thanksgiving Day (150), a conception more appropriate to a time of indoor plumbing and international imperialism than to the small southern town of the 1840s. Another plumber joke had appeared in *The Prince and the*

---

15 As early as 1894, Martha McCulloch Williams, "In Re 'Pudd'nhead Wilson,'" *Fetter's Southern Magazine*, IV (February, 1894), 99–102, complained that the story had been common in the South for seventy-five years and that the book was misleading and malicious in its treatment of the region. A variant of the story does appear in Longstreet's *Georgia Scenes* (1835). J. B. Hubbell, *The South in American Literature*, 835, has also commented that the joke should have been accepted by Wilson's audience.

16 Notebook Fourteen, p. 10, Mark Twain Papers, University of California, Berkeley.

17 *The Idler*, VI (August, 1894), 223, even begged for a complete edition of the "unrivalled almanac." Twain had proposed in October, 1870, a "Mark Twain's Annual—1871," composed of *Galaxy* contributions, as a Christmas volume that he thought would outpay Josh Billings' *Allminax* (*Letters to His Publishers*, 40), so an awareness of Billings' success in this format had been with him for some time.

Pauper with the same function and was more readily identified in the medieval context by Twain's reviewers. Similarly, a motto concerning Michelangelo in Rome, while it carries out the Italian motif of the burlesque preface, is more reminiscent of Twain the traveler in *The Innocents Abroad* than of Pudd'nhead Wilson's possible range of experiences. Twain, the literary comedian, was using this avenue into Wilson's mind as a means of creating a persona for him that approximated the personae at the center of his other major novels, and he is at least partly successful.

Jesse Bier calls Wilson's sayings "antiproverbialisms."[18] He finds them most pessimistic in entries such as the Columbus reference by Wilson for October 12, "It was wonderful to find America, but it would have been more wonderful to miss it" (201), which implies that "the chance at a right New World was doomed, for America should have been missed." Artemus Ward made much the same comment in the 1860s, remarking that Chris "put his foot in it" when he sailed for America.[19] Twain's supposedly *fin de siècle* despair in the calendar had more literary precedent in the irony of literary comedy than appears when the text is studied in isolation.

When Wilson's antiproverbialisms are used in the narrative they further divide Wilson from the residents of Dawson's Landing. The Capellos flattered the author by admiring his wit; but when Judge Driscoll showed Wilson's proverbs to the locals, they merely served to further discredit him (39–40), a process begun by the "shoot my half" story. The ironic wit of the literary comedians, and presumably the pessimistic response to social experience that is connected to it, are shown as out of keeping with a society that values its traditional concepts of honor and humanity. Even though Wilson is separated by his attitudes, there is some infusion of his proverbial *style* into the narrative. For example, Tom's sleep of the unjust thief is described in a phrase as "serener than any other kind" (141). However, the influence of the formula does not really pervade the novel and its

---

18 Bier, *The Rise and Fall of American Humor*, 148. Josh Billings' *Allminax* provides a number of analogs to Wilson's mottoes, frequently dealing with the same subjects in virtually the same words. M. Quod's *Brother Gardner's Lime Kiln Club* contains some proverbs which are also similar, and Bier sees this train of humor shared among the literary comedians.
19 Ward, *Works*, 133.

philosophy as it would if Wilson had been the narrator. His position is even more ambiguous due to this thematic and dramatic separation from the world around him.

Twain's viewpoints do appear in the novel's texture outside of the central figure, adding predictable social attitudes to the plot. Some of Twain's irony is directed at democratic institutions. Ward's burlesques of political rhetoric attacked hypocrisy; Pap in *Huckleberry Finn* had been partially affected by this mode in his "call this a govment" speech. Twain's verbal irony in *Pudd'nhead Wilson*, in the omniscient voice, however, throws a dubious light on the democratic process that is not moderated by burlesque overtones. Of Wilson's new name, "Pudd'nhead," Twain notes laconically, "Mr. Wilson stood elected" (7). Although this might appear no more than a conventional phrase, the extension of such diction to the problem of miscegenation is ironic. As Twain describes Roxy's condition: "To all intents and purposes Roxy was as white as anybody, but the one-sixteenth of her which was black outvoted the other fifteen parts and made her a negro. She was a slave, and salable as such. Her child was thirty-one parts white, and he, too, was a slave, and by a fiction of law and custom a negro" (12). The effect of this diction, which includes democracy in the problem of slavery, is heightened by its mathematical depersonalization. Twain's effect here may be compared with the treatment of miscegenation in Don Marquis' "The Mulatto," which is without any infusion of the diction of literary comedy: "Carter was not exactly a negro, but he was a 'nigger.' Seven drops of his blood out of every eight were caucasian. The eighth being African, classified him. The white part of him despised and pitied the black part. The black part hated the white part. Consequently, wherever Carter went he carried his own hell along inside of him."[20] The difference between the approach of the literary comedian and the unalleviated sterner realism of the revolt-from-the-village style lies in the comic insertion of social criticism. In the later story, the plot is resolved when Carter is murdered in a race riot as he tries to assert his equality with his white half-brother. For Twain, the ending of

20 *Harper's Monthly*, CXXXII (April, 1916), 726. The story is reprinted in Marquis' *Carter and Other People* (New York: D. Appleton & Co., 1921), 3–17.

the plot is almost as unpleasant, as Chambers is forced to lose the small comfort of his identity and Tom is sold as a slave. A milder-seeming protest through diction is available to the literary comedian. The closeness of Twain's passage to Marquis' bitter realism indicates the pessimism he felt, yet the comic voice cloaks his dissent from the discrimination that he feels to be inappropriate to an egalitarian society.

The references to business which characterized the Connecticut Yankee and Ward, the old showman, seem, like the democratic rhetoric, to become more bitterly ironic than in earlier novels when they appear in the authorial voice of an invisible narrator. Yet, they, too, continue to manifest the consciousness of the comedian rather than the sterner realist. The Yankee transmuted Arthurian England into a nineteenth-century business corporation by employing the terminology and the underlying concepts associated with his industrial and economic background. In *Pudd'nhead Wilson* the terms of business do not have such an organic relation to the hero's personality or to his social vision. What had appeared as enthusiastic rhetoric characterizing a naïve psychology becomes a matter of ironic tone: "Mrs. York Driscoll enjoyed two years of bliss with that prize, Tom —bliss that was troubled a little at times, it is true, but bliss nevertheless; then she died, and her husband and his childless sister, Mrs. Pratt, continued the bliss business at the old stand" (37). The comic language of a humorous showman has become in this passage a colloquial medium for suggesting the author's ironic view of his characters. The point of the criticism has become personal rather than social or moral and, in comparison to Twain's earlier writing, highly fictional but also relatively narrow in its application. Conditions of social and religious hypocrisy that earlier heroes dissented from are internalized in the personalities of Twain's secondary characters. Thus, the work shows Twain's comic techniques clearly but uses them to portray a gloomier (less externalized) view of human nature than had been represented in the first-person narratives.

More generally, the novel indicates a breaking down of responsibility that coincides with the altered use of diction. In *The Prince and the Pauper*, Miles Hendon had sworn to educate the young prince, a sentiment in keeping with Twain's own attitude toward professional development. Judge Driscoll reveals about his relation to Tom, "I have indulged him to his hurt, instead of training him up severely, and making a man of him" (118). For his part, Tom is described as complaining that his uncle thought paying Tom's two-hundred-dollar gambling debt expensive when it had cost Tom the whole of his uncle's fortune (107)—a revision of Ward's description of a debtor who, learning that his creditor would throw off half the debt, threw off the other half so as not to be outdone in liberality.[21] Tom's selfishness, the central feature of his "moral landscape," is not as good humored as the earlier joke, however, and the comic borrowing serves to establish the judge's failure to train Tom as a human being. Roxy shares in the breakdown of character, although her actions are largely excused through the melodramatized fear of being sold down the river. The comic sequence in which she readies herself for the tomb (19–20) is grotesque without being burlesque—slavery has distorted her conception of herself without granting her the naïve idealism of earlier characters. Her alignment of herself with the "Smith-Pocahontases" (124–26), carrying out the aristocratic theme established at the end of Twain's preface to the novel, further establishes her as a supporter of the feudal tradition which enslaves her.[22] In *Pudd'nhead Wilson* the antagonism between comic innocence and evil is by no means as clear as Twain elsewhere dramatizes it to be.

Earlier humorous contrivances by Twain are taken into *Pudd'nhead Wilson* with the purpose of providing "local color" in the Mississippi River milieu, again indicating the literary quality of Twain's regionalism. The blocking of the procession which forms to meet the Capello twins by a friendly and garrulous soul (48) is reiterated from "The Reception at the President's" from Twain's *Galaxy* "Memoranda."[23] The story of the humane negro prowler stealing a hen by putting a warm board under its feet appeared in "To Raise Poultry,"

---

[21] Ward, *Works*, 200–360. The joke in the Mormon's lecture uses the figure 200, as well.
[22] I have not discussed Roxy's dialect which shows some traces of cacography in formulations like "intrust" for "interest" and "throo en throo," because it appears that Twain's editors are partly responsible for the forms in which these renderings finally appeared.
[23] McElderry (ed.), *Contributions to "The Galaxy,"* 77–79.

in *Sketches, New and Old*.[24] In the original item it was part of the reversed ethics of the naïvely self-revealing thief; in the novel it becomes a justifiable response to slavery, the greater social theft, and thus a more serious assertion about the situation of the individual. Similarly, Judge Driscoll indicts the Capellos as "back-alley barbers disguised as nobilities" (148), recalling Twain's complaint about marriages in Washington, D.C., in *The Gilded Age*. Earlier the reference characterized the milieu, in the later novel the comment is factually untrue and is used maliciously to prevent the Capellos from gaining elective office; it takes an unpleasant place in the plot action rather than figuring as a generalized burlesque of a society. In each case, the social relevance of the joke as literary comedy is altered by its management as plot material. The nascent meanings inherited from the tradition are realigned so that the humor is more bitter in its revelation of the roots of meanness in individual characters. Twain's view of the world through humor has changed. Twain's view of slavery is still not as harsh-seeming as Don Marquis' or Charles Heber Clark's in *Captain Bluitt*; but *Pudd'nhead Wilson* is more pessimistic than are Twain's earlier novels, and part of the reason lies in the management of his humor.

Another way of phrasing the problem with *Pudd'nhead Wilson* as a work of literary comedy might be to identify it as a book about mental sickness and emotional bitterness. To the very end, Wilson holds this sense of imposition and intrusion into his own life by the community. His "compulsory" leisure is uppermost in his mind. Roxy, identifying her master's lack of love for Negroes (which is brutal enough in its own right), becomes the "dupe of her own deceptions" and finally acts out of a "crazed" parental instinct. Twain's terms, which blend into his prose style, make clear that this is a book about emotional malaise. Certainly this is part of the potency of the work despite its typically Twainian shambling plot. Giddy burlesque from *The Gilded Age* gives way to more serious ironies representing race and class conflicts. The literary comedians' social focus remains intact even though their sense of humor now disappears. Further-

---

24 Twain, *Sketches, New and Old*, 81.

more, the characteristic picaro figure has become helpless and largely shorn of his picaro traits and abilities. Huck Finn, Hank Morgan, and Mark Twain expressed most of their positive social sentiments in the comments and jokes woven through the picaresque narrative; Wilson has no such recourse.

The novel is less successful as a novel, however, because Pudd'nhead Wilson's interests are not in fact central to most of the action. Isolated and proverbial, Wilson does not have the melodramatic insight of the traveling heroes, and he sees no Yokels. Roxy's switching of the babies, Tom's maturation as a spoiled young man, the selling of Roxy down the river and her escape, and the Capello twins' visit are all free from Wilson's presence in any meaningful way as a major protagonist. He does add to the tension—and the final plot outcome—by his collection of fingerprints, and maintains a position as a local seer in Roxy's superstitious view, but this hardly integrates him into the bulk of the events in the novel. Tom manipulates the Driscolls by himself, and Chambers grows up offstage; the switching of the babies in their cribs remains an unknown until Roxy resurrects it. The nexus of character relations develops without the central figure's control. This powerlessness, described as stretching over twenty years, makes Wilson a far less positive figure than Miles Hendon, Huck, or Hank Morgan in their human relationships. Even in the denouemont there is a notable detachment from results, only temporarily masked by the emergence of Wilson in a new guise.

Wilson is transformed into a platform performer at novel's end, and his transformation throws more light on his status as Twain's hero. Like P. T. Barnum and Mark Twain the lecturer, Wilson is part showman, and, as with Hank Morgan, Twain's own platform manner is supposed to dramatize his power as a professional person. Although Wilson does not advance the progressive social theories of the Yankee, and is in fact regressive in his approval of the dueling code of the F.F.V. aristocracy, his courtroom conduct is like the Yankee's intellectual mastery over medieval monks. Twain's ideas concerning the value of a perfectly measured pause, its effect on the audience, and even his tendency to describe his technique theoretically appear in his description of Wilson preparing to expose Tom Driscoll:

Wilson stopped and stood silent. Inattention dies a quick and sure death when a speaker does that. The stillness gives warning that something is coming.... He waited yet one, two, three, moments, to let his pause complete and perfect its spell upon the house; then, when through the profound hush he could hear the ticking of the clock on the wall, he put out his hand.

. . . .

Stunned, distraught, unconcious of its own movement, the house half rose, as if expecting to see the murderer appear at the door, and a breeze of muttered ejaculations swept the place. (193-94)

Twain is describing a reaction in the audience that is essentially that of the crowd of Vassar College girls to his ghost story "The Golden Arm," the closing remark of which is preceded by a pause requiring the same accurate measurement that Wilson employs here with the ease of a practiced raconteur.[25] Wilson finally masters the yokels who labeled him "Pudd'nhead" through this dramatic timing. To insure that the reader understands the situation, Pudd'nhead even refers to his twenty years of compulsory leisure, recalling the initial experience (194). Twain's own ability is transferred to the dramatic figure, and it becomes his means of dominance over the confused society surrounding him, a society he has taken a large part in sustaining. Wilson is thus the humorist, related to Twain's other naïve heroes, but largely shorn of the power of his humor and the mobile perspective through which the traveler defied opposing social institutions and customs. The plot denies him; as Twain makes clear, social experience is not easily outdone. Like the Italian nobility, Virginians are unchanging. Chambers is free but with a slave's mind—he *cannot* be freed, in other words; Tom is enslaved—retribution certainly, but a poor showing after the antislavery tirades of Yokel and Hank Morgan. Passing time has mousetrapped Pudd'nhead's "victory" and made it into a grotesque reversal confusing the human condition rather than asserting it positively. The ending looks toward a second watershed in American experience as important, perhaps, as the changes occurring at the time of the American Civil War.

Pudd'nhead Wilson represents a departure from Twain's previous

[25] Bernard DeVoto (ed.), *Mark Twain in Eruption* (New York: Harper & Brothers, 1940), 225-27, dated October 10, 1907.

literary comedy—and perhaps even an abandonment of literary comedy as a form. The central figure is not as dominant as Twain's other heroes, advancing the tendency toward a disintegration of the naïve humorous viewpoint which began with *The American Claimant*. Twain's humor focuses around lesser figures like Roxy and the Driscolls without serving to characterize the psychology of the main figure. Hank Morgan and Huck Finn as comedian-narrators represented an alternative innocence to the corruption which was seen, frequently in burlesque, around them. Pudd'nhead Wilson is so divorced from the events of the plot that he does not fully provide the same alternative, although further analysis would show that he shares many traits with Huck and Hank. His "Calendar" identifies him as sharing the mentality of the literary comedian, the persona that underlies the American picaresque novel, which Twain contrives out of his own background and the literary tradition. Still, he remains isolated and powerless in his relation to his world, and his comic innocence is lost.

Perhaps this alteration indicates the approach of the modernist existential vision in American experience. The existential predicament, most typically seen in Theodore Dreiser's novels, calls for a form different from literary comedy as it wrestles with the ambiguities of individual experience. The conflict between the old ethics of individualism and the institutional complexity of the urban and industrial age is left behind.

ELEVEN

Conclusion

IN 1906, Mr. Dooley coolly lectured Mr. Hennessy, in "Royal Doings," about the charge that the eloping Princess Sophia was a crazy old woman: "Whin an ol' crazy-headed lunytic iv a woman skips out 'tis a crime; whin an ol' crazy-headed lunytic iv a duchess done it, it's a scandal; but whin an ol' crazy headed lunytic iv a princess does it, it's a romance."[1] The Connecticut Yankee offered up the same joke in a comparably democratic context. Artemus Ward and P. T. Barnum had treated royalty with an equivalent egalitarian condescension. And through this chain of humor the tradition of literary comedy can be roughly dated as flourishing between 1840 and 1910—essentially the dates of Mark Twain's originator, Samuel L. Clemens. These same dates may be taken as the outer limits of the era when the populist consciousness was most directly opposed to the growing corporate and business and governmental organization of the industrial age. The antislavery movement was a purer expression of the conflict, based on the earlier respect for the humanist premises of the Constitution. But the Civil War, historically, like the southwestern humorous tradition in literature, ought not to obscure the broader historical and ethical trends operating on the American consciousness.

Encountering a pirated edition of his *Library of Humor* in 1906,

---

1 [Finley Peter Dunne], *Dissertations by Mr. Dooley* (New York: Harper & Brothers, 1906), 15.

Twain commented that most of the humorists in the "mortuary" volume appealed by chance or through an odd trick of spelling. Yet, his position is close to Artemus Ward's, who believed that humorists should help the truth along without encumbering it with themselves:[2]

> The very things it (humor) preaches about, and which are novelties when it preaches about them, can cease to be novelties and become commonplaces in thirty years. Then that sermon can thenceforth interest no one.
> I have always preached. That is the reason I have lasted thirty years. If the humor came of its own accord and uninvited, I have allowed it a place in my sermon, but I was not writing the sermon for the sake of the humor. I should have written the sermon just the same, whether any humor applied for admission or not.[3]

Twain's statement of method is notably devoid of references to specific themes; he is stating a serious intention without defining its ethical direction, unless the word *sermon* is taken literally. Elsewhere, Twain broadens his definitions in such a way that this might be the case, when he comments, "The people who object to the backyard of Joseph of Arimathea being spoken of as if it were my own backyard, could not care if I spoke of a Mohammedan's backyard. There are so many curious notions in the world about irreverence."[4] Method and ideology join in this statement. The spiritual and the personal—the elevated and the common—are defined by the humorist in the same language. This is the egalitarian consciousness of Twain, and it is the source of the descriptions of royalty, churches, monuments, and cultural artifacts in Ward, Barnum, and Mr. Dooley as well. It is also the origin of their irony. The democratic "realist" describes his world in his terms, not in the terminology supplied by the conventions of social manners, literature or genealogy.

Twain took his moral truth seriously. In "Was it Heaven, or Hell?" a doctor, another of Twain's humanistic professional types, declares in his exaggerated role as "The Only Christian": "Is such a soul as

---

[2] Seitz, *Artemus Ward*, 238.
[3] *Mark Twain in Eruptions*, 202–203.
[4] Louis Budd, "Mark Twain Talks Mostly About Humor and Humorists," 16, interview from Sydney, Australia, dated September 17, 1895.

that *worth* saving? . . . Reform! Drop this mean and sordid and selfish devotion to the saving of your shabby little souls, and hunt up something to do that's got some dignity to it! *Risk* your souls! risk them in good causes; then if you lose them, why should you care! Reform!"[5] Compare this sentiment with Henry Ward Beecher's comment on morality and work, reprinted in 1887 in *Beecher as a Humorist*: "Abstract principles are like rivers in the wilderness, flowing night and day with power, but turning no mill. They come from the sea, they fall on the mountain, they run down through their channels back to the sea. Round and round they go in their perpetual circuit, doing nothing until civilization stops the water, and pours it over the wheel, and says 'Work for your living.' Then these forces begin to be productive."[6] Active Christianity, an American alternative to Muscular Christianity, replaces passive morality. Twain's personal risk is allowing humor itself into his sermon and vice versa. As his sermonizing became more pronounced, critics complained that his later short stories were wiser and wittier but less funny; the supporting techniques of literary comedy had given way to hurried jokes and cynicism.[7]

Values bear on reputation, and the argument over Twain's status as a literary writer continued throughout his career. Brander Matthews, in "The Penalty of Humor," gave one of the best analyses in 1894: "When we find that the man who wrote those chapters [referring to excerpts from *Tom Sawyer*, *Huckleberry Finn*, and *Pudd'nhead Wilson*], and so many more only a little less marvellous in their vigor and their truth, is set down in most accounts of American literature as a funny man only, when we see him dismissed with a line or two of patronizing comment, as though Mark Twain were only a newspaper humorist, a chance rival of John Phoenix or Artemus Ward or Orpheus C. Kerr as a vendor of comic copy, then we have it brought home to us that humor is a possession for which the possessor must

---

5 *The $30,000 Bequest and Other Stories* (New York: Harper & Brothers, 1917), "Author's National Edition," XXIV, 76.
6 *Beecher as a Humorist*, compiled by Eleanor Kirk (New York: Fords, Howard, and Hulbert, 1887), 109.
7 *The Academy*, LII (December 11, 1897), 519–20.

meet the bill. Mr. Clemens, having more humor than anyone else of his generation, has had to pay a higher price."[8] Such an analysis does much to justify Twain's own restlessness with comparisons between himself and other comedians who were incapable of sustaining their moral vision in an extended literary work. He had taken the nascent social and political positions of the comedians and integrated them in a significant world view. Even though his humor became less well integrated in his later works, his major achievements from the 1860s through the 1890s stand virtually alone in their application of the American egalitarian viewpoint in the comic mode.

On aesthetic grounds, Twain's own insistence on making judgments in moral terms has been condemned as intransigent absolutism interfering with balanced viewpoints toward the world around him.[9] The naïve exaggerations of the innocent traveler and Yokel's indictment of legalized inhumanity are equally parts of this distortion. Twain's humor is dependent on burlesque fabrications of ethical and realistic scenes both in the semifictional travel narratives and in the novels. As Twain put it in an interview, "'Get your facts first, and'—the voice died away to an almost inaudible drone—'then you can distort 'em as much as you please'."[10] The distortions are consistently dictated by the ethical vision.

Of course, there are related problems inherent in Twain's mode of writing. Warner Berthoff demonstrates that Huck Finn's peculiar idiom is almost completely debased in his callousness toward Jim in *Tom Sawyer Abroad* in 1894.[11] The significance of *Huckleberry Finn* does not lie merely in the vernacular voice in which Huck speaks or solely in what he says. Such a discovery clarifies Twain's debt to literary comedy, which deals with social issues more than local types *per se*. Many of the locals who appear in literary comedy, such as "Josiah Allen's wife," consistently treat a similarly socialized travel experience to that recorded in Twain's *Innocents Abroad*. This phenomenon probably derives from the regional differences that spawned the

---

8 Brander Matthews, "The Penalty of Humor," reprinted in *Aspects of Fiction, and Other Ventures in Criticism* (New York: Harper & Brothers, 1896), 56.
9 Bellamy, *Mark Twain as a Literary Artist*, 173.
10 Luke Sharp, "Mark Twain, A Conglomorate Interview Conducted by Luke Sharp," *Idler Magazine*, I (February, 1892), 86.
11 Berthoff, *The Ferment of Realism*, 70–71.

northern comic writer and his southwestern counterpart. The distinction is blurred by Twain's use of southern settings and dialect for many of his narratives.

To understand Twain's denunciation of literary comedians, it is necessary to understand the hardships which he endured as a serious humorist—due to his insistence on writing literary comedy. Throughout his career, critics urged him, as Harte and others had urged Ward, to write seriously, even though the burlesque mode is integrated into his most significant themes. The *Galaxy* criticized Ward in 1867 for jokes like "I am a early riser, but my wife is a Presbyterian,"[12] which became a standard Twain *non sequitur*, appearing in Aunt Polly's speeches in *Huckleberry Finn* and elsewhere in the canon.[13] Yet despite this uncomfortable similarity, Twain was a *Galaxy* columnist in 1871. Up until 1900 equally unpleasant confusions were occurring. One notebook entry by Twain records that Ben Butler expressed enthusiasm for Twain's work—and quoted three jokes from Josh Billings, showing that he did not really know who Twain was.[14] This would be ten years or more after the award of Twain's first Yale degree, yet Twain was still suffering confusion with other comedians.

Twain was recognized by many as important, particularly by the English. English critics saw Twain's unique employment of unconventional modes and his unconventional attitudes and found "abundant material for serious thought as [well as] for merry laughter."[15] Huck's refusal to take stock in dead people and Jim's rationalizations on "borrowing" were quoted to demonstrate the complexity of Twain. Offenses against good taste were seen as mitigated by the manner of narration, with its "prevailing dryness and sense of reality."[16] An aside in the *Saturday Review* in 1887 noted that the view of Ward and Harte as preeminent in their fields was taking "a short view of the author of *Huckleberry Finn*."[17]

---

12 *Galaxy*, III (January 15, 1867), 222.
13 "He turned blue all over and died in the hope of a glorious resurrection" (307). The reference to Joanna Wilks as having a harelip and giving herself to good works is similar.
14 Notebook 32b, 51, Mark Twain Papers, Berkeley.
15 *Congregationalist*, XIV (March, 1885), 251.
16 *The British Quarterly Review*, CXXXI (January, 1885), 465.
17 *Saturday Review*, CXIII (April 2, 1887), 495.

Twain's success is also reflected in the birthday messages which the *Critic* carried in 1885 on the occasion of his fiftieth birthday. Oliver Wendell Holmes, extending Brahmin recognition to a literary comedian once again, returned the favor of Twain's speech at the well-known Whittier dinner in 1877, placing his admiration on public record in a poem teasing Clemens' drinking habits.[18] Joel Chandler Harris added further recognition: "I know that some of the professional critics will not agree with me, but there is not in our fictive literature a more wholesome book than 'Huckleberry Finn.' It is history, it is romance, it is life. Here we behold human character . . . and, in the midst of it all, behold we are taught the lesson of honesty, justice and mercy."[19] He concluded that Twain had "the courage to have a distinctively American flavor to everything he has ever written." In comparison, Nasby had no success in sustained literature, and Kerr's attempt at a novel in 1884 was poor, although it received a scattering of kindly reviews. Opie Read and Max Adeler achieved popular successes but lacked the visionary dimension of Twain's voice and the social dimension of his humor.

Little has been made of Twain's contacts with literary humorists because of the prevailing tendency to see him as a "natural" rather than as a conscious literary man. He sought out or pursued contacts with Artemus Ward, Miles O'Riley, and Corry O'Lanus and Doesticks in the days before *The Innocents Abroad* established his reputation. He corresponded with B. P. Shillaber in the 1870s on publishing matters and other things, queried Nasby on the possibility of a joint lecture tour, and considered working with Thomas Nast on the platform. S. S. Cox, a now-vanished political humorist and anthologist, wrote to him. Among other letters preserved in the Mark Twain Papers at Berkeley are notes from Bill Nye, R. J. Burdette, J. W. Riley, J. W. DeForest, Josh Billings, and others. There is also a long series of letters from P. T. Barnum, the showman himself, who included batches of clippings for Twain and tried to interest Twain in joint publicity ventures. There were dinners with Nasby, Eli Perkins, Donn Piatt, George Ade, and, later, visits from Riley, Bill Nye, and Frank

---

18 "To Mark Twain," *Critic*, VII (November 28, 1885), 253.
19 Letter, *Critic*, VII (November 28, 1885), 253.

Stockton. In February, 1889, he introduced Riley and Nye to a Boston audience as the Chang-Eng Siamese twins of Barnum, joking that Riley had a high moral sense but "no machinery to work it."[20] Entries in his notebooks dealing with the *Library of Humor* include a variety of southwesterners and also Seba Smith, T. C. Haliburton, Joseph Neal and Mortimer Thompson, G. H. Derby and Francis M. Whitcher. Literary comedians listed were C. F. Browne, Newell, Henry Wheeler Shaw, C. H. Smith, Marietta Holley, James M. Bailey, R. J. Burdette, Charles Heber Clark, Samuel W. Small, and others.[21] He also thought of Burton's *Cyclopedia* as a source for forgotten humorists. The contacts were extensive.

Walter Blair has written that Mark Twain was essentially southwestern, and Bernard DeVoto has described him as a natural product of the Mississippi River Valley. It *may* be true that Twain's narrative impulse was southwestern or that Twain's desire to tell stories rather than jokes sprang from a Mississippi or western background. Such an ability to elaborate materials seems to be a characteristic of his writing, at any rate, from an early time. His elaborate narratives and highly individualized characters unquestionably build his positive statements up to the level of vision. To deny the significance of the tradition of literary comedy in the development of the Twain canon, however, is to deny most of the ethical and social basis of his philosophy. It is also to deny the relevance of much of his humor to the creation of his vision; yet, Mark Twain's jokes are crucial in posing his world view. Jennette Tandy has stated boldly that Ward "conferred on Mark Twain the ignorant traveler in Mormondom, as expanded in *Innocents Abroad*,"[22] but this is not needed to establish Ward's importance to Twain's career. Ward did confer on Twain a form of ethical statement through humor. Twain's declaration in 1900, in "Literature," that "You cannot have a theory without principles. Principles is another name for prejudices. I have no prejudices in politics, religion, literature, or anything else,"[23] paid homage to the old showman at Oberlin who originated the premise with an al-

20 Fatout, *Mark Twain on the Lecture Circuit*, 234.
21 Notebook 15, pp. 3–5, Mark Twain Papers, Berkeley.
22 Tandy, *Crackerbox Philosophers*, 146.
23 "Literature" (May 4, 1900), in *Mark Twain's Speeches*, 207.

most identical statement. Twain created his persona out of the materials of the tradition and brought the tradition to maturity, even while he surpassed it.

Twain's early humor, along with Ward's, shows the embryonic development of a major social viewpoint. Twain developed fully. Huck Finn, Hank Morgan, Miles Hendon, Mark Twain, and to some extent David Wilson and Jack Halliday of "Hadleyburg" all hold the same set of characteristics, comprised in the flexibility of language that marks the debt to and growth beyond the vulgar vision of the old showman. Politics and political rhetoric—the corporate versus the humane and individualized—provide the antagonistic milieu against which the hero asserts his naïve faith in the standing of individuals. *Huckleberry Finn* is most successful as a novel because it roots these concerns most completely in characterization and in the psychology of the narrator, and in the national ethos of antislavery. Yet other works show the same process. The synthesis is so unique that the absence of belletristic plot symmetry pales beside it, as it did for the millions who recognized Twain as the moral spokesman of their generation. And it partly explains the failure of some of his contemporaries in distinguishing him from other comic writers of his era.

There are also some problematic aspects of Twain's vision. The central figure—the comic narrator—is largely a dissenter. This is the same figure who is the platform speaker of the 1860s and 1870s, generally a posed naif, but with the addition of dramatic power. The stance of the dissenter from accepted social and political beliefs is appropriate to an egalitarian democracy but is nonetheless *outside* the norm. In fiction, this means only that a travel narrative format is best suited to the expression of comic commentary. Dramatically, it calls for the hero to play antagonist to a milieu that comprises popular or widespread practices. Nasby and Kerr, as would have Ward had he tried, found this development of literary comedy impossible, and later humorists like Marietta Holley (who never traveled at all) either stayed almost solely in the travel narrative format or, like Opie Read, downplayed humor in favor of conventional sentimentalized plotting and diction. Twain used his comedy to create a value-loaded environment and to suggest the contemporaneousness of his themes to his readers. The implications of the humor are vital to his cultural description. Yet his heroes remained rootless, awkward precursors of modern alienated heroes.

Twain's later pessimism may also relate to the comic tradition. Ward's old question of "how he stands as a man" becomes increasingly haunting as the later nineteenth century advances into the modern industrial age. Even though conventional dating of literary comedy ascribes it to the 1860s, its roots lie clearly in the economic changes taking place in the 1830s and 1840s in the Northeast; so, too, the overt recognition of twentieth-century industrial depersonalization in Dreiser's *The Financier* and the novels of Dos Passos and Farrell foreshadow modern social changes to a comparable extent. The increasing pessimism of Twain's works, particularly the later ones identified by John Tuckey in volumes of the Mark Twain Papers, may owe something to this enlargement of American culture beyond the personal scale. The standing of an individual is dubious as a touchstone of moral values when the individual is lost in a limitless world in which far larger powers outmatch his own personal force.

The aspirations expressed in Twain's humor are equally problematical. Examining Huck Finn's ethics, a reader might question the application of those ethics to the present world. The widespread and rather uncritical teaching of *Huckleberry Finn* indicates that it is a model, but it is flatly indifferent to the conformities that are most valued in institutions of higher learning and higher business, as well as government. Huck balances viewpoints and emerges with unforseen compromises. He rejects, as did Twain in *The Innocents Abroad*, the letter of the law in favor of its spirit. These are heretical principles when applied to the conventionalities that reap lip service from humanists. Lying, cheating, and stealing are Huck's method for asserting his standing as a man. His nonconformity is consistent with the anticorporate vision of the humorists as expressed in Barnum's humbug and the old showman and Jim Griggins, but it hardly equates with the established view of society. The abolitionists were involved in similar activities prior to the Civil War, of course. In

Hank Morgan's story, the logical outcome of such opposition is violent warfare, aptly labeled by Chadwick Hansen as "international gangsterism." Twain's novels seem to offer little cause for a more favorable relationship between the hero and his milieu. In the modern era, such dissent is met with resistance as massive as that which Twain dramatizes. Twain *also* had the advantage of externalizing evil in villains and melodramatic events, simplifying moral choices through burlesque.

Literary comedy, in relation to Twain's canon, offers two insights. First, a minor literary tradition appears to have become a major visionary phenomenon through a combination of literary and historical events that are generally ignored in interpreting Twain's work. The Americanness of Twain's writing is in great part expressed by materials from this tradition—the vulgar pose, ironic showmanship, pragmatic valuing of the individual over the bureaucracy. Second, recognizing the roots of Twain's beliefs, new ethical implications seem to appear in his canon. His viewpoint is further outside the conventionally accepted than is sometimes realized. The vision of corporate society as essentially corrupt is hidden in comedy and is difficult to bring out. Consequently, *Huckleberry Finn* and books like it are described as attacks on the antebellum South or on human nature too broad to be related to the social experience of the twentieth century in any personal way. Elsewhere the book is described as a new expression of American language; this may be an important aspect of the work, but it is subservient to content finally. Huck Finn would be expelled, jailed, or otherwise punished were he to appear in the world of his present-day readers. The literary comedians paid such prices. Ward was condemned in the North for giving a benefit for Confederate widows and orphans, and Twain in the 1890s expiated his guilt by traveling the world to pay back his business debts. Yearning for genteel acceptance, they were willing to take risks in carrying out the values they saw as paramount.

The ultimate difficulty was for Twain to relate the ethics of half a century to a modern world in which their place was at best ambiguous. Nineteenth-century writers do not seem to have resolved this problem any more successfully than pre–Civil War industrialism

CONCLUSION 199

was managed by Hawthorne, and Twain left many manuscripts unpublished or unfinished among his later undertakings. Artemus Ward said, "I'm in favor of the Union as it wasn't." This expression of unrealistic idealism is representative of the strength of the comedians in looking beyond actuality, but it can only be stretched so far. Their sense of the power of an egalitarian man was probably no more fully realized in any one era in American history than in any other; it is a vision of what *can* be hoped for. This was also Mark Twain's reality, for Mark Twain is a persona—a fictional intelligence whose psychology is beyond the norm. He is an embodied tradition and expresses through his novels an amalgam of effects, personality, vision, and philosophy: Mark Twain as a literary comedian. His last great statement of this theme, reversing reality and fantasy, is an appropriate final example:

During just one hour in the twenty-four—not more—I pause and reflect in the stillness of the night with the echoes of your English welcome still lingering in my ears, and then I am humble. Then I am properly meek, and for that little while I am only the MARY ANN, fourteen hours out, cargoed with vegetables and tinware; but during all the twenty-three hours my vain self-complacency rides high on the white crest of your approval, and then I am a stately Indiaman, ploughing the great seas under a cloud of canvas and laden with the kindest words that have ever been vouchsafed to any wandering alien in this world, I think; then my twenty-six fortunate days on this old mother soil seem to be multiplied by six, and *I* am the BEGUM of Bengal, one hundred and forty-two days out from Canton, homeward bound!²⁴

The literary comedian is once again the small-time outsider, freighted with a keen sense of his own social position. Translated into an American commercial image, he is of heroic proportions, an egalitarian apotheosis of the humanism of the common man and his psychology. Embedded in a richly resonant nautical image which is consistent with Twain's own unique personal history, the sentiment is localized, and thus freed from the limitless existential darkness which may be sensed lurking just beyond.

---

24 "The Last Lotus Club Speech" (January 11, 1908), *Speeches*, 374.

Bibliography

WORKS BY MARK TWAIN

The Autobiography of Mark Twain. Ed. Charles Neider. New York: Washington Square Press, 1961.
"Barnum's First Speech in Congress." New York *Evening Express*, March 5, 1867, p. 1.
"Chapters from My Autobiography," *North American Review*, CLXXXVI (July 5, 1907), 465–74.
Clemens of the "Call," Mark Twain in San Francisco. Ed. Edgar M. Branch. Berkeley and Los Angeles: University of California Press, 1969.
Contributions to "The Galaxy," 1868–1871 by Mark Twain. Ed. Bruce R. McElderry, Jr. Gainesville, Ga.: Scholar's Facsimiles & Reprints, 1961.
"Does the Race of Man Love a Lord?" *North American Review*, CLXXIV (April, 1902), 433–44.
"Doings in Nevada." *Territorial Enterprise.* January 4, 1864, in Scrapbook One, p. 71, Mark Twain Papers, University of California, Berkeley.
Europe and Elsewhere, with An Appreciation by Brander Matthews and Introduction by Albert Bigelow Paine. New York: Harper & Brothers, 1923.
"The Facts Concerning the Recent Important Resignation." New York *Tribune*, February 13, 1868, p. 2.
"Female Suffrage/The Iniquitous Crusade . . . ." St. Louis *Missouri Democrat*, March 15, 1867, p. 4.
"Female Suffrage/Petticoat Government." New York *Sunday Mercury*, April 7, 1867, p. 3.
"Female Suffrage/Views of Mark Twain." St. Louis *Missouri Democrat*, March 12, 1867, p. 4.

202 BIBLIOGRAPHY

"Female Suffrage/A Volley from the Downtrodden/A Defense." St. Louis *Missouri Democrat*, March 13, 1867, p. 4.
"Inspired Humor." Buffalo (N.Y.) *Express*, August 19, 1869, p. 4.
"Letter from Mark Twain/Another Bloody Massacre!" *Territorial Enterprise*. November 16, 1863, in Scrapbook One, p. 71, Mark Twain Papers, University of California, Berkeley.
Letter, dated June 8, 1867. Reprinted in "Letter Twain Wrote in Wee Hours Before Holy Land Trip Discovered," New Haven (Conn.) *Register*, November 29, 1964, n.p.
"Letter Read at a Dinner of the Knights of St. Patrick." *Rambling Notes of an Idle Excursion*. Toronto: Rose-Belford, 1878 (pirated edition).
"Letter 24." *Alta California*. Dated New York, June 2, 1867, in Scrapbook Seven, Mark Twain Papers, University of California, Berkeley.
The Love Letters of Mark Twain. Dixon Wecter, ed. New York: Harper & Brothers, 1949.
Mark Twain-Howells Letters. Henry Nash Smith, ed., with William M. Gibson. 2 vols. Cambridge: Harvard University Press, 1960.
Mark Twain in Eruption. Bernard DeVoto, ed. New York: Harper & Brothers, 1940.
"Mark Twain in Uncle Joe's Lair." New York *Herald*, June 30, 1906, p. 5.
Mark Twain of the "Enterprise"/Newspaper Articles & Other Documents, 1862–1864. Ed. Henry Nash Smith. Berkeley: University of California Press, 1957.
"Mark Twain Sees a Riot in the Vienna Parliament and Cables to the *World*," New York *World*, November 29, 1897, pp. 1–2.
Mark Twain to Mrs. Fairbanks. Dixon Wecter, ed. San Marino, Calif.: Huntington Library, 1949.
Mark Twain's Fables of Man. John S. Tuckey, ed. Berkeley: University of California Press, 1972.
Mark Twain's Letters. Albert Bigelow Paine, ed. New York: Harper & Brothers, 1917.
Mark Twain's Letters from Hawaii. Ed. A. Grove Day. New York: Appleton-Century, 1966.
Mark Twain's Letters to his Publishers, 1867–1984. Hamlin Hill, ed. Berkeley: University of California Press, 1967.
Mark Twain's Notebook. Ed. Albert Bigelow Paine. New York: Harper & Brothers, 1935.
Mark Twain's Satires & Burlesques. Ed. Franklin Rogers. Berkeley: University of California Press, 1967.
Mark Twain's Speeches. Ed. Albert Bigelow Paine. New York: Harper & Brothers, 1923.
Mark Twain's Travels with Mr. Brown. Ed. Franklin Walker and G. Ezra Dane. New York: Alfred A. Knopf, 1940.

BIBLIOGRAPHY 203

Mark Twain's "Which Was the Dream?" And Other Symbolic Writings of the Later Years. Ed. John S. Tuckey. Berkeley: University of California Press, 1967.
"Open Letter to Commodore Vanderbilt." *Packard's Monthly*, I (March, 1869), 89-91.
"A Reminiscence of Artemus Ward." New York *Sunday Mercury*, July 7, 1867, n.p.
Selected Mark Twain-Howells Letters. Frederick Anderson, William Gibson, Henry Nash Smith, eds. New York: Athenaeum, 1968.
"Stirring Times in Austria," *Harper's Monthly*, XCVI (March, 1898), 530-40.
"Those Extraordinary Twins." Manuscript, Berg Collection, New York Public Library.
Traveling with the Innocents Abroad. Ed. Daniel Morley McKeithan. Norman: University of Oklahoma Press, 1958.
The Washoe Giant in San Francisco. Ed. Franklin Walker. San Francisco: George Fields, 1938.
"The White House Funeral." New York *Tribune*. (Exists in galley proofs in Mark Twain Papers, University of California, Berkeley, dated Washington, March 4, 1869.)
The Writings of Mark Twain. "Author's National Edition," 24 vols. New York: Harper & Brothers, n.d.

REVIEWS OF MARK TWAIN'S WORKS

"The Adventures of Huckleberry Finn." *British Quarterly Review*, LXXXI (January, 1885), 465-66.
"The American Claimant." *Spectator*, LXIX Supplement (November 19, 1892), 714.
"Among the New Books." *Book Buyer* (New York), XII (March, 1895), 92.
Anderson, Frederick, ed. *Mark Twain: The Critical Heritage*. New York: Barnes & Noble, 1971.
Angert, Eugene H. "Is Mark Twain Dead?" *North American Review*, CXC (September, 1909), 319-29.
Appleton's Journal, XII (October 3, 1874), 446.
"Artemus Ward." *Chamber's Journal*, XLII (June 10, 1865), 357-61.
"Artemus Ward's Travels." *North American Review*, CII (April, 1866), 586-92.
"Barnum." *Fraser's Magazine*, LI (February, 1855), 213-23.
"The Book Hunter." *Idler*, VI (August, 1894), 223.
"Christmas Books." *Saturday Review*, LII (December 24, 1881), 801.
"Contemporary Literature." *British Quarterly Review*, LXXV (January, 1882), 118.
"Current Literature." *Congregationalist*, XIV (March, 1885), 251-52.
"Current Literature." *Congregationalist*, XL (March, 1882), 259-60.

"Facts *versus* Fun." *Academy*, LII (December 11, 1897), 519-20.
"The Gilded Age." *Old and New*, IX (March, 1874), 386-88.
"The Gilded Age." *Saturday Review*, XXXVII (February 14, 1874), 223-24.
"The Gilded Age: A Tale of To-day." *Galaxy*, XVII (March, 1874), 428.
[Harte, Bret]. "The Genial Showman." *Overland Monthly*, V (October, 1870), 388-90.
Hingston, E. P. "Reviews and Literary Notice." *Atlantic Monthly*, XXVI (October, 1870), 511.
Howells, W. D. "The Bigelow Papers." *Atlantic Monthly*, XIX (January, 1867), 124.
"*The Innocents Abroad.*" *Athenaeum*, No. 2239 (September, 1870), 395-96.
"*The Innocents Abroad*," *Nation*, IX (September 2, 1869), 194-95.
"*The Innocents Abroad*; or the New Pilgrim's Progress." *Nation*, IX (September 2, 1869), 194-95.
"*Life on the Mississippi* by Mark Twain." *Athenaeum* (London; June 2, 1883), 694-95.
"Literary." *Appleton's Journal*, XI (January 10, 1874), 59.
"Literature." *Athenaeum*, No. 2739 (April 24, 1880), 529-30.
"Mark Twain's 'Frozen Truth' Lecture." Washington (D.C.) *Evening Star*, January 10, 1868.
"New Novels." *Graphic*, IX (February 28, 1874), 199.
"Novels of the Week." *Athenaeum* (London), No. 2411 (January 10, 1874), 53.
"Novels of the Week." *Athenaeum*, No. 2539 (June 24, 1874), 851.
[Perkins, F. B.]. "The Gilded Age." *Old and New*, IX (March, 1874), 386-88.
Perry, T. S. "American Novels." *North American Review*, CXV (October, 1872), 366-88.
"*The Prince and the Pauper*." *Critic*, I (December 31, 1881), 368.
"Revelations of a Showman." *Blackwood's Magazine*, LXXVII (February, 1855), 187-201.
Sedgwick, Arthur George. "Artemus Ward's Travels." *North American Review*, CII (April, 1866), 586-92.
Southern Literary Messenger, XXI (January, 1855), 59.
Stead, W. T. "Mark Twain's New Book." *Review of Reviews*, I (February, 1890), 144-45.
Saturday Review [London], LXIII (April 2, 1887), 495.
"The Stolen White Elephant." *Nation*, XXXV (August 10, 1882), 119.
"The Stolen White Elephant." *Critic*, II (June 17, 1882), 163.
Trent, W. P. "Mark Twain as an Historical Novelist." *Bookman* (New York), III (May, 1896), 207-10.
"Twain's Yankee Knight." *Weekly Gate City*, November 25, 1886, n.p., in Scrapbook Twenty, pp. 62-63, Mark Twain Papers, University of California, Berkeley.

Williams, Martha McCulloch. "In re Pudd'nhead Wilson." *Fetter's Southern Magazine*, IV (February, 1894), 99–102.
"Yankee Humor." *Quarterly Review*, CXXII (January, April, 1867), 212–37.

BOOKS AND ARTICLES

[Ade, George]. *The America of George Ade*. Jean Sheperd, ed. New York: Capricorn Books, 1962.
Adeler, Max [Charles Heber Clark]. *Captain Bluitt*. Philadelphia: Henry T. Coates, 1901.
Andrews, Kenneth R. *Nook Farm, Mark Twain's Hartford Circle*. Hamden, Conn.: Archon Books, 1967.
"Artemus Ward." *Harper's Weekly*, XI (March 23, 1867), 188.
"Artemus Ward." (London) *Times Literary Supplement*, XXXIII (April 26, 1934), 289–90.
"Artemus Ward Among the Printers—They Meet in a Body and Receive Him." St. Louis *Missouri Republican*, March 23, 1864, p. 3.
"Artemus Ward, Patriot." *Littell's Living Age*, CCLXXXVIII (March 18, 1916), 763–66. Reprinted from the (London) *Spectator* (January 29, 1916), 154–55.
Austin, James C. *Artemus Ward*. New York: Twayne, 1964.
Baetzhold, Howard. *Mark Twain and John Bull: The British Connection*. Bloomington: Indiana University Press, 1970.
Baldanza, Frank. *Mark Twain: An Introduction and Interpretation*. New York: Barnes & Noble, 1961.
Baldwin, Joseph G. *The Flush Times of Alabama and Mississippi*. New York: Sagamore Press, 1957 [1853].
[Barnum, Phineas T.]. *The Life of P. T. Barnum, Written by Himself*. New York: Redfield, 1855.
Barr, Robert. "Samuel L. Clemens, 'Mark Twain' (A Character Sketch)," *McClure's Magazine*, X (January, 1898), 246–51.
[Beecher, Henry Ward.] *Beecher as a Humorist*. Eleanor Kirk, ed. New York: Fords, Howard, and Hulbert, 1887.
Beer, Thomas. *The Mauve Decade*. New York: Alfred A. Knopf, 1926.
Belknap, P. H. "Our Unique Humorist: Artemus Ward." *Dial*, LXVII (1919), 433–34.
Bellamy, Gladys C. *Mark Twain as a Literary Artist*. Norman: University of Oklahoma Press, 1950.
———. "Mark Twain's Indebtedness to John Phoenix," *American Literature*, XIII (March, 1941), 29–43.
Benson, Ivan. *Mark Twain's Western Years*. Stanford: Stanford University Press, 1938.
Benton, Joel. *The Life of Hon. Phineas T. Barnum*. N.p.: Edgewood, 1891.
———. "Reminiscences of Eminent Lecturers." *Harper's Monthly*, XCVI (March, 1898), 603–14.

Bentzon, Th. "Les Humoristes Américains/I: Mark Twain." *Revue de Deux Mondes*, CCIV (July 15, 1872), 313–35.

———. "Les Humoristes Américains/II: Artemus Ward, Josh Billings, Hans Breitmann," *Revue de Deux Mondes*, CCIV (August 15, 1872), 837–62.

Berthoff, Warner. *The Ferment of Realism/American Literature, 1884–1919*. New York: Free Press, 1965.

Bicknell, Percy H. "Mark Twain." *Dial*, LIII (October 16, 1912), 290–92.

Bier, Jesse. *The Rise and Fall of American Humor*. New York: Holt, Rinehart and Winston, 1968.

[Josh Billings.] *The Complete Works of Josh Billings*. New York: G. W. Dillingham, 1876.

———. *Josh Billings: His Sayings*. New York: Carleton, 1866.

———. *Josh Billings' Old Farmer's Allminax*. New York: G. W. Dillingham, 1902 [1870–1879].

Blair, Walter. "Burlesques in Nineteenth-Century American Literature," *American Literature*, II (November, 1930), 236–47.

———. *Horse Sense in American Humor*. Chicago: University of Chicago Press, 1942.

———. *Mark Twain & Huck Finn*. Berkeley: University of California Press, 1960.

———. *Native American Humor*. San Francisco: Chandler, 1960 [1937].

———. "The Popularity of Nineteenth-Century Humorists." *American Literature*, III (May, 1931), 175–94.

———. "The Structure of Tom Sawyer." *Modern Philology*, XXXVII (August, 1939), 75–88.

Boatright, Mody C. *Folk Laughter on the American Frontier*. New York: Macmillan, 1949.

Bone, J. H. A. "St. Simon Stylites and the Flea." *Knickerbocker Magazine*, XLIII (March, 1854), 243–44.

Branch, Edgar M. *The Literary Apprenticeship of Mark Twain*. Urbana: University of Illinois Press, 1950.

———. "'My Voice is Still for Setchell': A Background Study of 'Jim Smiley and His Jumping Frog.'" *PMLA*, LXXXII (December, 1967), 591–601.

Brashear, Minnie M. *Mark Twain: Son of Missouri*. New York: Russell & Russell, 1964 [1934].

Bridges, William. "Family Patterns and Social Values." *The American Culture*. Hennig Cohen, ed. (Boston: Houghton Mifflin, 1968), 248–56.

Bridgman, Richard. *The Colloquial Style in America*. New York: Oxford University Press, 1966.

Brooks, Van Wyck. *New England: Indian Summer 1865–1915*. N.p.: E. P. Dutton, 1940.

Browne, J. Ross. "Washoe Revisited." *Harper's Monthly*, XXXI (June, 1965), 1–12.

Budd, Louis J. *Mark Twain: Social Philosopher*. Bloomington: Indiana University Press, 1962.
——. "Mark Twain Talks Mostly About Humor and Humorists." *Studies in American Humor*, I (April, 1974), 4-22.
Cady, Edwin H. *The Light of Common Day: Realism in American Fiction*. Bloomington: Indiana University Press, 1971.
Carter, Paul J., Jr. "Mark Twain and the American Labor Movement." *New England Quarterly*, XXX (September, 1957), 582-88.
Cary, Edward, *George William Curtis*. Boston: Houghton Mifflin, 1894.
Cash, W. J. *The Mind of the Old South*. New York: Random House, 1969.
Cassady, Edward E. "Muckraking in the Gilded Age." *American Literature*, XIII (May, 1941), 34-41.
Clemens, J. R. "Some Reminiscences of Mark Twain." *Overland Monthly*, LXXXVII (April, 1929), 105, 125.
Clemens, Will M. *Famous Funny Fellows*. New York: John W. Lovell, 1882.
Cohen, Hennig, and William B. Dillingham, eds. *Humor of the Old Southwest*. Boston: Houghton Mifflin, 1964.
——. "Mark Twain's Sut Lovingood." *The Lovingood Papers*, ed. B. H. McClary. Knoxville: University of Tennessee Press, 1962, pp. 19-24.
Covici, Pascal, Jr. *Mark Twain's Humor*. Dallas: Southern Methodist University Press, 1962.
Compton, Charles H. "Who Reads Mark Twain?" *Who Reads What?* New York: H. W. Wilson, 1935, pp. 15-34.
Cox, James M. *Mark Twain: The Fate of Humor*. Princeton: Princeton University Press, 1966.
Cox, Samuel S. *Why We Laugh*. New York: Harper & Brothers, 1880.
Cozzens, Frederic S. *The Sparrowgrass Papers: Or Living in the Country*. New York: Derby & Jackson, 1856.
[Curtis, George W.] *The Potiphar Papers*. New York: G. P. Putnam, 1854.
Dahl, Curtis. "Artemus Ward: Comic Panoramatist." *New England Quarterly*, XXXII (December, 1959), 476-85.
Da Ponte, Durant. "American Periodical Criticism of Mark Twain, 1869-1917." Ph.D. dissertation, University of Maryland, 1953.
DeQuille, Dan [William Wright]. "Artemus Ward in Nevada." *California Illustrated Magazine*, IV (August, 1893), 403 406.
——. "Reporting with Mark Twain." *California Illustrated Magazine*, IV (July, 1893), 170-78.
DeVoto, Bernard. "Introduction." *The Portable Mark Twain*. New York: Viking, 1946.
——. *Mark Twain's America*. Boston: Houghton Mifflin, 1967.
——. *Mark Twain at Work*. Cambridge: Harvard University Press, 1942.
Dickens, Charles. *Hard Times*. New York: Holt, Rinehart, and Winston, 1963.

Dickinson, Leon T. "Mark Twain's Revisions in Writing *The Innocents Abroad*." *American Literature*, XIX (May, 1947), 139–57.
Dilke, Sir Charles W. *Greater Britain*. London: Macmillan, 1885.
Doesticks, Q. K. Philander [Mortimer N. Thomson]. *Doesticks, What He Says*. New York: Edward Livermore, 1855.
Doesticks, Q. K. Philander [Mortimer N. Thomson], and Knight Russ Ockside [E. F. Underhill]. *The History and Records of the Elephant Club* . . . . New York: Livermore & Rudd, 1857.
Duckett, Margaret. *Mark Twain and Bret Harte*. Norman: University of Oklahoma Press, 1964.
[Dunne, Finley Peter]. *Dissertations by Mr. Dooley*. New York: Harper & Brothers, 1906.
"Editor's Table." *Knickerbocker Magazine*, L (August, 1857), 194–97.
Emberson, Francis G. *Mark Twain's Vocabulary: A General Survey*. "University of Missouri Studies," Vol. X. Columbia, 1935.
Falk, Robert. *Victorian Mode in American Fiction, 1865–1885*. East Lansing: Michigan State University Press, 1965.
Fatout, Paul. "Artemus Ward Among the Mormons." *Western Humanities Review*, XIV (Spring, 1960), 194–99.
———. *Mark Twain in Virginia City*. Bloomington: Indiana University Press, 1964.
———. *Mark Twain on the Lecture Circuit*. Bloomington: Indiana University Press, 1960.
Ferguson, DeLancey. *Mark Twain: Man and Legend*. Indianapolis: Bobbs-Merrill, 1943.
Ferris, George T. "Mark Twain." *Appleton's Journal*, XII (July 4, 1874), 15–18.
Fisher, Henry W. *Abroad with Mark Twain and Eugene Field*. New York: N. L. Brown, 1922.
Ford, James L. "A Century of American Humor." *Munsey's Magazine*, XXV (July, 1901), 482–90.
Forester, Frank [Henry W. Herbert]. *The Warwick Woodlands: Or Things as They Were There Twenty Years Ago*. Philadelphia: T. B. Peterson, 1850.
Foster, Edward F. "*A Connecticut Yankee* Anticipated: Max Adeler's *Fortunate Island*." *Ball State University Forum*, IX (1968), 73–76.
French, Bryant M. *Mark Twain and the Gilded Age*. Dallas: Southern Methodist University Press, 1965.
Ganzel, Dewey. *Mark Twain Abroad*. Chicago: University of Chicago Press, 1968.
"Gath" [G. A. Townsend]. "An Interview with 'Josh Billings.'" Philadelphia *Free Press*, January 31, 1878.

Gerber, John C. "Mark Twain." *American Literary Scholarship/1967*, ed. James Woodress. Durham: Duke University Press, 1969.
———. "Mark Twain's Use of Comic Pose." *PMLA*, LXXVII (June, 1962), 297–304.
Gilder, Richard Watson. "Mark Twain: A Glance at His Spoken and Written Art." *Outlook*, LXXVIII (December 3, 1904), 842–44.
Gohdes, Clarence. "Mirth for the Millions." *The Literature of the American People*. Arthur Hobson Quinn, ed. New York: Appleton-Century-Crofts, 1951.
Grimm, Clyde L. "*The American Claimant*: Reclamation of a Farce." *American Quarterly*, XIX (Spring, 1967), 86–103.
Hanchett, William. *Irish/Charles G. Halpine in Civil War America*. Syracuse: Syracuse University Press, 1970.
"Hardcoal Sketch, No. 2." *Carpet-Bag*, I (January 7, 1851), 7.
Harris, George Washington. *Sut Lovingood's Yarns*. New Haven: College and University Press, 1966 [1867].
Harris, Joel Chandler. "Letter." *Critic*, VII (November 28, 1885), 253.
Harris, Neal. *Humbug: The Life of P. T. Barnum*. Boston: Little, Brown, 1973.
Harrison, John M. *The Man Who Made Nasby: David Ross Locke*. Chapel Hill: University of North Carolina Press, 1969.
Harte, Bret. "American Humor." *Stories and Poems and Other Uncollected Writings*. Ed. Charles M. Kozlay. Boston: Houghton Mifflin, 1914.
———. "Artemus Ward." *Stories and Poems and Other Uncollected Writings*. Ed. Charles M. Kozlay. Boston: Houghton Mifflin, 1914.
———. "The Genial Showman." *Overland Monthly*, V (Octuber, 1870), 388–90.
Hauck, Richard, "The Dickens Controversy in the *Spirit of the Time*." *PMLA*, LXXXV (March, 1970), 278–283.
Hazard, Lucy L. *The Frontier in American Literature*. New York: Thomas Crowell, 1927.
Heffernan, Michael [Samuel Ferguson]. *Father Tom and the Pope: Or a Night in the Vatican*. "Ante-Preface" by Frederic S. Cozzens. New York: Moorhead, Simpson, & Bond, 1868.
Henderson, Archibald. *Mark Twain*. New York: Fredcrick A. Stokes, 1910.
Hill, Hamlin. "Barnum, Bridgeport, and *The Connecticut Yankee*." *American Quarterly*, XVI (Winter, 1964), 615–16.
———. "Introduction." *A Connecticut Yankee in King Arthur's Court*. San Francisco: Chandler, 1963.
———. *Mark Twain and Elisha Bliss*. Columbia: University of Missouri Press, 1964.
Hingston, Edward P. *The Genial Showman*. New York: Harper & Brothers, 1870.

———. "Introduction." *The Innocents Abroad*. London: John Camden Hotten, 1872.
Holland, J. G. "Lecture-Brokers and Lecture-Breakers." *Scribner's Monthly*, I (March, 1871), 560–61.
———. "Triflers on the Platform," *Scribner's Monthly*, III (February, 1872), 489.
Holmes, Oliver Wendell. "To Mark Twain." *Critic*, VII (November 28, 1885), 253.
[Howard, Joseph.] *Corry O'Lanus: His Views and Experiences*. New York: G. W. Carleton, 1867.
Howe, M. A. DeWolfe. "Bret Harte and Mark Twain in the 'Seventies,' Passages from the Diaries of Mrs. James T. Fields." *Atlantic Monthly*, CXXX (September, 1922), 341–48.
———. "Some Humorists." *American Bookmen*. Dodd, Mead, 1898.
Howells, W. D. "First Impressions of Literary New York." *Harper's Monthly*, XCI (July, 1895), 62–74.
———. "Introduction." *Artemus Ward's Best Stories*. New York: Harper & Brothers, 1912.
———. *My Mark Twain*. Baton Rouge: Louisiana State University Press, 1967 [1910].
Hubbell, Jay B. *The South in American Literature*. Durham: Duke University Press, 1954.
Hudson, Frederic. *Journalism in the United States, from 1690 to 1872*. New York: Harper, 1873, pp. 688–96.
James, George Wharton. "Mark Twain and the Pacific Coast," *Pacific Monthly*, XXIV (August, 1910), 115–34.
Jennison, Keith W. *The Humorous Mr. Lincoln*. New York: Bonanza Books, 1965.
Johnson, Clifton. "Biographical Notes." *Artemus Ward's Best Stories*. New York: Harper & Brothers, 1912.
———. "Recollections of Artemus Ward." *Overland Monthly*, Second Series, LXVII (January, 1916), 28–33.
Jones, Joseph. "Josh Billings: Some Yankee Notions on Humor." *University of Texas Studies in English*, 1943, pp. 148–61.
Josephson, Matthew. *Victor Hugo*. New York: Doubleday, Doran, 1942.
Keeling, Anna E. "American Humor: Mark Twain." *London Quarterly Review*, XCII (July, 1899), 147–62.
Knight, Enoch. "The Real Artemus Ward." *Overland Monthly*, XVIII (July, 1891), 54–60.
Landon, Melville D. "Travelling with Artemus Ward." *Galaxy*, XII (September, 1871), 442–45.
———. *Eli Perkins: Thirty Years of Wit, and Reminiscences of Witty, Wise, and Eloquent Men*. New York: Cassell, 1891.

Langford, Gerald. *The Richard Harding Davis Years: A Biography of a Mother and Son*. New York: Holt, Rinehart and Winston, 1961.
Leacock, Stephen. *The Greatest Pages of American Humor*. London: Methuen, 1937.
Leisy, Ernest E. "Mark Twain's Part in *The Gilded Age*." *American Literature*, VIII (January, 1937), 445–47.
Leland, Charles Godfrey. "Artemus Ward and *Vanity Fair*." *Memoirs*. New York: Appleton, 1893.
———. *Meister Karl's Sketch-book*. Philadelphia: T. B. Peterson & Brothers, 1872.
Liljegren, S. J. *The Revolt Against Romanticism in American Literature as Evidenced in the Works of S. L. Clemens*. New York: Haskell House, 1970 [1945].
Livingston, Luther S. "The First Books of Some American Authors." *Bookman* (New York), VIII (February, 1899), 563–67.
Long, E. Hudson. *Mark Twain Handbook*. New York: Hendricks House, 1957.
———. "Sut Lovingood and Mark Twain's *Joan of Arc*." *Modern Language Notes*, LXIV (January, 1949), 37–39.
Longstreet, A. B. *Georgia Scenes*. New York: Sagamore Press, 1957 [1835].
Lorch, Fred W. "'Doesticks' and *Innocents Abroad*." *American Literature*, XX (January, 1949), 446–49.
———. "Mark Twain's 'Artemus Ward' Lecture on the Tour of 1871–1872." *New England Quarterly*, XXV (September, 1952), 327–43.
———. "Mark Twain's Lecture from *Roughing It*." *American Literature*, XXII (November, 1950), 290–307.
———. *The Trouble Begins at Eight: Mark Twain's Lecture Tours*. Ames: Iowa State University Press, 1968.
Lowell, James R. "Introduction" (The Bigelow Papers, Second Series), *The Poetical Works of James Russell Lowell*. Boston: Houghton Mifflin, 1882.
Lucy, Sir H. *Sixty Years in the Wilderness*. New York: E. P. Dutton, 1909.
Lukens, Henry Clay. "American Literary Comedians." *Harper's Monthly*, LXXX (April, 1890), 783–97.
Lynn, Kenneth S. *Mark Twain and Southwestern Humor*. Boston: Little, Brown, 1959.
Macy, John. "Mark Twain." *The Spirit of American Literature*. Garden City: Doubleday, Page, 1913.
M'Alpine, Frank. *Our Album of Authors*. Philadelphia: Elliott & Beezley, 1886.
"Mark Twain." *Dial*, XLVIII (May 1, 1910), 305–307.
"Mark Twain as a Plagiarist." *Critic*, New Series, XXI (March 31, 1894), 221.

"Mark Twain Number." *Bookman* (London), XXXVIII (June, 1910).
"Mark Twain Number." *Bookman* (New York), XXXI (June, 1910).
"Mark Twain Number." *Overland Monthly*, LXXXVII (April, 1929).
Mark Twain's Library of Humor. New York: Charles L.Webster, 1888.
"Mark Twain's Pessimistic Philosophy." Anonymous essay, *Current Literature*, XLVIII (June, 1910), 643-47.
Marks, Barry A. (ed.). *Mark Twain's Huckleberry Finn*. Boston: D. C. Heath, 1959.
Marquis, Don. *archy and mehitabel*. Garden City, N.Y.: Doubleday, n.d.
———. *Carter, and Other People*. New York: D. Appleton, 1921.
———. "The Mulatto." *Harper's Monthly*, CXXXII (April, 1916), 726-30.
Marvel, Ik [Donald G. Mitchell]. *Fudge Doings: Being Tony Fudge's Record of the Same*. New York: Charles Scribner, 1855.
Marx, Leo. "The Pilot and the Passenger: Landscape Conventions and the Style of *Huckleberry Finn*." *American Literature*, XXVIII (May, 1956), 120-46.
Mason, Laurens D. "Real People in Mark Twain's Stories." *Overland Monthly*, LXXXIX (January, 1931), 12-13, 27.
Mathews, Brander. "The Penalty of Humor." Reprinted in *Aspects of Fiction, and Other Ventures in Criticism*. New York: Harper & Brothers, 1896.
M.B.C. "Mark Twain as a Reader." *Harper's Weekly*, LV (January 7, 1911), 6.
"McArone" [George W. Arnold]. "The American Waterloo." *Vanity Fair*, VI (October 18, 1862), 183.
McKee, Irving. "Artemus Ward in California and Nevada." *Pacific Historical Review*, XX (February, 1951), 11-24.
McKeithan, D. M. "Mark Twain's Story of the Bulls and the Bees." *Tennessee Historical Quarterly* (September, 1952), 246-53.
Meine, Franklin J. "American Comic Periodicals: No 1—The *Carpet Bag*." *Collector's Journal*, IV (October-November-December, 1933), 411-13.
———. "American Comic Periodicals: No. 2—*Vanity Fair*." *Collector's Journal*, IV (January-February-March, 1934), 461-63.
Merrill, W. H. "When Mark Twain Lectured." *Harper's Weekly*, L (February 10, 1906), 199-209.
Morris, George P. "'The Monopoly' and 'The People's Line.'" Reprinted in William E. Burton, ed., *The Cyclopedia of Wit and Humor* (New York: Appleton, 1875 [1859]).
Moore, O. H. "Mark Twain and Don Quixote." *PMLA*, XXXVII (June, 1922), 324-46.
Moore, William Edgar. "Mark Twain's Techniques of Humor." Ph.D. dissertation, George Peabody College for Teachers, 1946.
Mott, Frank Luther. "The Beginnings of Artemus Ward." *Journalism Quarterly*, XVIII (June, 1941), 146-52.

———. *A History of American Magazines*. Cambridge: Harvard University Press, 1938.
Nadal, E. S. "Artemus Ward." *Scribner's Monthly*, XXI (November, 1880), 144–40.
Nasby, Petroleum V. [David Ross Locke]. *"Swingin Round the Cirkle."* Boston: Lee and Shepard, 1867.
Neal, Alice. "Introductory." *Widow Bedott Papers*. New York: Derby & Jackson, 1956, ix–xix.
Neal, Joseph C. *Charcoal Sketches*. Philadelphia: Carey and A. Hart, 1838.
"Nebulae," *Galaxy*, III (January 15, 1867), 222.
[Newell, Robert H.] *The Cloven Foot*. New York: Carleton, 1870.
———. *The Orpheus C. Kerr Papers*. New York: Carleton, 1866.
———. *Versatilities*. Boston: Lee & Shepard, 1871.
Nock, Albert Jay. "Artemus Ward's America." *Free Speech and Plain Language*. New York: William Morrow, 1937.
———. "Preface." *Selected Works of Artemus Ward*. New York: Albert & Charles Boni, 1924.
Northcroft, George J. H. "Artemus Ward." *Littell's Living Age*, CLXXVII (May 5, 1888), 301–304. Reprinted from *Time*, XVIII (1888).
Nye, Edgar W. *Remarks by Bill Nye*. Chicago: A. E. Davis, 1887.
Pain, Barry. "The Humor of Mark Twain." *Bookman* (London), XXXVIII (June, 1910), 107–11.
Paine, Albert Bigelow. *Mark Twain: A Biography*. New York: Harper & Brothers, 1912.
———. "Mark Twain. Some Chapters from an Extraordinary Biography." *Harper's Monthly*, CXXIV (March, 1912), 583–97.
———. *A Short Life of Mark Twain*. Garden City: Garden City, 1925.
Pattee, Fred Lewis. *The Feminine Fifties*. New York: D. Appleton-Century, 1940.
———. *A History of American Literature Since 1870*. New York: Century, 1915.
Phelps, William Lyon. "Mark Twain." *North American Review*, CLXXXVI (July 5, 1907), 540–48.
Phillips, R. E. "Mark Twain: More than Humorist." *Book Buyer* (New York), XXII (April, 1901), 196–201.
Phoenix, John [George Horatio Derby]. *Phoenixiana: Or, Sketches and Burlesques*. New York: D. Appleton, 1873 (1855).
———. *The Squibob Papers*. New York: Carleton, 1865 (1859).
Pond, Major J. B. *Eccentricities of Genius*. New York: G. W. Dillingham, 1900.
Quad, M. [Charles B. Lewis]. *Brother Gardner's Lime-Kiln Club*. Chicago: Belford, Clarke, 1889 [1883].
Read, Opie. *Mark Twain and I*. Chicago: Reilly & Lee, 1940.

Reed, John Q. "Artemus Ward: A Critical Study." Ph.D. dissertation, State University of Iowa, 1955.

———. "Artemus Ward's First Lecture." *American Literature*, XXXII (November, 1960), 317–19.

Regan, Robert. *Unpromising Heroes: Mark Twain and His Characters*. Berkeley: University of California Press, 1966.

Rideing, William H. "Mark Twain in Clubland." *Bookman* (New York), XXXI (June, 1910).

Rodney, Robert M. "Mark Twain in England: A Study of the English Criticism of and Attitudes Toward Mark Twain, 1867–1940." Ph.D. dissertation, University of Wisconsin, 1945.

Rogers, Franklin R. *Mark Twain's Burlesque Patterns as Seen in the Novels and Narratives 1855–1885*. Dallas: Southern Methodist University Press, 1960.

———. *The Pattern for Mark Twain's "Roughing It."* Berkeley: University of California Press, 1961.

Rourke, Constance. *American Humor: A Study of the National Character*. Garden City: Doubleday, 1953 [1931].

Rowlette, Robert. "'Mark Ward on Artemus Twain': Twain's Literary Debt to Ward." *American Literary Realism: 1870–1910*, VI (Winter, 1973), 13–26.

Ruthrauff, C. C. "Artemus Ward at Cleveland." *Scribner's Monthly*, XVI (October, 1878), 785–91.

"Samuel L. Clemens" [anon.]. *Littell's Living Age*, CCLIV (July 6, 1907), 60–62. Reprinted from *Spectator* (London, May 25, 1907).

Schmidt, Paul. "Mark Twain's Satire on Republicanism." *American Quarterly*, V (Winter, 1953), 344–56.

Seitz, Don C. *Artemus Ward: A Biography and Bibliography*. New York: Harper & Brothers, 1919.

———. "Artemus Ward: His Home and Family." *Scribner's Monthly*, XXII (May, 1881), 46–53.

———. "Relics of Artemus Ward." *Century Magazine*, XLVI (May, 1893), 132–35.

"Serious Humorists" [anon.] *Nation*, XC (June 30, 1910), 645–46.

Sharp, Luke. "Mark Twain. A Conglomorate Interview Conducted by Luke Sharp," *Idler Magazine*, I (February, 1892), 79–80, 83–92.

Shaw, Archer H. "Artemus Ward." *The Plain Dealer: One Hundred Years in Cleveland*. New York: Alfred A. Knopf, 1942.

Shillaber, B[enjamin] P. *Life and Sayings of Mrs. Partington, and Others of the Family*. New York: J. C. Derby, 1854.

———. *Lines in Pleasant Places*. Chelsea, Mass.: the author, 1874.

———. Letter to Mark Twain dated January 1, 1870 [1871], in Mark Twain Papers, University of California, Berkeley.

Smith, Henry Nash. *Mark Twain: The Development of a Writer.* Cambridge: Harvard University Press, 1962.

———. *Mark Twain's Fable of Progress: Political and Economic Ideas in "A Connecticut Yankee."* New Brunswick: Rutgers University Press, 1964.

———. "The Morality of Power." Clarence Gohdes, ed. *Essays in Honor of J. B. Hubbell.* Durham: Duke University Press, 1967.

Smith, Seba. *The Life and Writings of Major Jack Downing.* Boston: Lilly, Wait, Colman, & Holden, 1834.

[Smith, Sydney.] *The Wit and Wisdom of Sydney Smith.* New York: G. P. Putnam's Sons, n.d.

Stampp, Kenneth M. *The Causes of the Civil War.* Englewood Cliffs, N.J.: Prentice Hall, 1959.

Stewart, George R., Jr. *John Phoenix, Esq.: The Veritable Squibob.* New York: Henry Holt, 1937.

Stone, Albert E. *The Innocent Eye: Childhood in Mark Twain's Imagination.* New Haven: Yale University Press, 1961.

Tandy, Jennette. *Crackerbox Philosophers in American Humor and Satire.* New York: Columbia University Press, 1925.

Thompson, Charles Miner. "Mark Twain as an Interpreter of American Character." *Atlantic Monthly*, LXXIX (April, 1897), 443–50.

Trent, W. P. "A Retrospect of American Humor." *Century Magazine*, LXIII (November, 1901), 45–64.

Twitchell, Joseph H. "Mark Twain." *Harper's Monthly*, XCII (May, 1896), 817–27.

Vale, Charles. "Mark Twain as an Orator." *Forum*, XLIV (July, 1910), 1–13.

Vogelback, A. L. "The Literary Reputation of Mark Twain in America, 1869–1885." Ph.D. dissertation, University of Chicago, 1938.

———. "*The Prince and the Pauper*: A Study in Critical Attitudes." *American Literature*, XIV (March, 1942), 48–54.

———. "The Publication and Reception of *Huckleberry Finn* in America." *American Literature*, XI (November, 1939), 260–72.

Walker, Franklin. *San Francisco's Literary Frontier.* New York: Alfred A. Knopf, 1939.

Ward, Artemus [Charles F. Browne]. "Morality and Genius." *Artemus Ward in London and Other Papers.* New York: G. W. Carleton, 1867.

———. "Artemus Ward's Lecture [*Robinson Crusoe*]." St. Louis *Missouri Republican*, March 27, 1864, p. 3.

———. "Artemus Ward Letters," ed. Don C. Seitz, *American Collector*, III (February, 1927), 195–98.

———. "Brigham Young." Cleveland *Daily Plain Dealer*, February 2, 1858, p. 3.

———. "City Facts and Fancies." Cleveland *Daily Plain Dealer*, March 4, 1858, p. 3.

———. "City Facts and Fancies." Cleveland *Daily Plain Dealer*, February 15, 1859, p. 3.
———. *The Complete Works of Artemus Ward*. London: Chatto & Windus, 1922.
———. "Letter from Artemus Ward." Cleveland *Daily Plain Dealer*, February 14, 1859, p. 3.
———. "Our Local Heard From." Cleveland *Daily Plain Dealer*, February 2, 1859, p. 3.
Warner, Charles Dudley. *Backlog Studies*. Boston: James R. Osgood, 1873.
Watson, Aaron. "Artemus Ward and Mark Twain" and "Mark Twain's Own Account." *The Savage Club*. London: T. Fisher Unwin, 1907.
Watson, J. W. "How Artemus Ward Became a Lecturer." *North American Review*, CXLVIII (April, 1889), 521–22.
Watterson, Henry. "Mark Twain—An Intimate Memory." *American Magazine*, LXX (July, 1910), 372–75.
Weber, Carl N. "A Connecticut Yankee in King Alfred's Country." *Colophon*, New Series, I (Spring, 1936), 525–35.
———. "A Ghost from a Barber Shop." *New Colophon*, I (April, 1948), 185–89.
Wecter, Dixon. *Sam Clemens of Hannibal*. Boston: Houghton Mifflin, 1952.
———. "Mark Twain." Robert Spiller *et al*, eds. *The Literary History of the United States*. New York: Macmillan, 1968.
Werner, M. R. *Barnum*. New York: Harcourt, Brace, 1923.
Wharton, Henry M. "The Boyhood Home of Mark Twain." *Century Magazine*, LXIV (September, 1902), 675–77.
White, Frank Marshall. "Mark Twain as a Newspaper Reporter." *Outlook*, XCVI (December 24, 1910), 961–67.
Wiggins, Robert A. *Mark Twain: Jackleg Novelist*. Seattle: University of Washngton Press, 1964.
Williams, Stanley T. "Artemus the Delicious." *Virginia Quarterly Review*, XXVIII (1952), 214–27.
Winter, William. "Artemus Ward." *Old Friends*. New York: Moffett, Yard, 1909.

Notebooks and Scrapbooks in Mark Twain Papers, University of California, Berkeley, and various papers in the Berg Collection of the New York Public Library have been consulted.
Files of *Vanity Fair, Knickerbocker Magazine*, and *Carpet-Bag* have also been used.

Index

Ade, George, 194
Adeler, Max. *See* Clark, Charles Heber
Aldrich, Thomas Bailey, 37, 51, 114
Altgeld, John, 101*n*
Ament, Joseph, 59
American Humor: G. H. Derby called father of, 19; and Joseph C. Neal, 10–12; B. P. Shillaber's place in, 14; English and Irish sources of, 4–7, 28*n*, 55, 134
Americanism, 12, 33, 96–97, 152, 198
American traits in England, 55–56, 117–27, 146–67
Apprenticeship: Connecticut Yankee on, 151–52; Miles Hendon, 126, Tom Driscoll, 183–84; Mark Twain on, 60–61; Ward, 30
Arp, Bill. *See* Smith, Charles Henry

Bailey, James, M. (Danbury News Man), 180, 195
Baldwin, Joseph G.: Ovid Bolus, 109; mentioned, 1
Barnum, P. T.: *Blackwood's* review of, 33; career of, 14, 31–35; and *A Connecticut Yankee*, 146–49; and "shoot my half" story, 178–79; stance of, 20, 43–44; as traveler, 49, 55; in Mark Twain's sketches, 77, 86–90, 110; mentioned, 6, 36*n*, 68, 83, 90*n*, 92, 97–98, 122, 126, 139, 186, 189–90, 195. *See also* Browne, Charles F.
Beard, Dan, 164
Beecher, Henry Ward, 191
Bellemy, Edward, 148
Bible, King James, 68
Bierstadt, Albert, 96
Billings, Josh. *See* Shaw, Henry Wheeler
Bixby, Horace, 63
Bliss, Elisha, 78, 80, 105

Bone, J. H. A., 150*n*
Boucicault, Dion, 38
Brackenridge, H. H., 5
Breitmann, Hans: in Mark Twain scrapbook, 61; mentioned, 37. *See also* Leland, C. G.
British and Irish humor, 4–7, 12
Browne, Charles F. (Artemus Ward):—place in American literature: relation to Barnum, 31–35, 44, 49–50, 87, 90*n*; career, 29–44; as literary comedian, 25–28, 73; ethics, 45–57; idealism, 50, 198–99; interest in Mark Twain, 65, 69–72; lectures, 37, 40–43, 53 79–71, 74; compared to Mark Twain, 52–53, 62, 72–73, 79*n*, 103, 183–84, 195; "A Man," 22, 27–28, at Oberlin with Prof. Peck, 26, 195; on railroads, 48, 112; San Francisco opinion of, 73
—Mark Twain's works and Ward: *American Claimant*, 174; *Connecticut Yankee*, 154–56, 163; *Gilded Age*, 108, 111; *Huckleberry Finn*, 130–31, 135*n*; *Innocents Abroad*, 99–101; *Pudd'nhead Wilson*, 181–84
—Ward's works: *Among the Mormons*, 50–53; "In Canada," 50; "In London," 54–57; "In Washington," 90*n*; "The Green Lion and Oliver Cromwell," 56, 100; "High Handed Outrage in Utica," 39; "Robinson Crusoe," 42, 53, 74; "Soliloquy of a Low Thief" (Jim Griggins), 38–39, 45, 48–49, 88, 99, 100, 112, 121–22, 165
—and other writers: Seba Smith, 40, 98; B. P. Shillaber, 15, 30, 40; John Phoenix, 20, 40, 173*n*
—mentioned, 3, 13, 15, 58, 64, 66, 68, 85, 86, 91, 92*n*, 94, 95, 110, 118, 124, 133, 135, 137, 139, 140, 142, 147, 148, 159, 163, 165–66, 170, 172–75, 190–91, 193–96

Browne, J. Ross, 63
Burdette, Robert, 83, 180, 194
Burlesque, 6, 12, 17, 24, 38, 42, 48, 90–95, 103, 106, 110, 115, 121, 140–42, 146, 152–53
Burlingame, Anson, 76
Burton, William E., ed., *Burton's Cylopedia of Wit and Humor*, 10n, 195
Bushnell, Horace, 14
Business, 2, 33, 47, 148, 151, 183
Butler, Ben, 193

Cable, George W., 158
Cacography, 28n, 36, 45–46, 64, 111, *passim*
Carleton, G. W., 78
Carpet-Bat, 14–15, 17, 30, 35, 142.
Cervantes, Miguel, 63, 73
Chang-Eng Siamese Twins, 35, 195
Christianity and the church, 17, 97–99, 101–102, 116, 135, 140, 147, 159, 164, 191
Church, 5–6, 26, 34, 39, 99, 102, 122–23, 131, 140, 150, 159, 164
City types, 10–11, 25
Clapp, Henry, 72
Clark, Charles Heber (Max Adeler), 57, 116, 133, 139, 158, 185, 195
Clay, Henry, 47, 173
Clemens, Jane, 59
Clemens, Orion, 15, 63–65, 82
Clemens, Samuel Langhorne (Mark Twain):
—and Artemus Ward (C. F. Browne), 4n, 29, 34, 43–44, 46–47, 50–55, 69–73, 76, 79, 81, 124–25, 128
—development, 58–*103*
—later career, 189–99
—lecturing, 79–81
—as narrative writer, 86–103, 136
—platform voice, 75, 118, 131–32, 186–87
—*Quaker City* voyage, 77
—sources, 12, 19, 33–34, 39, 49–50, 55, 79, 97, 108, 112, 115, 124–25, 130, 138, 150, 156, 158, 172–73, 179, 184, 195, 197
—travel humor, 18–19, 34, 50, 136
—works by Mark Twain: *Adventures of Huckleberry Finn*, 46, 128–45, 147, 149, 159, 165, 170, 191, 193, 197–98, *passim*; *Adventures of Tom Sawyer*, 106, 114–47, 191; *American Claimant*, 92, 138–39, 168–77; "American Vandal," 17, 79, 131; "Another Bloody Massacre," 66–68; *Autobiography*, 59, 131n; "Barnum's First Speech in Congress" and "How Are the Mighty Fallen," 89–90, 103, 110; "The Bloody Massacre at Dutch Nicks," 65–66; "Cannibalism in the Cars," 76, 93–94; *The Celebrated Jumping Frog of Calaveras County*, 76, 78; *A Connecticut Yankee*, 33, 83, 139, 141, 146–68, 170, 177; "The Dandy Frightening the Squatter," 59–60; "Female Suffrage" and "Petticoat Government," 90–93; "Forty-three Days in an Open Boat," 76: *The Gilded Age*, 88, 90–93, 104–14, 117–18, 136, 139, 170, 173, 175, 177, 185; *Innocents Abroad*, 50, 77, 80–81, 95–103, 104, 128, 156, 162, 181, 197; *Joan of Arc*, 13; "The Last Lotus Club Speech," 199; "License of the Press," 61n; "Memoranda" (in *Galaxy Magazine*), 81, 93, 158, 180n; "The New Dynasty," 160; *Prince and the Pauper*, 27–28, 117–27, 139, 147, 159; *Pudd'nhead Wilson*, 83, 167, 177–88, 191; "A Reminiscence of Artemus Ward," 70n; *Roughing It*, 64, 92, 106, 132–33, 136, 146, 155–56, 175; "The Second Advent," 96; "Snodgrass" letters, 62; *Sketches, New and Old*, 77, 185; *A Tramp Abroad*, 56–57, 156; "Those Extraordinary Twins," 179n; "The Tournament in A.D. 1870," 158
—mentioned, 1, 15, 23–24, 39, 43–44, 46–48, 57
—*See also*: Barnum, P. T.; Browne, C. F.; Burlesque; Clarke, C. H.; Cosmopolitan; Deadpan; Locke, D. R.;
Congress, 47, 86–88, 90, 94–95, 107, 111, 173
Cooper, James Fenimore, 5, 64
Corporate society, 2, 10, 13–14, 16–17, 48, 50–53, 95, 99, 113, 117, 161, passim. *See also Railroads*
Cosmopolitan, 7, 15–17, 41, 49, 70, 98, 129
Cox, Samuel S., 55n, 194
Cozzens, Frederick S., 6n
Crayton, Goeffrey, 10
Crockett, Davy, 7–8
Cromwell, Oliver, 56
Curtis, G. W., 5, 7. *See also* Potiphar

Danbury News Man. *See* Bailey, James M.
Darwinism, 14, 48, 57
Deadpan, 28, 94, 118, 125, 137, 154, 162
Derby, G. H. (John Phoenix), 15, 19–20, 40, 70, 173n, 195
DeForest, John W., 83, 112, 128, 194
DeQuille, Dan (William F. Wright), 65–70
Dialect and diction, 5–6, 8–9, 16, 29, 41, 46, 56, 68, 70, 90, 130–31, 147–52, 184n. *See also* Vernacular figure; Voice and viewpoint; Vulgar voice
Dickens, Charles, 4–5, 28, 44, 61, 102, 102n
Dodge, Ossian E., 37n
Doesticks, Q. K. Philander (Mortimer Thompson), 77–78, 80n, 96, 194
Dos Passos, John, 197
Downing, Major Jack, 4, 8. *See also* Smith, Seba
Dreiser, Theodore, 188, 197
Duke and dauphin, the, 130, 136–38
Dunne, Finley Peter (Mr. Dooley), 170, 189–*90*

Ealer, George, 63
Egalitarian viewpoint, 12, 18, 26–28, 33, 50,

INDEX 219

54, 57, 85, 95, 117, 159–60, 163–64, 173–76, 189–99
Ethics, social, 2, 10–14, 16–18, 23–26, 36, 45–57, 103, 109, 133–35, 143–44, 152, 166–67, 185, 192, 197. *See also* "A man," moral humor
Existentialism, 124, 197–97

Fairbanks, "Ma," 78
Farrell, James T., 197
Father Tom and the Pope, 6, 134
Feejee Mermaid, 32
Fields, James T., and Annie, 41–42

Galaxy Magazine, 60, 81, 93n, 158, 180n, 184, 193
"Gath"(G. A. Townsend), 70n
Genteel, 18–19, 52–53, 126, 128, 152, *passim*
George, Henry, 148
Goldsmith, Oliver, 63
Goodman, Joseph, 65, 82, 119
Grant, U. S., 109
Gray, Joseph W., 31
Greeley, Horace, 26, 31, 63, 73, 154
Griggins, Jim. *See* Browne, Charles F. "Soliloquy of a Low Thief"
Grimke sisters, 14

Haliburton, T. C., 7, 195. *See* Slick, Sam
Halpine, C. G. (Miles O'Reilly), 15, 22, 35, 40, 60, 77, 194
"Hard Cases" (Joseph Neal), 11, 135
Harris, George W., 1, 3, 17
Harris, Joel Chandler, 194
Harte, Bret, 17, 19n, 38, 46, 60, 72–73, 81, 83, 125, 193
Hawthorne, Nathaniel, 198–99
Hay, John, 63
Herbert, Henry William (Frank Forrester), 9–10, 16, 117
Heth, Joice, 32
Hingston, E. P., 35, 40, 54, 69–70, 78
Historical institutions: in Ward, 43, 49, 54–57; in Mark Twain, 75, 97, 118–89, *passim*
Hoaxes: and Artemus Ward, 31; and Mark Twain, 65–69, *passim*
Holley, Marietta, 14, 170, 195–96
Holmes, Oliver Wendell, 42, 46, 50, 80, 83, 194
Hood, Tom, 6, 63, 78
Hooper, Johnson J., 1, 17
Horses, 52–53, 74, 102, 162–63
Howard, Joseph W. (Corry O'Lanus), 77, 194
Howells, William Dean, 27, 30, 38, 51, 66, 77, 80, 83, 109, 128, 159, 165–66, 170, 176
Humanism, 1, 14, 17, 21–22, 27, 50–53, 122, 124, 129, 143, 160, 164–67, 174, 199

Irreverence. *See* Reverence
Irving, Washington, 7, 10

John Bull, 12n
Johnson, Andrew, 89
Jokes: "First-class corpse in Congress," 47, 172–73; "Is he dead?" 56, 100–101, 101n; "Ladies and children not admitted," 134; "Man of Boston dressin'," 52; "Owe two million dollars," 108; "Red hair," 162; "Shoot my half," 178; "Spoon stealing," 56, 99–100

Kennedy, J. P., 9
Kerr, Orpheus C. (Richard Henry Newell), 13, 24–25, 28, 54, 95, 139, 191, 194–96
Knickerbocker Magazine, 11–12, 19, 150

Landon, Melville D. (Eli Perkins), 43–44, 70, 194
Langdon, Jervis, 81, 94n
Lanier, Sidney, 106
Law, 2, 21, 48, 102, 112, 118, 120, 165
Lecturing, 24, 40–43, 70, 76, 85, 114, 164
Leland, Charles G., 22, 37. *See also* Breitmann, Hans
Lemon, Mark, 6, 43
Lincoln, Abraham: "A Man," 21–22; burlesqued, 26, 37, 46n; Emancipation Proclamation, 39; as humorist, 20–22, 26, 28; and Ward, 22–26; mentioned, 109
Lind, Jenny, 32–33, 87, 149
Lippard, George, 61
Literary comedy, 3–4, 12, 15–16, 29, 47, 58–83, 134–35, 165, 189–99
Localism, 23, 59, 68, 104–106, 114, 118–19, 134–35, 145, 160, 165, 167
Locke, David Ross (Petroleum V. Nasby), 8, 13, 23–4, 28, 44, 54, 71, 79, 81, 95, 109–10, 194, 196
Longstreet, A. B., 1, 8, 11, 60, 180n
Lowell, James R., 8–9

Maelzel's chess player, 21
"Man, A," 18, 21–22, 27, 79, 122, 124–26, 144, 147, 161–64, 184, 197
Mann, Horace, 13
Marquis, Don, 182, 185
Marvel, Ik. (Donald G. Mitchell), 14
Matthews, Brander, 191–92
Menken, Adah, 24
Michelangelo, 181
Middle class, 10, 20, 25, 46
Mississippi River, 62–63, 73, 106, 128, 134, 153
Monarchy, 26–27, 50, 54, 118, 124–25, 136–40, 159–60, 164, 169, 174, 189
Moral stance of comedians, 17, 26–28, 31–33, 37, 66, 69, 73, 86, 137, 190–96
Mormons, 42–43, 133
Morris, George P., 10
Moulton, Louise Chandler, 15

Naif, 16, 19–20, 26, 51, 99, 101n, 110, 120–21, 124, 132, 143, 167, 178, 188, 192
Nasby, Petroleum V. *See* Locke, D. R.
Nast, Thomas, 194
Newspapers, 22, 30–31, 59–63, 64, 155–56
Northeastern humor, 7–12
Neal, Joseph C., 10–12, 35, 49n, 135, 195
Newell, Richard H. *See* Kerr, Orpheus C.
Nye, Bill, 53–54, 71, 83, 195

Oberlin, Professor Peck, 26, 195
O'Lanus, Corry *See* Howard, Joseph

Panorama, 34, 42
Partington, Mrs., 12n, 15–17, 18, 20, 25, 36, 40, 79, 114, 117, 133. *See also* Shillaber, B. P.
Perkins, Eli. *See* Melville D. Landon
Persona, 44, 79–80, 85, 87–95, 98, 108, 129, 131, 175, 181. *See also* Voice and viewpoint
Phoenix, John (George Horatio Derby), 13, 15, 40, 51, 60–61, 68–70, 79, 96, 125, 191. *See also* Derby, G. H.
Piatt, Don, 194
Pilgrims, 99–102, 162–63
Poe, Edgar Allen, 61
Political humor, 4, 6–7, 10–12, 20–22, 47, 56–57, 90–95, 105–14, 135, 159–61, 169–74
Pope, the, 5–6, 122–23
Populism: of Jim Griggins, 39; of Dan Beard, 164; mentioned, 12
Porter, William T., 2, 4, 179n
Pragmatism, 21, 38, 127, 133, 135, 162
Prince Napoleon, 38
Prince of Wales, 26–27, 54, 156, 163

Quad, M. (Charles B. Lewis), 15, 114, 133, 181n
Quaker City, voyage of, 77–79

Railroads, 9, 15–17, 48, 92–94, 112–13
Ramsbottom, Mrs., 12n
Read, Opie, 101n, 194, 196
Realism, 17, 113–14, 131, 134–35, 157, 160, 190
Redpath, James, 81
Regionalism, 134–35. *See also* Localism
Reverence and irreverence, 54–55, 80–81, 119, 149–50, 190
Riley, James W., 83, 194
Routledge's *Broadway Magazine*, 82

St. Simon Stylites, 150
San Francisco, 19, 37, 73, 84–85, 133
Sandwich Islands, 39, 73–76
Saxe, John G., 15, 38, 40
Sedgwick, Arthur George, 43
Sellers, Captain Isaiah, 62
Shakers, 26, 37

Shakespeare, William, 24, 55, 68
Shaw, Henry Wheeler (Josh Billings), 22–23, 36, 70–71, 85, 91n, 102, 180, 194–95
Shillaber, B. P., 13, 15–22, 25, 30, 36–37, 40, 60, 79, 82, 133, 142, 158, 198. *See also* Partington, Mrs.
Showman, 29–57, 128, 134, 147, 157, 170, 186
Slavery, 8, 88–89, 122, 144, 159, 182–87
Sleery (in Dickens' *Hard Times*), 28, 102n
Slick, Sam, 14, 10. *See also* Haliburton, T. C.
Slote, Dan, 94n
Small, Samuel W., 195
Smith, Albert, 6–7, 34
Smith, Charles Henry (Bill Arp), 26, 46, 195
Smith, Seba, 4, 8, 40, 195
Smith, Sydney, 7, 15
Smollett, Tobias, 63
Southwestern humor, 1–3, 12, 17, 60, 79, 109, 119–20, 179n, 195
Spike, Ethan (Matthew Whittier), 15, 37
Stead, W. T., 148
Sterne, Laurence, 4, 63
Stockton, Frank, 194–95
Stoddard, R. H., 38
Sublime, 74–75, 94, 96
Suggs, Simon, 2, 17, 97
Swain, Mark, 76

Thackeray, William M., 5, 7, 19, 38, 60, 61, 81
Thompson, William T., 2
Thomson, Mortimer. *See* Doesticks
Thorpe, Thomas Bangs, 2
Thumb, Tom, 32
Travel narrative, 34, 44, 49–51, 71, 78–80, 95–103, 125, 147, 157, 160, 169, 196
Twain, Mark. *See* Samuel L. Clemens

Union, 22, 28, 39, 199
Urban setting, 10–11, 25, 133n

Vanity Fair, 37. *See also* Browne, Charles F.
Vernacular figure, 43, 52, 56, 141–42, 178, 192. *See also* Vulgar voice
Vignettes, 98, 121–22, 162–63
Voice and viewpoint, 16–17, 29, 36, 53–56, 73–74, 80, 84, 87–88, 94, 99, 102, 117, 119, 136
Vulgar voice, 16, 29, 56, 86–87, 100, 111, 131, 136, 152, 174. *See also* Browne, Charles F.

Wakeman, Ned, 86, 90
Ward, Artemus. *See* Browne, Charles F.
Warner, Charles Dudley, 18, 51, 81, 83, 105, 112, 162n
Webb, Charles H., 38, 72, 78
Western humor, 19, 120. *See also* Harte, Derby
Whitcher, Francis M., 195

Whittier dinner, 66, 194
Whitty, Edward M., 5

Yankee: dialect, 8–9, 46; humor, 7–8, 32, 44, 80, 151, 179*n*, 180; irreverence, 55, 80, 146–67; myth, 33–34, 44. *See also* Barnum, P. T.; Clemens, Samuel L., *A Connecticut Yankee*
Yokel, 121, 169, 186, 192
Yokels, 147, 187
Young, Brigham, 26, 38, 79*n*, 133
Younge, Charlotte, 118

For Product Safety Concerns and Information please contact our EU
representative GPSR@taylorandfrancis.com
Taylor & Francis Verlag GmbH, Kaufingerstraße 24, 80331 München, Germany

www.ingramcontent.com/pod-product-compliance
Lightning Source LLC
Chambersburg PA
CBHW071834300426
44116CB00009B/1544